D1520999

Candid Comments

Candid Comments

Selected Columns from
The Eufaula Tribune,
1958–2006

JOEL P. SMITH

NewSouth Books
Montgomery | Louisville

NewSouth Books
105 S. Court Street
Montgomery, AL 36104

Library of Congress Cataloging-in-Publication Data

Smith, Joel P.
Candid comments : selected columns from the Eufaula tribune, 1958-2006 /
Joel P. Smith.
p. cm.
Includes index.
ISBN-13: 978-1-60306-068-4
ISBN-10: 1-60306-068-5
1. Smith, Joel P. 2. Eufaula (Ala.)—History—Anecdotes. 3. Eufaula (Ala.)—
Biography—Anecdotes. 4. Eufaula (Ala.)—Social life and customs—Anecdotes. 5.
Newspaper editors—Alabama—Eufaula—Biography. 6. Journalists—Alabama—
Eufaula—Biography. I. Eufaula tribune II. Title.
F334.E84S64 2011
976.1'32—dc22
2011005308

Design by Randall Williams
Printed in the United States of America by Sheridan Books

Thanks to Media General Corporation for its permission under 2006 license agreement for the use of the author photograph and images on pages 28, 44, 55, 59, 110, 133, 142, 150, 154, 204, 214, 221, 238, 242, and 270 as published in the *Eufaula Tribune* between the years of 1958 and June 26, 2006. The image on page 83 is courtesy the *Columbus Ledger-Enquirer*. All other images courtesy the Smith family.

ACKNOWLEDGMENTS

The Smith family is indebted to loyal readers of the *Eufaula Tribune* and to the people of Eufaula for sharing their stories with us for almost five decades. You have our heartfelt appreciation. Special thanks go to each *Tribune* staff member over the years that made it happen "twice a week every week"; to current staff members who assisted us in gathering correct dates and photocopies; and current General Manager Ed Trainor for access to *Tribune* photo files. Thanks go to Jack Smith for his role in selection and editing; to Barclay Smith for typesetting, to Joel Smith Jr. for his sound counsel and to Bill Smith for his encouragement and advice. We appreciate the sensitivity and expertise of Brian Seidman of NewSouth Books as he guided us through the publishing process. — ANN SMITH

Contents

Foreword / 7

1 Gracious Ladies & Colorful Characters / 13

2 Eufaula's Priceless Treasures / 39

3 Eufaula as Symbol, Old and New / 69

4 War and Peace in an Old South Town / 103

5 Barbour's 'Fighting Little Judge' / 136

6 Family: The Ties that Bind / 163

7 Reflections of a Lifetime / 182

8 Presidents, Politicians & Other Notables / 203

9 The Chattahoochee: A River's Story / 230

10 Hot Type, Heartache & Happiness / 248

11 Buck Dancing & Sunsets / 273

12 Santa, Cedar Trees & Christmas Spirit / 291

13 Fatherhood / 307

14 Cuba, Cairo & Points Between / 325

Index / 343

Foreword

By Abb Jackson Smith II

Dad was an encourager. That wonderful trait defined who he was as a father, a husband, brother, friend and editor. As I learned in the painful days following his death, Dad made those he knew feel better about who they were. He made them believe they could be something bigger, something better, than they had been before.

Dad did the same for Eufaula, Alabama, the town that he loved with all of his heart. For almost fifty faithful years, he challenged and encouraged Eufaula to be the best town it could be on the pages of the *Eufaula Tribune*, the newspaper he loved almost as much as his adopted hometown.

Eufaula would not be what it is today if Joel P. Smith had not taken the job as Editor and General Manager of the *Tribune* in 1958. He championed many causes through his coverage and commentary, from education and historic preservation to open government and community progress. He encouraged and cajoled, pressed and prodded Eufaula to reach her full potential, to be a choice community with a sense of place.

To be candid, as Dad would be, Eufaulians too often took his contributions and the importance of a locally-owned paper for granted. Dad never let the cocktail party criticisms and barbershop barbs that he said were "part of it" deter him, though. I never once saw him back down when the truth had to be told, or when others, even his friends, chided him for his editorial positions.

The *Eufaula Tribune's* editorial page, which he rightly insisted should be exclusively local in focus and content, won numerous state and national awards in the many years that he labored over it. His remarkable newspaper career paralleled the evolution of the once sleepy town he loved so much, from the days of hot metal type and Linotype machines to the modern era of computers and "pagination."

Later in his career, after I came home to join him in the family business, he marveled at our ability to automate the once painfully laborious process of publishing a newspaper. He was more comfortable cutting, pasting and waxing narrow columns of copy than he ever was with a mouse in his hand. Yet up until the last newspaper we published before selling the business in 2006, when Dad was seventy-seven years old, he was still the best in the building at writing headlines that fit just right on scraps of paper that he would fish out of the trash can. (As a child of the Great Depression, Dad wasted nothing.)

DAD BELIEVED THE editorial page is the soul of any good newspaper. If that's true, then his award-winning "Candid Comments" column was the *Tribune's* heart. It was in this cherished space that he made a personal connection with his readers every week. He often wrote about them, too.

Through his columns, Dad also shared openly and freely about his family and his children, and about how he never got over the death of his mother when he was just a boy. He wrote about his devotion to and love for his wife, Ann, my Steel Magnolia mother who was instrumental at the newspaper and in the publication of this book.

Dad wrote those personal columns because he knew all parents could relate to them, whether it was a column about the birth of his three sons or a poignant letter he wrote to each of us when we graduated from high school.

He wrote hundreds of columns about Eufaula's character, as well as her characters. Dad had a real talent for capturing the essence and personality of the people he wrote about. The first two chapters in this book are a small sampling of the people portraits he painted on his trusty typewriter. They are first because that's where he would have wanted them. He understood decades ago what some dying daily newspapers have finally come to realize: Local news about local people that can't be read anywhere else in the world is what makes a news market.

Dad genuinely loved people. He also loved history—Eufaula's, Alabama's and the South's. We had the unenviable task of eliminating for consideration countless columns on Eufaula's rich history because of space limitations in this book. (If we ever recover from the birth of this long-overdue book, perhaps we will compile a second edition.)

THIS BOOK IS a collection of his columns, but it is really just a sampling. After all, Dad wrote more than 2,700 "Candid Comments" without ever missing a week—even when surgeons in Birmingham cracked open his chest to repair a congenital heart defect in 1995. (Looking back on Dad's life and legacy, I am convinced his heart failed because he loved so hard for so long.)

As anyone who has ever worked at a community newspaper knows, such a streak of deadlines never missed is hard to fathom. Dad was the Cal Ripken of community newspaper columnists. The publication of this book was a dream of his for many years. In retirement, he spent countless hours sifting through old columns, marking some as "must for book," either because he believed they were an important part of Eufaula's history or they were about the people he loved. Dad also dreamed of publishing other collections, including one just for his family. One day, we might do just that.

Numerous times before his death in 2009—a loss that left a hole in the heart of his family and his town that won't ever be filled—Dad told me to make sure the readers of this book knew that virtually all of these columns were written on tight deadlines. If journalism is literature in a hurry, then community journalism is literature in a hurry while your hair is on fire.

In the process of selecting columns for this book, an excruciatingly difficult task given the sheer volume of material, we made some edits and fixed a few typos, but the style we left unaltered and the imperfections we left unpolished. It is essentially his work as his work appeared in print.

THOSE WHO READ this book will be reminded that Dad was indeed an encourager, but he was much more than that. He was a devoted husband, a loving father, a fearless leader, a man of great faith and a patriot who loved his town, his country and his profession.

Those who knew Dad miss him every day, as does the town that did not always love him back when the tough stories had to be written or the truth had to be told. I thank God that he was my father and that he bequeathed to me and to my children, to my brothers, niece and nephews a wonderful legacy of love and devotion on the pages that follow.

Dad, we miss you and we love you. This book is for you.

Candid Comments

Chapter 1

Gracious Ladies & Colorful Characters

CASHIER MISTAKES CANDIDATES FOR ROBBERS

June 11, 1964

B y now, some folks have probably had their jug full of politicking, so I'll not attempt to give you a dissertation on "An Anatomy of an Election." But fortunately, Eufaula's politicians—on the whole—don't take the great American game too seriously.

George Gingell, WRBL-TV's genial public affairs director, was impressed with the friendly attitude Eufaula's four candidates for mayor had toward each other when he interviewed them Friday. Usually opposing candidates, who appear on *Viewpoint*, a Sunday afternoon show moderated by Gingell, drive to the television studio in separate cars and leave by separate doors after the program is taped.

Gingell was a little surprised to learn that Marvin Edwards, Hamp Graves, Willie Ross and Willard Smith all drove up to Columbus together for taping the show. This was unusual enough, but the political rivals invited me to come along, too. True, I had to sit on the hump between the bucket seats, but nevertheless they let me go along for the ride—and what a ride it was!

From the minute we all packed into Willard's T-Bird for the trip to

Columbus, the jovial candidates ribbed each other. Road riding with such good company is an experience at any time, but when they're all on their toes, vying for votes, it's a riot. Believe it or not, we didn't have a single fistfight during the entire trip.

The TV narrator was so impressed that he commented, while on camera, that "a friendlier bunch of candidates I've never seen." The cameramen, too, commented that their latest edition of *Viewpoint* was one of the best they'd filmed.

After making their pitch on camera, a quick tour of WRBL's impressive facilities, and a round of handshakes, the four candidates and I loaded up and were motoring our way back home via the River Road. Somebody suggested that we stop for a Coke. Willard, taking the cue, pulled in rather abruptly into a filling station at Fort Mitchell. One by one, we filed into the station.

"What's this, a hold-up?" a lady behind the cash register asked rather nervously. "No, lady," I replied, "These are Eufaula's four candidates for mayor!" And Mayor Edwards added, "And he's the editor of our paper!"

Mrs. Louise Calhoun, the wife of the station's owner, looked mighty relieved when we all headed for the drink box and started opening up Cokes. "Well, I'm scared of men dressed up with ties on," she admitted. "You just can't tell about strangers these days."

As we pulled back into town, we parked in front of the Bluff City Inn and asked a newspaper boy to run into the poolroom and tell William Head to look out front.

Of course, a short time later each candidate "put on his gloves" again and the political fight was back on that night at the rally. By now they've probably congratulated each other and are once more drinking coffee together and swapping tales about the campaign.

Emmett Keeps His Pliers Handy

April 1, 1963

If Emmett Jones never got to be a Boy Scout, he should have been. Boy Scouts believe in being prepared, and so does this genial service station operator.

He always carries a pair of pliers in his left hip pocket and is always ready to fix anything. You might see him at a Mardi Gras dance or some other dress-up occasion, but chances are good that Emmett's got those pliers sticking out of his back pocket. "Suppose I wuz sitting in church and the organ broke down," Emmett tells folks who kid him about his pliers.

All sorts of characters gather at his place on the corner of Broad and Orange. Young high school boys get a bang out of "Mr. Emmett" and his capers. And so do lots of men around town.

They come by to buy a little gas or for a grease job, but mostly they drop in to rib Emmett. He's real ticklish and he gets up in the air when some joker gooses him. Take the time he was stooped over greasing a car when some character slipped up behind him and tickled him under the arms. He threw up his hands and squirted oil across the side of the station. And when he pinches his hands with a tool, he's liable to sling it through the air. One youngster recalls several incidents when he threw a tire tool on top of the icehouse down the street because he pinched his hand changing a tire.

Emmett hates cold weather worse than the Yankee snow birds do. He gives Yankee tourists heading for Florida a hard time—maybe it's because he envies 'em. Anyhow, his answers to some of the Northern travelers' questions are priceless.

Take the time two female Yankee tourists pulled their car up to his station and wanted to know what the town was celebrating. It was Friday afternoon, and the high school band was parading up and down Broad Street to whoop up enthusiasm for a big home football game that night. "Ladies, we've just had one lynching and we're celebrating that. Then later on this afternoon we're gonna have another one," Emmett, with a straight face, explained.

And Sammy Mann, who worked off and on at Emmett's station since he was fifteen-years-old, recalls the time when he sold some citrons for watermelons to some Yankee passers-by.

Emmett calls Sammy "Cabbage Head," because he says that if you would pull all the leaves off his "cabbage head" you'd wind up with nothing. His nickname for Sammy's younger brother, Billy, is "Zero," and he calls Little Al Molnar "Zero Minus."

Although Emmett's well known as a practical joker, he has a serious side, too. While he's done such things as give a snake bite kit to a fellow who was "snake bitten" and a pair of false teeth to a kid one Christmas, he's given some good fatherly advice to more than one fellow who'd gotten into a jam and was having trouble at home.

Emmett has about the greenest thumb in town. His garden each summer produces some of the finest vegetables around, and Emmett's always giving somebody some corn or a mess of turnip greens. Take the other day, for instance. He had just chugged up to Dutch Town in his ole fishin' car to pull some tender ears of corn for his friend, Dr. Ed Comer.

Carrying an armload of corn, he walked into the wrong house on the hill and blared, "Guess what I've brought you?" To his surprise he was in the wrong house, but he grinned, sheepishly, and handed the folks the corn.

MEN'S COFFEE CLUB DOESN'T WALLOW IN GRIEF

November 24, 1991

The Ten O'Clock Coffee Club won't be the same without Ray Blackmon. His good nature and delightful conversation made him a welcome member around that back table at the Holiday Inn. He was fun to be around.

These last two years Ray was also an inspiration. He kept driving down for coffee and he continued to play dominoes with friends at the Country Club. The good soldier that he was, he faced his terminal illness with determination and optimism. Members of the coffee crowd scheduled times to drive him to a Columbus hospital for treatments.

His friends who gather religiously to drink coffee and to chat each weekday morning provided moral support. There are few long faces around the table when those long-time friends congregate. Like male counterparts of those Steel Magnolias, they are supportive when illness or death or tragedy strikes one of the crowd. Sometimes they show their support in rather peculiar ways, but they're supportive.

They don't wallow in grief nor do they condone self-pity. They do keep on keeping on as members of long standing depart. They do celebrate and remember their departed friends, from time to time.

The play *Steel Magnolias* which the Eufaula Little Theatre now has in the casting stage, warmly captures the struggles of Southern women as they meet time after time in Truvy's beauty shop. If I were a playwright, I would peck out on my typewriter a wonderful script about Southern men, like those in that coffee club.

One central, thinly-veiled character would bear a striking resemblance to our departed friend Ray. He would be lovable, yet tough as steel. He would handle life's disappointments and joys with equal aplomb. He would do some really great things to lift some in the community who had fallen. He would be the most loyal and supportive, non-judgmental friend imaginable.

True, we won't sing many sad songs for Ray Blackmon at the Ten O'Clock Coffee Club, but you can bet his presence will be missed.

He's still alive in the hearts and minds of that congenial group of friends who gather with the punctuality of a non-chartered civic club. With wit and fondness, we'll talk about him from time to time: Just as we do about Ross, Dad Grubb, Sam and Yates, among others.

We won't dwell on what a great friend and a great American Ray really was. If we all could play instruments like Dooley used to play the trombone in the Three Notch Symphonic Band, we'd probably strike up a tribute a little akin to a New Orleans jazz dirge.

Make no mistake, nobody in that aging crowd was more beloved or appreciated than Ray Blackmon. The coffee crowd just handles life's struggles and disappointments in anything but a melodramatic way.

Still, years from now we'll all miss him. He'll live in our hearts and minds.

TRULY ONE OF THE TALLEST TREES
IN THE FOREST FELL

April 28, 1983

Eufaula said goodbye last week to one of the greatest ladies ever to live in the Bluff City of the Chattahoochee. Truly, one of the tallest trees in the forest fell when "Miss Caro" Clayton died Monday, April 18.

The beloved centenarian was born Caroline Elizabeth Copeland on May 23, 1882, in the house on the northeast corner of Broad and Sanford. She was as much a part of Old Eufaula as the few century-old Monarch Oaks that still stand in that historic neighborhood, scarred somewhat by the ravages of time but grand just the same.

It has been said an oak spends fifty years of its long life growing and fifty years dying. This was no parallel to "Miss Caro's" long and fruitful life. She was the town's historian, often writing articles for the *Tribune* or providing historical perspective. She was a walking encyclopedia when it came to Old Eufaula. Miss Caro was a prolific letter writer, and until the last two years of her remarkable life she averaged three letters a day.

Whenever visitors came to town seeking missing links to their family genealogy, they usually made a beeline to Miss Caro's house on Cherry Street or later to her room at the Eufaula Geriatric Center.

But Miss Caro was much more than Eufaula's link with history—much of which she experienced during her long lifetime. She was an exemplary Christian lady who loved Eufaula and its people. She often welcomed newcomers to town by baking them loaves of delicious bread. Whenever any of her friends' families had an emergency of any kind she often sent them two loaves of bread, her son Preston Clayton, the distinguished attorney and former State Supreme Court justice, recalls.

Until she decided it was time for her to close up her home and move to the Geriatric Center only a couple of years ago, she cooked lunch for her two sons, Preston and Lee Clayton, a former postmaster. As a bachelor, it was my good fortune to be her friend and put my feet under Miss Caro's table with her boys. Rocking on the front porch after a hearty dinner at midday and enjoying the company of the Claytons was memorable. And so was my twenty-five-year association with Miss Caro. That bright, gracious lady, while appreciative of Eufaula's rich heritage, didn't live in the past. She was vibrant and attuned to current happenings.

Well do I recall a much appreciated telephone call from her at a time when the editor's office was almost under siege. To my astonishment, Miss Caro was aware of the community problem involving our youth and drugs.

Perhaps I should have known Miss Caro knew more about young people than I would ever learn from rearing three sons. She was the mother of five children, and the Clayton house was always a child's paradise where all the neighborhood children felt at home.

Her home and her church were close to her. Baptized in St. James's Episcopal Church when only a few months old, she faithfully attended services there until her death. Last year the church presented a little brass plaque in honor of her one-hundredth birthday. It was simply engraved: "In Love and Thanksgiving, Caro C. Clayton, for 100 years of service to St. James Episcopal Church."

She was close to her father, Dr. William Preston Copeland, who was also a native Eufaulian. Her mother was Mary Fontaine Flewellen, daughter of Col. Williams T. Flewellen, solicitor general of the Pataula Circuit in neighboring Georgia.

She read *Gray's Anatomy* from cover to cover, and on one occasion when an emergency operation on one of the blacks at a country farm house was necessary, young Caro gave the chloroform while her father performed the operation in the light of a kerosene lantern.

As a vivacious young lady, she was sponsor of the Eufaula Military Co. which was Company G of the Second Regiment of Alabama Militia, and when she married on June 4, 1902, the company gave her as a wedding present a replica of three stacked rifles with bayonets attached with a clock in the shape of a drum.

Miss Caro, by popular vote, was chosen to reign over Eufaula's Sesquicentennial festivities in 1973. What a grand sight it was—Miss Caro, with an old fashioned parasol in her hand, riding in an antique carriage down Broad Street.

Miss Caro was a warm, witty and wonderful queen, and devoted Eufaulians were her willing subjects.

Truly, one of the tallest trees in the forest fell when Mrs. Lee Johnston Clayton died.

WE'LL WATCH CEDAR PLANTED IN LEE'S HONOR GROW

March 6, 1997

The Bluff City's heart is as big as beautiful, boundless Lake Eufaula. I've known that for some time, but the outpouring of people attending the special service and dedication in memory of "Little Lee" Clayton gladdened my heart.

We live in a town where we take time to bury the dead with reverence and respect. Eufaulians know how to rally and support such simple things as planting a cedar tree in memory of a little boy who died tragically on March 5, 1951.

As I listened to remarks by Little Lee's childhood friend, Justice Gorman Houston, my mind gave flight to fantasy: I wondered what kind of man Lee Johnston Clayton III would be had he enjoyed the normal life expectancy. Having Clayton blood in his veins, he could very well have been a U.S. senator, a general or the president of the University of Alabama.

Looking at the picture of the All-American little boy in the memorial program, I wondered how in the world could his loving family and the town have sustained such a loss. No wonder his father's face seldom broke into smiles.

Justice Houston agreed to speak at the dedication with the realization "that it is in our Christian mysteries, that we can rejoice and mourn at the same time for the same reason."

Quoting John Greenleaf Whittier, the Alabama Supreme Court Justice said: "Love can never lose its own."

"The death of children has been a philosophical and theological problem through the ages. In an attempt to explain the why of it, Meander in the third century B.C. wrote: "Whom the gods love die young.""

"In the book of Wisdom found in the Apocrypha, this is written of the death of a child: 'He, being made perfect in a short time, fulfilled a long time; for his soul pleased the Lord: therefore, hastened he to take him away from the world.'"

Justice Houston recalled the sad time in Eufaula forty-six years ago when Lee Clayton III died.

"Our town was shaken. There had been a fire, a disastrous fire that had caused serious personal injury and great destruction.

"I slept facing east and downtown, and I woke during the night thinking that a cruel dawn was breaking, until I realized that a huge fire was raging. From the charred remains of the fire some dynamite was obtained, and as if the Ides of March came early that year, this was the instrument of Little Lee's death and another young boy's injury."

On personal reflection, he recalled standing on a ladder stocking shoes at Jay's Department Store (now Watson's) when he heard that some boys had been injured or killed in an explosion in the Cherry Street alley behind his home.

"I froze. I literally could not move for a period of time, for I feared I knew who the boys were."

For years after Lee's death, when he heard *The Littlest Angel* read, Justice Houston says he pictured Lee as the littlest angel, with his "box of things that a boy would collect."

Russell Irby and Bill Grubb, two more of Lee's friends, dedicated benches placed in the parkway on the crest of College Hill. Robert Owen, another of Lee's friends who experienced the tragedy, stood quietly on the hilltop during the dedication. Today, this is a peaceful spot to sit and enjoy the lovely streetscape below.

And as Justice Houston says, we will all watch the native cedar grow that Margaret Lee Russell planted in memory of her brother.

Little Lee, "Eufaula's Eternal Little Boy," is remembered today by his childhood friends who have made their mark. Other Eufaulians who never knew him know of his spirit and climbing that tall cedar in front of Kendall Manor to touch a lighted star to win the approval of his friends, Bill and Russell.

EUFAULA'S GREATNESS FOUND IN HER PEOPLE

June 8, 1972

Eufaula's greatness does not lie in its past, as glorious as it was. The Bluff City is one of the greatest little cities anywhere not because of its spectacular antebellum homes built by the prosperous planters and rich merchants during the golden plantation era. True, Lake Eufaula and the fabulous Chattahoochee Waterway are tremendous assets to the community.

But the thing that really makes Eufaula great is its people—its present citizens. Many great individuals before us have helped build the firm foundation upon which we stand, but it's the caliber of the average Eufaulian that is the key factor in making Eufaula the proud and outstanding community it is today.

Eufaulians love their hometown, they love each other, but they also by their very nature are outspoken—sometimes almost to a fault. Now, they may put up with a little too much back-scratching, some corruption from time to time, and sometimes it looks like the citizenry is just not interested in good government, improving economic conditions or in moving the community forward.

But then stouthearted individuals don't mind speaking out. In short, they "tell it like it is," to quote the young folks. While this approach is sometimes tough on politicians, a preacher every now and then and even the local press, it is quite refreshing and it is part of the reason for Eufaula's greatness.

Eufaulians generally don't like to play follow-the-leader as they do in so many small cities. They are self-confident, they have faith in their own ability and in their community generally.

Yes, it's people who make the difference in Eufaula. We have more fine people per square block than any little city anywhere. True, many of our people are real individuals, characters, if I may say so. But this is what gives individuality to Eufaula. This is part of our town's make-up, our character.

I believe we have more real individuals than any small place around. When I say individuals, I mean people who are their own man or woman, their own selves.

Such great individuals as Jan Lee, Mary Foy, Fonnie Strang, Mildred Houston, Lib Logue, Lois Mooty and countless other gracious and lovely Eufaula ladies add real character to Eufaula. Such dependable men as Bill Long, Yank Dean, Sam LeMaistre, Bill Roberts, Dick Boyette, Earl Laing, Billy Moorer, Donald Comer III, Gene Parker, Jimmy Clark, Waters Paul, Gaston Hester, Joe Neal Blair, Fred Bachman and Lawton Riley give real stature to Eufaula.

Of course, the list could go on and on. And there are many, many outstanding young people who do more than their share to make Eufaula great. Gals such as Mary Gray, Martha Houston, Jane Boyette, Toni Houston, Jacque Chapman, Sherry Harrison, Eleanor Hinton, Ann Mitchell, Janice Smith, Becky Graddy, Anna Neville and many, many others also give real character, real substance to Eufaula. They also give freely of their time, whether it's working for the Pilgrimage, singing for civic groups or teaching Sunday school.

Yes, Eufaula people stack up against the best. They're first class, and that's why the Bluff City is a first-class community.

If we published all the great Eufaulians we know personally, it would fill up the *Trib*. I'd have to include such great individuals as my aunts, Babe and Sally Smith, Sis Perry, Mary Wallace Martin, Mrs. Louise Petry, Elizabeth Upshaw, Archie Grubb, Lois Little, John Hagood, Robert Motley, Mac Reeves, Mrs. Caro Clayton, Hazel Mann, Dan Parker and Neal Logue.

No, the greatness of Eufaula does not rest in its past. True, the city's built on a very firm foundation and has a goodly heritage, but it's the present people, the people of today, who make Eufaula great.

WORLD NEEDS MORE SALLY SMITHS

January 16, 1986

A n unheralded Eufaula lady, who has meant so much to countless Eufaulians, observed a quiet, yet milestone birthday Wednesday, Jan. 15. Miss Sally Smith, a retired school teacher and my devoted aunt, is so publicity shy the *Tribune* didn't even make her picture when she retired from the classroom in 1968.

Miss Sally, as her former pupils call her, is a most unusual person. Not only was she an exemplary teacher, thoroughly teaching her young charges the basics as well as instilling morals and principles in their lives, but she has been a remarkable aunt to her brother Abb's five sons and a daughter.

Sally, who has the same birthday as Martin Luther King, readily accepted the challenge when the Eufaula city schools became the first to be integrated in Alabama. She worked hard—in the classroom and at home —to teach her black pupils in the second grade. Many of them were far behind in their academic progress. She was excited at how fast many of them learned during a special remedial class she taught one summer. She was a splendid choice for this challenging task because during her long career she never got away from stressing the basics.

When modern principals urged their teachers to quit wasting time with phonics, she kept right on being old-fashioned and taught her young charges to read by learning the usual sounds of certain letters.

The "Johnnies" in her room could read by golly—and they could spell and work math problems, too.

Sally Smith was well suited to be a teacher. When she graduated from the little high school in Coffee Springs with distinction, the principal of her school had her unusually bright class stand the State Teachers Examination. As a young girl she was soon teaching in the Geneva County schools, before earning a degree years later at Troy State Teacher's College.

When she was only seventeen, her professor at Troy "guaranteed" her qualifications, and she accepted a job in Eufaula teaching under the supervision of Professor Thomas Wilkinson, an educator whose high ideals and dedication to education she shared. After teaching since 1926, she retired in 1968.

A fantastic teacher, she has also been an aunt without equal. A real taskmaster, nonetheless, she knows what real love is all about. She has generously shared her life with my brothers and my sister and me. She and her sister Lydia, who is recuperating from a heart attack, complicated by heart failure, made a wonderful home for my younger brother, Douglas, and sister, Sarah, after our lovely mother died when Doug was six months old.

Their antique-furnished home has also been family headquarters for my other brothers and me. She has been a powerful influence on the lives of her niece and five nephews, all of whom it can be said enjoy an uncommon degree of success.

Sally Pierce Smith, a descendant of Pierce Butler, who signed the Constitution, has many sterling qualities. She has generously shared her life, her brilliant mind, her sense of humor and her love with countless fortunate children, including the five Smith boys and their sister Sarah. She has touched our lives and the lives of her former pupils in such a way we can never repay our debt of gratitude.

What the world needs now is more "Aunt Sallys."

'White Russian' gave Eufaula color

April 10, 1986

Old timers here often bemoan the loss of the town's characters. Some contend Old Eufaula has lost some of its personality due to the loss of numerous, delightful individuals who simply die of old age.

The Bluff City recently lost a charming gentleman, Ben Blinov, who gave color and character to our town. A White Russian, who immigrated to America in 1926, Veniamin Dmitri Blinov added a dimension to Eufaula's diverse, ethnic background.

He was one of the best read members of my coffee club, who managed to be jolly and congenial, even when he faced adversity. Distinguished looking, he often wore a Greek-style fishing cap and he used a cane after having a leg amputated.

His many hobbies included extensive reading in Russian and Soviet culture, economics and trade, and keeping up with national and world affairs. During his retirement years he has especially enjoyed listening to classical music, writing poetry, singing songs of Old Russia, and he loved good, spirited conversation. Football, turkey hunting and the usual coffee table conversation interested him, but he loved to tell the latest jokes on the Red hierarchy, which he read regularly in his White Russian newspaper.

Mr. Blinov came from Slavic people, who lived in the ancient walled city of Novgorod. Family legend, heard from his babushka, or grandmother, is that the name Blinov is derived from blini, a holy pancake made in the shape of the sun. The Blinovs were blessed by the local priest, and in every generation of Ben's family there have been priests. He was descended on his mother's side from Volga Germans, who came to Russia with Catherine II, wife of Peter the Great. The descendants were the landed gentry and lesser nobility, and they became known as White Russians, who fought for the Tsar and later the legally elected Duma.

His parents died of typhus fever during the Revolution. The local Bolshevik government turned the family estate into a collective farm, but allowed Ben, his sister and her two children to leave Russia. They crossed Siberia during the summer of 1922 in a freight train, arriving in Harbin, Manchuria. After a short stay at an orphanage, he was taken in by Methodist missionaries who were responsible for him coming to America on a scholarship to Emory University.

Some of Ben's fondest memories were of his association with Dr. Dewey and the Emory Glee Club. He sometimes sang for his supper, and did such interesting things as tree surgery and turning cadavers in the medical school to support his studies.

Mr. Blinov met Mary Lou Methvin of Eufaula, while they were students at the Atlanta Conservatory of Music, and they married in 1955. At one time they moved with their children, Natasha, Jimmy and Tanya to a small cattle farm at the foot of the Blue Ridge Mountains of Virginia. During his farming years, he earned his B.S. degree from Lynchburg College and he did graduate work at The University of Virginia, where he translated Russian and did research in Soviet trade.

In 1959, he and Mary Lou and their children moved to Eufaula where they bought and managed the Roberts Dress Shop. They retired in the early 1970s.

Listed in the *Who's Who in the South and Southwest*, Ben Blinov was a man of many talents with impressive credentials. This interesting, scholarly Eufaulian, who was born in 1909 in Kazan, Russia, added color and depth to his adopted hometown. He will be missed.

EUFAULA HONORS HER GRACIOUS LADIES

September 20, 1973

The Bluff City has many attributes that put our lovely little city into a class of its own. Not the least of these exemplary traits is our unusually large number of gracious, hospitable ladies.

During one of those first Pilgrimages, a general's wife, who was afforded

Eufaula's gala celebration of its Sesquicentennial in 1973 included a court of eight ladies who had to be at least 75-years-old to be chosen. Attending a media luncheon honoring the court were, left to right, Louise Foy Petry, Sesquicentennial queen Caroline Copeland Clayton and Bertha Moore Merrill.

VIP treatment, observed how younger Eufaulians respect and pay unusually close attention to their elders. How true this is. No other small town I've ever known has the rapport between the younger generation and our older citizens. Our younger men and women admire our beloved senior citizens, and the feeling is mutual.

Certainly Eufaula has more gracious ladies per capita than any city in America. It was fitting the Sesquicentennial Steering Committee chose to honor the seventy-plus set by naming a queen and court from their ranks.

This group of gracious ladies was presented to the press Wednesday, officially kicking off a series of Sesquicentennial events. I've always marveled at our lively elderly ladies, but yesterday they came through with flying colors. The going was a little tough.

The day before, a member of this select court of honor had died. Charming, friendly Mrs. Montine Comer was sorely missed, but her close friends of long standing met the challenge.

"This is part of life," one member of the honor court remarked when asked if she wished to attend the press day and luncheon. They simply felt this was an official function, something they owed their beloved Eufaula, and since it was too late to postpone, too late to notify the invited out of town press, then it was their duty to shore up and meet their responsibilities.

Not only did each of them meet the press but they were gracious and even witty. They showed once again something of the strong fiber that characterizes their generation of Eufaulians.

Beloved "Miss Caro" Clayton, the queen, was her usual charming self. Typically, she had baked some small cakes for the morning coffee at Shorter Mansion. Miss Caro has lived all but two years of her ninety-plus years in Eufaula. Eufaula's unofficial historian, Mrs. Clayton says, "My father, Dr. William Preston Copeland, imparted to me many historical facts and I try to keep these facts alive within the minds of the younger generations."

Lively Mrs. Louise Sparks Flewellen, age eighty-seven, also has a sense of history. Each year, she opens her antebellum home, which she once shared with her brother, Gov. Chauncey Sparks, during the Pilgrimage.

Mrs. Mary Ross Foy, who has lived her lifetime in Eufaula, keeps on the go, too. The mother-in-law of Adm. Thomas H. Moorer visits Tom and Carrie frequently in Washington and keeps scrapbooks on her illustrious son-in-law and daughter. Eighty-five years young, her grandfather, Dr. Hamilton Weedon, first came to Eufaula during the War Between the States to help care for the wounded soldiers.

When the youthful Chamber secretary, newcomer Jo Ann Reifenberg, was informed Mrs. Marie Holleman Kendall was on the golf course, she exclaimed to someone in the office, "Oh, I've made an awful mistake!" She hadn't. Mrs. Kendall briefed the press on her latest tournament victory and confided at sevety-six she also won an award for being the oldest golfer in the tournament.

The press was also told Mrs. Janet McDowell Lee, eighty-six, is a lifelong Eufaulian. And would you have guessed, she says "church and people" are her special interest. Indeed, Miss Jan loves people, and people love her in return. Mrs. Bertha Moore Merrill, age seventy-seven, was overheard explaining to a visiting reporter that she was one of the younger ladies in the court. Her interests include "reading, music, people, driving, making scrapbooks and working in the RSVP program." She also loved to tell that she made her debut in Atlanta.

Then pretty, talkative "Miss Louise" Foy Petry is another lifetime Eufaulian. At eighty-two, she enjoys visiting with members of her family and keeping up with her former pupils whom she taught for thirty years in the first grade.

Forbes features Elton B. Stephens's success story

July 4, 1993

Barbour County has been touted as the home of governors, but Imperial Barbour has also produced outstanding businessmen. Gov. William D. Jelks founded Protective Life Insurance, and Gov. B.

B. Comer purchased controlling interest in Birmingham's City National Bank and became its president and established Avondale Mills. Elton B. Stephens, who was born in Clio, founded EBSCO Industries, which has $650 million in sales.

Alabama's octogenarian magazine salesman-turned-banker is subject of an article in the May edition of *Forbes* magazine. "If age is a state of mind, eighty-one-year-old Elton B. Stephens is perhaps approaching fifty," writes Brigid McMenanmin. "Eleven years ago Stephens was just hitting his stride. He had built up a successful family owned company called EBSCO Industries, Inc., which sold an odd mixture of magazine subscriptions, fishing lures, carpets and pool tables. But he was still feeling spry and wanted to try something new. So Stephens, who had turned EBSCO over to his eldest son, went into banking."

The Barbour native, who was almost born selling, says bankers have a tendency to sit on their "you-know-whats." So, he taught bankers a thing or two since buying Citizens Bank in Leeds for two million dollars. He opened the bank on Saturday mornings, served coffee and made the officers leave their desks and call on potential customers.

The bank now has $46 million in assets, and Stephens has bought other banks and formed Alabama Bancorp. He organized Highland Bank in Birmingham with assets of nearly $70 million. Now, Alabama Bancorp is in seven locations with $165 million in assets and earned $1.6 million last year for a sixteen percent return on equity.

Stephens says his enthusiasm for selling is responsible for his success, along with routinely ignoring his wife Alys's advice not to diversify beyond magazines. "Behind every successful man," Stephens quips, "is a woman telling him he can't do it."

Just the same, he and his lovely wife have been great partners ever since they met as students at Birmingham-Southern College.

During the Depression, money was scarce when Stephens went off to college with few clothes and $125. He milked six cows and bottled and sold the milk before school when he was a lad in Clio. He sold newspapers, suits, sandwiches and Cloverleaf Salve. He also raked leaves and shined shoes to save for college. His father was a highly respected banker who, legend has it, paid all his depositors who lost their money when the bank went broke. In Birmingham he worked forty hours a week selling socks and shirts at a dry goods store. He sold subscriptions to Butterick's Delineator magazine. In 1930, he and five friends hitchhiked to Michigan to sell subscriptions door-to-door. He also hired students George Wallace and Charlie Weston from Barbour County.

After graduation from Southern, he earned a law degree from Alabama. He said "no" to a lawyer's sevety-five dollars a month salary and earned ten times that amount selling magazines. With a franchise from Keystone Readers Service as middleman, he managed thirty-nine salesmen selling twenty magazines such as *Saturday Evening Post* and *Ladies Home Journal* in the Southeast. In 1943, he formed EBSCO with $5,000, selling pool tables and personalized stationery at military bases.

In 1964, while Wallace was governor, he ran the only warehouse distributing textbooks to the public schools. Publishers still pay him a cut of the twelve million dollars worth of books the state orders every year.

Jane Stephens Comer, Elton's business and arts-minded daughter, married Donald Comer III, who managed Cowikee Mills while they were newlyweds. In Birmingham, some called their marriage a merger, but in Eufaula we knew it was one of the best things to happen to Eufaula as we struggled to move our town forward.

Jane was responsible for moving the Wellborn House to the bluff and restoring the first Greek Revival mansion built here to house the Eufaula Arts Council, which she helped found. Donald made his civic contributions, too, rescuing The Tavern and restoring it as a showplace.

In the meantime, Elton Stephens didn't forget tiny Clio, pop. seven hundred. He contributed heavily to the restoration of the Barbour County School building where he and Wallace were classmates. He also funded the Elton B. Stephens Library, which operates inside the well maintained George C. Wallace Museum and auditorium.

Today, Stephens is one of Birmingham-Southern's most generous benefactors, having funded a science wing and a conference center. He is also one of the Magic City's greatest philanthropists. The Elton B. Stephens Expressway honors his contributions.

Eufaula's 'Top Ten Characters' named

December 18, 1968

This time of year newspapers and magazines are full of articles listing the ten best this or the ten worst that. The Ten Best Dressed Women, the Ten Most Admired Men and even the Ten Worst Actors are selected and publicized.

While we noted with interest Barbour Countian George C. Wallace made the Gallup Poll's Ten Most Admired list, some of the other top ten lists are more amusing than newsworthy.

As a spoof on this practice of the national news media, the "Fishwrapper" staff started choosing Eufaula's Ten Best Dressed Men, but it soon got to be serious business, and last year we dropped it. It made amusing copy for this column back when only a few men about town wore ties to work.

As a substitute for the Ten Best Dressed list, I've stuck tongue in cheek and whipped up a list of Eufaula's Ten Biggest Sports or Ten Biggest Characters—take your pick for a title. They appear, not necessarily in the order of their selection:

Archie Grubb	Ben Blinov	Bill Jackson
N. G. Barron	Tom Posey	Edward Comer
Dick Williams Sr.	A. M. Rudderman	Bobby Lockwood
Glenn Griffin		

Perhaps the one thing these colorful individuals, with their own unique personalities, have in common is the fact they are all generally well liked and are an addition to any gathering. But there the similarity ends.

Archie Grubb, known to the Holiday Inn coffee drinkers as "Dad," has one of the keener senses of humor. He likes jawing with his partner, Sam LeMaistre, and making jokes about politicians. "Dad" has one of the keenest legal minds in town and enjoys local politics.

Blinov, the White Russian, is without a doubt one of the most colorful individuals in the Bluff City. He gets his clever jokes out of a White Russian newspaper—which I'm sure he gives liberal translation—and he loves to sing. Only in Eufaula do you find a Ben (Vin) Blinov.

Called "General Jackson" by his friends, Bill is one of the gentlemen who perks up the conversation at the Country Club or the poolroom domino games. He's done everything and been everywhere—from serving in the foreign legion to acting on stage and designing championship golf courses.

The Rev. Mr. N. G. Barron—initials really do not stand for No Good—is a man who is hard to back into a corner. His conversation, when not from the pulpit, is full of wit and sprinkled liberally with puns. He's at his best during the Rotary Club fellowship hour when he swaps barbs with Dooley Cole, another great local character.

Posey would make anybody's list of Eufaula characters. This genial grocery man has a word for everyone shopping at A&P. "Isn't it a lovely day?" is his favorite greeting, whether the sun's shining or storm warnings are up.

One of the brightest medicine men, Dr. Comer can charm the birds right out of the trees. He quotes poetry and is a master of the English language—as well as another tongue or two. The tale is told he lost an entire portable hospital during his military travels in Europe during the war. A scholar and Southern gentleman, he nevertheless, is one of the town's delightful characters.

Dick Williams is known to his golfing buddies as "Big Coon." He is also chairman of the Country Club's "Y'all Committee."

Ruddy is perhaps the town's number one character. Cigar-puffin' Ruddy steps high and gets things done when he has a civic duty to perform. He can collect more money for crippled children than anybody around. People like his jokes and his jawing.

Lockwood, alias Lock, is one of the more delightful personalities around. He's one of the younger characters with a tremendous sense of humor and a pretty good repertoire of gestures he uses to entertain with when he converses on everything from Auburn football to the Atomic Energy Commission and Alabama Power Company operations.

Dr. Griffin, the vet, is known far and wide for his professional manner. He is also a big game hunter of note and a big fisherman. Ask Son Hasty about the duck-hunting story when Dr. Griffin misread the depth of the lake—his paddle touched the top of a submerged stump—and he stepped into deep water over his head. Better still, ask Glenn. He's good company. Some others who should at least make the second list include: Murray Greer, Sam Robinson, Ben Reeves, T. C. Cole, Charlie Archibald, Hizhonor Hamp Graves, Tom Culpepper, Jule Schaub, George M. Mangum and Bob Methvin.

HERE'S LIST OF COUNTY'S
20 GREAT LEADERS OF CENTURY

January 9, 2000

Why have Eufaula and Barbour County—a small town in a small county—produced so many leaders?

We believe it was because this was Alabama's last frontier and that the settlers moving into the Indian village Eufaula and the area enjoyed a degree of prosperity. They farmed the rich soil in Virginia, the Carolinas, and Georgia until the fertility wore out. When they moved here, to the fertile Chattahoochee basin, many already had a stake. Those pioneer leaders were sometimes well educated, too.

The number of outstanding leaders in the first half of the twentieth century multiplied from the 1820s' survivors who built a prosperous plantation region. We're fascinated with the unusually large number of leaders, both local, state and national, who called Barbour County home.

Many of these could have made the cut when Alistair Cooke wrote his new book, *Memories of the Great & Good.* They were public men, for the most part, some linking the Lower Chattahoochee Basin of the Civil War with the nuclear age. Some were sons of Confederate officers. The following are twenty of our greatest leaders from the twentieth century:

Gov. WILLIAM DORSEY JELKS (1901–1907) began a new century providing leadership, becoming the second governor from Barbour, after John Gill Shorter (1861–1863) who served during the Civil War. In June of 1901, after only six months in office, Gov. Samford died and Jelks, as president of the Alabama Senate, became governor. The Old Confederate captains respected him, and he ran for office himself in 1902. He was largely responsible for a five-month minimum school term and created a textbook commission. Child labor legislation also passed in his term.

BRAXTON BRAGG COMER succeeded Gov. Jelks (1907–1911), the "storm that followed the calm," after his fellow Barbour countian. He was a man of "vision, compassion, courage and integrity." His political achievements were great and his business enterprises were colossal. The Comer family moved from Virginia to Georgia in the early nineteenth century, then to Barbour County, where Gov. Comer's father established a large plantation and lumber business. Born in Barbour County in 1848, Comer enrolled at the University of Alabama during the last year of the Civil War. His many contributions were perhaps topped by his contributions to the education system. After his term, he was appointed to succeed Sen. J. H. Bankhead.

LT. GOV. CHARLES S. MCDOWELL was elected the first president of the Eufaula Country Club in 1915 and chaired the powerful Judiciary Committee in the Legislature. He led the campaign to build roads, using the slogan, "McDowell or Mud." He also spearheaded construction of the metal cantilever bridge, connecting Eufaula and Georgetown. At its dedication in 1925, the bridge was named in his honor.

ARCHIBALD M. MCDOWELL was a respected lawyer who served on the Eufaula City Council and was elected to the Alabama Senate, where he was an exemplary leader. He was Lt. Gov. Charles S. McDowell's brother.

CONGRESSMAN HENRY D. CLAYTON JR. served seven terms, resigning to accept President Woodrow Wilson's appointment as U.S. District Judge for the Middle District of Alabama. He died in 1929. He was author of the Clayton Anti-Trust Act. In 1908, he succeeded in passing a bill authorizing $50,000 to build the U.S. Post Office (1912) in Eufaula.

REV. MORTON B. WHARTON's leadership in 1907 spearheaded the fund drive to rebuild First Baptist Church after a fire. He had served as consul to Sinneburg, Switzerland, and ambassador to Saxe-Coburg in Germany. The town erected the statue at the intersection of Barbour and Randolph in his honor in 1912.

Col. George Legare Comer, who died in 1933, witnessed the burning of the University of Alabama by Gen. Croxton's federal troops during the Civil War. He was long-time mayor in Eufaula and helped organize the first cotton mill in 1888.

Gov. Chauncey Sparks served (1943–1947) during World War II and was "the guiding force behind establishment" of Alabama Medical College. He was conservative and left money in the treasury and came home to Eufaula to practice law. However, soon afterwards, he left for Germany to serve as a consultant to Gen. Lucious Clay, the military governor of U.S. occupied zone.

Lt. Col. Robert McKenzie commanded Battery D, 104th Coast Artillery (AA), Separate Battalion during World War II. The Eufaula unit was mustered into federal service Nov. 23, 1940, with a full wartime strength of 154 eventually. Proud citizens gave them a sendoff downtown on Feb. 18, 1941.

Congressman George Andrews, a native of Clayton, spend more than twenty-five years in Washington. He was one of the big advocates for impounding the Chattahoochee and was instrumental in Eufaula's development after it became an inland port in 1963, when industries upstaged the agricultural economy.

Adm. Thomas H. Moorer was Chairman of the U.S. Joint Chiefs of Staff during President Richard Nixon's administrations, climaxing a life-long career in the U.S. Navy and graduation from Annapolis. He was a World War II hero.

Brig. Gen. Franklin A. Hart, born in Eufaula, provided leadership for the Allies. Days before the Japanese delegation boarded the battleship USS *Missouri* on Sept. 2, 1945, to sign the formal surrender ending WWII, Hart received the Bronze Star Medal for meritorious achievement on Iwo Jima. After playing on the Auburn football team, he enlisted in the U.S. Marine Corps with inspired leadership, advancing in rank. He received the Navy Cross presented by Adm. Chester W. Nimitz "for extraordinary heroism while serving as commanding officer of a regimental team." He later became Marine commandant.

Vice Adm. Joe Park Moorer, the Joint Chief chairman's brother, also followed in his steps with a distinguished Naval career after graduating from the United States Naval Academy.

PRESTON C. CLAYTON, who served in the Alabama Senate, was defeated for re-election by youthful George C. Wallace. Gov. Gordon Persons later appointed Clayton an associate justice on the Alabama Supreme Court.

REP. SIM THOMAS served four terms in the Alabama House of Representatives and was a member of the Auburn University Board of Trustees. He chaired the State Mental Health Board.

JAMES S. CLARK has served as state senator and three terms as speaker of the Alabama House of Representatives. His leadership was largely responsible for building Lakepoint Resort State Park and four-laning U.S. 431. He has greatly influenced state government, often impacting the governor's leadership.

GOV. GEORGE C. WALLACE served an unprecedented four terms as governor of Alabama. In 1968, he formed the American Independent party, drawing fifteen percent of the electorate eventually. Historian Dan T. Carter contends: "More than any other political leader of his generation [he] was the alchemist of the new social conservatism that reshaped American politics in the 1970s and 1980s." He was Alabama's greatest politician.

LT. GOV. JERE BEASLEY made history when he qualified in the lieutenant governor's race while former Gov. George C. Wallace ran for a second term in 1970. He won in a runoff and he and Wallace became the only governor and lieutenant governor from the same hometown to serve simultaneously. He served twice.

GOV. LURLEEN BURNS WALLACE qualified to run as governor in 1966 when the Constitution prohibited Gov. Wallace from succeeding himself in office. She won without a runoff and was inaugurated Jan. 16, 1967. Her term was short-lived, and she died of cancer in May 1968. However, she became chief executive in her own right, impacting state mental health and the state parks program.

GORMAN HOUSTON JR. won three statewide elections to the Alabama Supreme Court and continues to serve (2000). He chaired the Eufaula Sesquicentennial in 1973.

Chapter 2

Eufaula's Priceless Treasures

Grandmother inspired Rev. Houston's faith

February 1, 1998

"Everything I ever needed to know about the Christian faith," says the Rev. Gorman Houston III, "I learned from my grandmother."

"Seminary was helpful, I guess, but the real basic understandings of the Christian faith I learned at an earlier age from a seasoned faith, taught and lived in wonderful consistency—the way of love, the power of Christian hope and the endurance of faith. Basic lessons like, 'love covers a multitude of sins,' like 'trust in the Lord with all your heart and lean not on your own understandings,' and 'it is more blessed to give than to receive.'"

I don't know how the articulate young minister held his composure; how he could speak such comforting words at his beloved grandmother's funeral, but he did. Mildred Vance Houston, Eufaula's lovely, gracious lady, was so modest she never sought honors, or recognition for the many good things she did for others.

As her devoted grandson says, the gathering of her family and her friends—who filled her beloved First United Methodist Church—would have embarrassed her. So many of the things she cherished most deeply were "wrapped up" in the gathering. "It ran against her modest ways." Yet, there were represented so many things she loved, as her grandson said so eloquently.

She loved her three children: Gorman Houston Jr., the respected associate justice and scholar on the Alabama Supreme Court; Celeste Houston, the retired high school counselor who helped countless high school students find their bearings; and Billy Houston, the bank president and civic leader.

Her children called her blessed. Mildred Houston was a devoted mother who reared three remarkable children following the tragic death of her husband, Gorman Houston. She was "a living sermon," living an exemplary life without resorting to theatrics or orations.

Her husband, who acquired the nickname of "Demop" when a student at the University because he was an avid football fan who followed the highly successful Demopolis High School team, was the life of the party. And Mildred was the gracious hostess. Her beautiful home was the scene of holiday parties and social gatherings, including the Symposium Club and the Christ Child Circle, not to mention countless church circle meetings.

She was also one of Eufaula's most marvelous cooks. Her caramel cakes and oyster dip were superb.

The daughter of Ernest Word and Lucia Edwards Vance was one of the Bluff City's kindest, most generous ladies. She was a stalwart, life-long member of First United Methodist Church. She sat on the fourth pew with members of her family every Sunday, until a relentless illness sidelined her. Though small in frame, this lovely lady fought to survive—not selfishly but to serve others.

The youths at the former Eufaula Adolescent Center perhaps never knew it, but for many years she collected gifts and money for the troubled youngsters who didn't have homes to go to for the holidays. She carefully shopped for Christmas gifts they could use, knowing somebody out there loved them.

Mildred Houston loved the less fortunate just as she loved her affluent friends. This little lady couldn't saw or hammer but she helped repair places for poor families to live. She assisted the local Habitat for Humanity in its noble work. She was a long-time active member of RSVP.

Mildred Vance Houston was one of our town's finest ladies: She was a role model for her church and community, as well as her grandson, the minister, and all her family and many friends.

We are blessed for having known her.

James D. Murphy's heart was
as big as his shoes

March 5, 2000

American industry lost a giant, and Eufaula lost one of the best friends our town ever had in the death of Jim Murphy.

In this day when the company CEO often lives out of town and unexpected mergers or buy-outs appear to happen over night, I look back and recall some of the many things James D. Murphy, giant of the metal buildings industry, did for our town and Alabama.

My bride and I were living in one of "Dad" Grubbs's new apartments on Malone Alley (renamed Circle) when in 1967 the "Lee Iacocca of the metal building business" and a group of investors purchased fledgling American Buildings Company. Some of those investors and company officials temporarily lived in an apartment in the same complex.

This was a turning point not only in the *Eufaula Tribune's* operations, but in the town's future and my personal fortune as well. American Buildings personified my hopes for a bright future for Eufaula and my dreams of the town's revitalization after sleeping pleasantly the previous twenty-five years. Yes, the town's success with locating American Buildings in the new State Docks Industrial Park was a dream come true.

The likable chief honcho in my coffee club chuckled when the crowd at the Broad Street Café first talked about plans for a new industrial park in Old Eufaula. "You mean," he'd say, "they're going to tell a new industry they will have to locate in the industrial park?"

Why, they could have put a plant anywhere they pleased.

American Buildings' moving to town from Columbus was a turning point indeed. I have a mental picture of dapper Willard Joy, who founded the company in 1947, stepping out of his Rolls Royce at Eufaula's new Holiday Inn. But the company had unknowingly (to industry hungry Eufaula) fallen on hard times. Enter Jim Murphy, the entrepreneur. Things turned around dramatically for American Buildings—and the Bluff City of the Chattahoochee.

Murphy didn't drive a Rolls Royce, but he did later buy a restored vintage Bentley and sometimes drove it just for fun.

He was a gregarious, big man who filled big shoes in his adopted hometown. The day he and his charming, vivacious wife Maria, a native of Puerto Rico, moved to town was a red letter day. She became the Eufaula Art Association "president for life."

The town's aristocrats were somewhat taken aback when Jim erected steel beams for his huge house on St. Francis Point. Not since Kendall Manor was completed after The War had such an imposing house been built in Eufaula.

But Murphy's heart was as big as his shoes. He embraced his company and Eufaula with all of his strength. American Buildings grew and prospered. It was sold several times and bought back, making rich men out of several investors.

Jim Murphy was a friend to Eufaulians. He employed many who either lost their jobs or their businesses and needed a job. He was the mentor of many who learned how to succeed in the metal buildings industry. And all the while he was a good citizen who paid his civic rent daily.

The roof at Shorter Mansion probably would have fallen in on the Oriental rugs if he hadn't been elected president of the Eufaula Heritage Association.

When the veterans came home from Vietnam, Jim Murphy donated the handsome eagle sculpture that tops their monument on North Eufaula Avenue. During an unfortunate controversy over the placement of the monument, the editor (me) was caught in a political cross fire for taking a stand on Mayor George Little's playing politics with the monument's placement. When I came under fire, Jim Murphy quietly called me one night and offered his support to a beleaguered editor. I never felt such warm, personal support from a devoted reader during a controversy at the newspaper.

All of Eufaula has lost a wonderful friend. Jim Murphy was more than a friend to humanity—he was a visionary who loved Eufaula and lived to watch his associates and friends succeed.

The day Jim Murphy and associates bought American Buildings Company was a turning point in Eufaula's industrialization and my personal lot as well.

I shall never forget my friend James D. Murphy Jr. nor will many, many, many others.

BLONDHEIM'S PERSONA CAST IN BUILDINGS, IN OUR HEARTS

February 15, 1998

How do you say goodbye to a long-time friend like Charlie Blondheim? Eufaula's Gothic-style First Presbyterian Church was filled with people from all walks of life from throughout Alabama and many other places Tuesday, Feb. 10. They were there to comfort his family and to celebrate the life of the talented, lovable architect.

Charlie, with his mischievous smile, loved legions of people—and they loved him in return. Each person who mourns his untimely passing at age sixty-four has at least one "Charlie story" they're anxious to share. I have mine.

As his minister and friend John Boyer reminded the congregation, Charlie grew up in the post-bellum church on North Randolph that was built in 1869, fashioned after English parish churches from bricks imported from Holland. He loved the church and its historic architecture. It had a profound impact on his all-too short, but enormously productive life.

As a sometimes-devilish little boy, he attended Sunday school in the

Charlie Blondheim traded life in the big city to return to his beloved hometown to establish his architectural practice, Blondheim and Mixon. The firm's offices eventually found a home in the classic old Eufaula Post Office, which they adapted to suit their use.

church where he later became Sunday school superintendent. He received his Eagle Scout badge there in a court of honor before proud family and friends. He grew up to be one of Eufaula's outstanding young sons. He quickly found his niche, after attending Auburn for two years, transferring to Georgia Tech to study architecture and preparing for a career that would utilize his many talents and earn him national recognition, while winning him friends from every point on the compass.

The AIA in 1957 recognized Charlie was a comer: They awarded him the Langley Graduate Scholarship, opening doors to prestigious MIT, where he earned the faculty's respect and a master's degree in architecture, his first love.

It didn't take Charlie long to win recognition for his good taste and exceptional organizational ability. Although dearly loved and coached by an elocution teacher, his delightful, extroverted mother, Martha, he found it a little intimidating to speak to a room full of ladies with hats on their heads when he moved back home to practice architecture.

Charlie Blondheim was one of those native sons who jumped at the chance to move back home when the Chattahoochee River was impounded, creating magnificent Lake Eufaula. Those were golden days because Eufaulians like Charlie loved their hometown and "always wanted Eufaula to be the best it could be," as Mayor Jay Jaxon says.

I didn't worry about the young lawyers like Gorman, Ben, Albert and Bill nor Charlie's classmate, Dick, who left a big city firm to set up an accounting practice here. However, as excited as I was about Eufaula's future prospects, I was concerned like some others that Charlie left a promising Atlanta position—where he brushed shoulders with the likes of architect John Portman—to come home.

Never mind, it wasn't long before Charlie Blondheim and his associates were designing and building monumental structures all over Alabama and several other states. He was licensed in eight states.

Barbour countians utilize numerous buildings every day designed by the Blondheim and Mixon firm. Not only did Charlie name Lakepoint, but his firm also designed the lodge and convention center. Children and adults benefit daily from educational buildings, not only in Barbour but also at Alabama, Auburn and UAB, too. The Bevill Center and the Sparks State Technical College, most Eufaula schools and several in the Barbour County system have his imprint. And so do Eufaula City Hall, Eufaula Post Office and Alabama Power's handsome buildings.

Politics, like architecture, was a passion: Charlie was a tremendously effective campaigner during fellow Barbour countian George Wallace's forays into California. Charlie spent weeks in Bakersfield, Calif., to get petitions signed to get Wallace's name on the presidential primary ballot.

Remarkably, he understood why I decided not to continue endorsing our friend for governor. He understood my simple explanation that "all I want is good government." My groomsman and I remained good friends and reveled in preserving historic buildings and building local landmarks. We were also soul mates in city beautification and in planting and caring for Eufaula's venerable oaks and elms.

We also shared an interest in art. We joined Donald and Jane Comer and others in planning the first Lake Eufaula Festival Sidewalk Art Show. Auburn's art department professors didn't think much of our idea for an outside show, but with the Rotary Club's sponsorship, and Charlie's expertise, Eufaula began a great tradition.

Another influential, close friend of Charlie's was Speaker Jimmy Clark, who utilized his considerable clout to help him land major building projects around Alabama. "He was a very innovative and creative architect," says Rep. Clark, "and the legacy of his projects and buildings all over the state are recognized now and will be recognized in the future."

Like the Speaker says, people liked to work with Charlie—whether it was planning and designing a building or planning another Eufaula Arbor Day.

I mean no disrespect when I say he was a "good time Charlie." Charles Alexander Blondheim, Jr. loved to have fun, along with his hard work. Few men earn so much respect or so much love as our Charlie did. His hallmark, his persona are indelibly cast in those handsome durable buildings and in the hearts and minds of those who knew and loved him.

DIAMOND LIL' HAD MANY NICKNAMES, FRIENDS

May 19, 2002

I called her Belle. Her nephew called her Chick. Her grandchildren called her Grand. One called her Miss Auburn and another Diamond Lil' Lillian McKenzie had many friends and scads of nicknames.

It hurt to say good-bye to this delightful, long-time friend who always made you feel better because you ran into her. "Lillian would have loved to be here among us," Dr. Gorman Houston said in his graveside eulogy at Fairview Cemetery Addition. "Lillian loved us all. Lillian had a way of honoring all of us. She would make a child feel special.

Her family and many friends remember Lillian Luke McKenzie, a Miss Auburn during her college days, for her upbeat spirit and ready smile. Pictured with her is her daughter, Jane McKenzie Human.

"It honors me to be here when we celebrate Lillian's home going. 'I've come that you may have life and have it abundantly,'" Dr. Houston quoted the Lord. "Lillian took Him up on it."

She lived life fully. Life was never designed to be dull.

"Jesus's first miracle was turning water into wine at the wedding at Cana. That was Lillian's kind of miracle."

Five years ago, the doctor discovered this lovely, convivial lady had cancer (melanoma). She was a trouper and chose not to burden her friends. A few weeks ago, the doctor told her she was dying. She responded she wanted to "take the express train home." Just as her friend Dr. Houston ended his most fitting eulogy, a train whistle was heard in the background. "It's the express train," a friend standing nearby exclaimed.

Lillian Luke McKenzie's joyous disposition and her beautiful smile and laughter made her beloved hometown Eufaula a more enjoyable place. She and her late husband, Trip, made this a better place, a friendlier place. They loved life and extended hospitality to their many friends. Well do I remember the dinner party she hosted for Bobby Jennings when he returned home after a long absence. When he returned to California, he wrote descriptively about his hometown and some of its characters for a story in *Playboy* magazine.

Lillian had a wonderful philosophy: When someone encountered a glitch, she would say, "Do the best you can with what you've got to do with." Dr. Houston recalled stopping at the McKenzies's green house when he saw the front door open. He discovered they had installed a storm door and had opened the door "to let the light in and the love out."

I can't think of many friends of long standing whom I've loved or enjoyed any more than Lillian McKenzie. As Gorman says, she had a town full of close friends.

Lillian was a family friend I inherited—along with her jovial mother, Big Lukie—before I moved to town forty-four years ago.

She was the kind of friend who arranged the flowers for my sister's wedding reception. Lillian was creative with flowers. She kept her scissors and other tools and supplies in a basket that was ready on a moment's notice. She and Trip also beautifully maintained the spacious grounds around their home.

It touched me when I heard her kinsman Dan McKenzie and his wife, Martha, at Lillian's behest, dug up three of her specimen boxwoods and transplanted them to her lovely daughter Jane Humann and husband Phil's Atlanta home, where she took refuge during her terminal illness.

I dubbed Lillian "Belle" during the United Daughters of the Confederacy's War Between the States' Centennial Ball at the old armory.

That was a memorable evening when "Miss Jennie" Dean directed the tableau, and many of us had been invited, no, told, to portray various illustrious characters from Eufaula's colorful history. I was Edward Courtney Bullock, one of the "fire-eaters of Southeast Alabama" who led the strong Southern rights group, principally lawyers from Eufaula.

I don't remember who Lillian played, but she was magnificent in her

Southern belle dress. And did we have fun as Miss Jennie directed us like we were all in kindergarten. Another memorable evening was the party at my bachelor cottage after my sister's wedding. Jim Wilson, who would become a shopping center mogul, directed us in a game of "Ned is dead." That is when Lillian nicknamed me "Ned."

This town will miss our beloved friend Lillian McKenzie. We'll miss her laughter, her counsel, funny jokes and her charming company. She made this a more enjoyable place to live.

Mr. Clark made Eufaula better place

November 3, 2002

Businessman, banker, builder, city coucilman, churchman, major player on the local political scene, Fred M. Clark left his impact on his hometown Eufaula. Our town lost a good citizen in the death of Mr. Clark on Oct. 22.

Years before the impoundment of the Chattahoochee River and the Eufaula Renaissance, businessman Clark was paying his civic rent as charter member of the Eufaula Housing Authority board in 1952 and charter board member on the Eufaula Planning Commission in 1953.

The latter was appropriate, because he planned his endeavors well and saw them through to fruition. Eufaula languished for twenty-five years before the U.S. Army Corps of Engineers set up headquarters in the Bluff City Inn and began to survey the river basin and to acquire land for the reservoir.

After the lock and dam was completed in 1963, Mr. Clark and his brother, Senator James S. Clark, worked untiringly to help Eufaula reach its full potential. They were sparkplugs that moved the town forward. Their drive and their personalities figured prominently to motivate other budding leaders.

The Brothers Clark would have made a great evangelistic team. Fred had the charisma and Jimmy had the zeal. They saw the opportunity at hand—both personal and for the community.

Fred founded First Federal Savings and Loan of Eufaula at a time when banks were tightfisted with their construction loans. His friends dubbed him "First Fred." He partnered with his brother to secure a state charter to organize the very successful Citizens Bank of Eufaula, forerunner of the local Compass branch.

One of the highlights of Fred Clark's long, successful career—in which he wore many hats—was his election to the Eufaula City Council in 1964.

He added vision and foresight to city government. His personality, his wit and his drive invigorated the city fathers during his two terms from 1964 to 1972.

He chaired the street and sanitation department masterfully. The sandspurs thriving in the city's medians were eradicated. He was sometimes a little impatient with city garden clubbers who were "long on planting and short on cultivating." But they became a winning team when they paid for the fledgling Live Oaks in the historic district and "Captain" Clark's city crew did the planting and maintenance.

He lead the urban forestry movement in his beloved Bluff City with a tree-planting program that helped restore the canopy along North Eufaula and North Randolph. Mayor Jay Jaxon correctly describes Clark as a man who "always saw the big picture and at the same time took care of the details," such as keeping streets cleaner.

Tourism and retiree attraction may or may not have been his cup of tea, but he fostered them by his beautification efforts. He was a builder and a banker, and it was his desire to build new homes and businesses to "catch up" with other progressive towns in the state. He never was a leader in historic preservation, but "First Fred" financed our old house purchase and restoration and we suspect many others. He kept the city parkways and rights-of-way manicured, reflective of his careful and personal grooming. He and his devoted wife, Dottie, were a striking couple.

"Fred was strong in character and protected his family," his minister, Dr. Al Harbour, said in his eulogy. "Dot had to temper that when Fred leaned toward overprotection. A wife of over sixty years, she knew Fred best. Fred's family has a house of good memories."

He tended to the "Clark Compound" with the same tenacity as he did the city's real estate. When he left a note, "Dottie, I've gone to play golf!" you would find him in the cornfield. His grandchildren loved riding on the tractor with him "at rabbit speed rather than turtle speed. And when the hay was gathered there were bales left and moved over to the road for hayrides or for the children to play on," his preacher says. "People in the work world noticed his gifts and skills of supervision, delegation and leadership. Good people worked for him," Dr. Harbour says. "With his skills in networking and connecting, he could get things done."

These qualities served him well in business. As an International Harvester dealer, he sold some of the first cotton pickers and harvesters in the Lower Chattahoochee Basin. He also operated the Pontiac-Cadillac dealership for a time, and he was a Texaco distributor.

His leadership also played a role in his church, First United Methodist, where he chaired the board, was a trustee and a faithful member of the venerable Adams Bible Class.

Fred Morgan Clark lived a productive eighty-two years. He helped shape our town. His son, Mac Clark, followed in his footsteps, as a banker and city councilman. His brother, Jimmy, the powerful Alabama Speaker of the House, often sought his advice.

Old Eufaula is a better and more beautiful place because Fred Clark cared passionately for his hometown.

CIVIL RIGHTS ACTIVIST HELPED
LEAD FIGHT FOR EQUALITY

January 12, 2003

Civil Rights activist and local historian David Frost Jr.'s home-going celebration will be held on Saturday, Jan. 11, at noon.

The author of *Witness to Injustice*, a candid and controversial memoir, was born Jan. 22, 1917, in Eufaula and died Jan. 3, nineteen days before his eighty-sixth birthday.

The life and times of this prominent African-American are part and parcel, a necessary part, of the Civil Rights Movement in Barbour County. He and I became friends through his letters to the editor he wrote over the years. "I am asking you to editor [sic] my letter," he wrote in a note clipped to a letter he had typed April 30, 1997, on his manual typewriter.

He trusted me to edit his letters, and I welcomed those intelligent, frank observations and opinions from an African-American reader. During the Civil Rights Movement, the 1950s and 1960s, there were few letters from the black community. I had difficulty finding a dependable black columnist, and I welcomed Dave Frost's letters, which added a dimension to the editorial page.

Witness to Injustice, published by the University Press of Mississippi in 1995, "provides an important perspective on life in the Deep South during a period of political struggle and dramatic change in a hard and previously hidden world that should be acknowledged as part of the American past," Louise Westling, University of Oregon professor, writes in her editor's preface.

"David Frost provides a local context of black community activism for those nationally significant events, and he does so as a kind of African-American Everyman—not a doctor or a lawyer or a minister—but instead a former moonshine maker and a small night club operator who just happens to be a dedicated longtime member of the NAACP."

Oddly enough, Frost voted for George Wallace "back yonder because I knew that he didn't mean all that stuff he was saying. He was saying that to get elected. But the other folks didn't know. They believed when he got up there and stood in the schoolhouse door and all that stuff. Every colored person and every white person thought he could stop the federal government. They thought it but I knew better. He knew better, too."

Frost had developed a respect for Wallace when he was a circuit judge, and he had a brush with the law and was treated more than fairly in court.

Frost wrote candidly about the impact on his life of watching his parents make moonshine in their back yard in a wash pot and listening to them tell "how the Peterson boy was lynched here in Eufaula."

He also recalled in 1956 Alabama outlawed the NAACP, which met secretly at the Masonic hall and encouraged blacks to register to vote. He and two others had volunteered in 1949 to try to register. He was the only one to pass the test on Alabama history and government and American government. The board let him register.

When his wife couldn't answer the registrars' silly questions and failed to register in the late 1950s, Frost wrote the Justice Department.

He met Martin Luther King in Montgomery when he and several Eufaulians were there hiring attorney Fred Gray to represent them when their Flake Hill property near the white school was condemned by the city.

He never gave up "trying to get colored people registered to vote," and "the law never gave up harassing me."

The former organizer and president of the Barbour County Improvement Association was also keenly interested in family history. Like Alex Haley, author of *Roots*, he traced his family history back to Africa. His grandfather was Anderson Frost, who swam to freedom across the Chattahoochee River (circa 1865) with his former master—who could not swim—on his back during Reconstruction Days. His great grandfather was Major Frost, born a slave in 1818.

His family history, accompanied with pictures of Major Frost, the first (1818–1905), and Anderson Johnson (1852–1925), his great-grandfather, is printed in *The Heritage of Barbour County, Alabama*.

No doubt, a highlight of this published historian's life was his trip to the College of Saint Rose in 1997 to lecture on living history to students in Albany, N.Y. The college selected his autobiography, *Witness to Injustice*, as a book of the semester.

The book is still in circulation and available from University Press of Mississippi, Jackson, Miss., 39211, or by calling 1-800-737-7788. Some of its content is shocking and questionable but it is an "exceptional memoir, a fresh, previously unheard voice [that] reveals cultural complexities that most historians have neglected," to quote the University Press.

David Frost Jr. will be eulogized at his "home-going celebration" Saturday at the New Birth Center Church of God in Christ on Fox Ridge

Road. His son, Elder Fred C. Frost, pastor, will officiate.

I'll miss his letters to the editor and his brief visits. We have lost a prominent African-American leader who persevered for decades in the face of adversity. He found God and peace among his fellow man—black and white.

'Miss Fonnie' epitomizes
good citizenship

February 2, 2003

Florence Foy Strang has been the epitome of a good citizen ever since she returned home from college to accept a position with the *Eufaula Tribune* during its founding in 1929.

After graduating from Hollins College, she attended Columbia University School of Journalism, interrupting her college career to become society editor and advertising manager.

Friday, Jan. 31, has been proclaimed Florence Foy Strang Day in Eufaula by his honor Mayor Jay Jaxon. It is indeed appropriate because this bright, articulate lady has not only been a joy to her family and her beloved hometown for ninety-five years, but she has continuously served Eufaula diligently and with exceptional foresight.

The *Tribune* has always been indebted to Fonnie Strang for her contributions that began with the publication of its first edition. She has been a leader throughout the years, contributing time, talent and knowledge to the betterment of the Bluff City and to humanity.

The bound volumes of the *Tribune* and the local history book, "Along Broad Street," have chronicled much of her civic, religious and cultural contributions to the community because she has played such a vital role in our town. We are all indebted to her for her unselfish contributions of her time and expertise. Eufaula is a far better place because she was born Jan. 31, 1907, to good parents and good citizens who also cared deeply for Eufaula and humanity.

The Kiwanis Club honored itself and Fonnie Strang in 1961 when they named Mrs. Carl J. Strang the Citizen of the Year. Historian Robert Flewellen documented: "For years Mrs. Strang had given freely of her time to her church, community and state. She was a member and past president of the Christ Child Circle, the Garden Club of Eufaula, the PTA, the Pierian Club and The Alabama Federation of Women's Clubs.

In 1961 she was also chairman of the Eufaula Carnegie Library Board, and under her leadership Barbour County became a member of the Choctawhatchee Regional Library Service which provided bookmobile service to rural citizens. A graduate of Hollins College, Mrs. Strang was an active member of the Alabama Citizens' Committee for Better Schools and of Eufaula's First Methodist Church where she taught a Sunday school class.

Of course, she continued to contribute to the community. She was a

Florence Foy Strang returned to Eufaula in 1929 and became the Eufaula Tribune's first advertising salesperson and society editor. For the ensuing eight decades, she has been one of Eufaula's foremost citizens and a significant force in the town's preservation efforts. In January, 2010, she celebrated her one hundred and second birthday.

cofounder and a driving force in organizing the Eufaula Heritage Association, chairing the first Eufaula Pilgrimage in 1966. She also spearheaded the campaign to expand Carnegie Library, resulting in the architectural award-winning addition.

Fonnie Strang is a Eufaula treasure. It is not possible to properly appraise her value to the community. Since marrying her managing editor, Carl Strang, she has contributed continuously to Eufaula, to Alabama and her country. She has been a role model to generations of Eufaulians.

In a remarkable memoir printed in this edition, Mrs. Strang shares her memories of growing up in Eufaula. Published first in the September 1990 Alabama Historical Association Newsletter, she writes, "I found growing up in Eufaula in the early 1900s to be a warm, happy, secure experience."

The *Tribune* extends warmest congratulations to Eufaula's first citizen, Florence Foy Strang.

MAJ. MITCHELL AN AMERICAN HERO

April 11, 2004

S hortly before Sept. 11, 2001, more than one national columnist lamented America was short on heroes.

This dilemma was quickly remedied when that fine young man on the flight over Pennsylvania commanded, "Let's roll!" Several new heroes stopped the terrorists' attack and gave their lives to save the targeted U.S. Capitol.

"If you want to define 'hero,' you don't need to look in Webster's Dictionary," says Maj. Gen. Ron Stokes, speaking at the 1128th Transportation Company's happy homecoming in Clayton. "You just need to look around here."

Operation Iraqi Freedom would not have been possible without the work of the 1128th, he adds.

It did my patched heart and soul good to welcome Capt. James Cruise and the 1128th home on their arrival early Sunday morning, March 7, at Ft. Benning after a year's deployment and three wartime missions in Iraq.

Maj. Logan Mitchell of Eufaula, another hero in our midst, is home after serving a year in Kuwait with the National Guard's 226th Area Support Group out of Mobile. It was my pleasure and some other "old folks" at the First United Methodist men's breakfast Wednesday to hear our hero speak words of faith and wisdom.

"Fourteen months ago, I was sitting in my office at home on a Monday working when the phone rang. The person on the other end told me that my services were required by Uncle Sam that coming Saturday," says Maj. Mitchell. "Two months later I was on a plane to Kuwait City which would mark the beginning of my eleven-month tour of duty in Kuwait and Iraq."

The war was only a few days old when his unit arrived.

In his introduction, retired banker Harry Nelson remarked the bunch of old folks have a short attention span. Perhaps we do, but not during this fine young officer and gentleman's pre-Easter devotional.

"While on the airplane flying over, I penned my first two letters . . . one to my wife and another to my mother. I knew that they were concerned about my safety as I was. In both those letters I included a short scripture:

"I can do all things through Christ who strengthens me" (Phillipians 4:13).

Over the next few months Mitchell repeated this scripture "over and over and over again" as he encountered many different situations—"some operational in nature and some personal in nature."

Mitchell and his unit arrived in April, just in time for the latter part of the sandstorm season that was followed by one-hundred-plus degree heat.

"I have grown up in south Alabama and experienced many August days of one hundred degree heat and one hundred percent humidity, so I figured that I would be pretty well suited for the desert heat. Fellows, I have never been so wrong about anything in my life. Those next four months that followed were probably the toughest part of my tour."

Nine August 2003, the day his cousin Blake Mitchell got married back home in Alabama, was memorable. He and eight to 10 others drove up to one of the Forward Operating bases located in a camp outside Nazariah, Iraq, right on the Euphrates River.

Their Humvee broke down just after crossing the border. It took two and a half hours for the mechanics to repair the vehicle.

"All the while we had locals kind of lurking around checking us out. The temperature continued to rise. It was a pretty tense period of time but somewhere in between, I just remembered Phillipians 4:13, and I repeated it to myself and at that moment everything was as calm and as clear as a bell to me."

There were two heat casualties that day.

"Overall the Army had more heat casualties on that day than any other day up to that point. That day was a long day, but by God's grace I got through it and several more like it."

In closing, Mitchell says, "I would encourage all of you that if you ever feel that you're hitting a brick wall or that you're reaching the end of your rope, read Phillipians 4:13 and have faith in this message."

In an informal chat, following Al Harbour's "prayer for peace," Logan added, he didn't have time to think about the political positions in the Iraq war. Leaders should give it the clarity that the soldiers need.

"They can do anything they tell them to do. They'll make it happen," he says. "Those kids, 18–22, they do the heavy lifting. Keep all of them in your prayers."

'Booty' was priceless treasure to his beloved Bluff City

February 27, 2005

It's hard to lose a friend to whom you were a friend in the true sense of the word. That was the connection between "Booty" Flewellen and me.

My association with historian Robert H. Flewellen got off to a rocky

Robert "Booty" Flewellen, left, chats with attorney Preston Clayton.
another distinguished Barbour County resident. Flewellen wrote for
the Eufaula Tribune *after retiring from a long teaching career.*

start back in 1958 when I became editor and general manager of the
Tribune. The history and American government master teacher was sponsor of the *Eufaula High Times*, which our back shop printed. There was a
problem with meeting the publication deadline: With Booty, you didn't
miss a deadline.

He summed that up when he autographed a copy of his definitive,
well-researched book, *Along Broad Street: A History of Eufaula, Alabama
1823–1984*, in 1992 for the "*Trib* staff—meet all the deadlines and never
flinch!"

I could depend on him to tell me the unvarnished truth, such as Barbour
County is neither the Wiregrass nor the Black Belt and that I printed too
much farm news for the small number we had.

Immediately, I learned to respect Robert Flewellen.

In 1989, when he autographed a copy of his book, *Eufaula's Gracious
Lady: Caroline Copeland Clayton*, he wrote on the fly leaf, "To Joel—A

friend in the true sense of the word." I valued that just as I valued his long friendship.

I also treasure that book not only because it was a labor of love for him but also because "Miss Caro" was also a close friend who soon became my ready source for local history, before Flewellen was commissioned by the City of Eufaula to write the well-indexed, local history, *Along Broad Street*. Losing Booty Flewellen was like losing a library, says my B. W. (Beautiful Wife), who was also a close friend of his.

After his retirement from teaching, I was fortunate to have him join the *Tribune* staff as a staff writer and columnist. A collection of his Alabama Press Association prize-winning columns, *From the Bluff*, was published in a limited edition. How fortunate we were to have him on the staff.

I was honored to write the foreword for *From the Bluff* and *Along Broad Street*, which I was pleased to copy-read. I observed first-hand his diligent research through the bound volumes of the *Eufaula Tribune*.

"His knowledge and willingness to research Eufaula's history will benefit generations to come," says Mayor Jay Jaxon, one of many good citizens influenced by Flewellen's teaching in American government and history classes. My intention with this personal column is to remind you, Gentle Reader, that Eufaula and Alabama have lost a remarkable man, a scholar and a storehouse of knowledge.

It was an honor to present one of many accolades to Booty in 2002 when the Eufaula Rotary Club went outside its membership to name him a Paul Harris Fellow. In making the presentation at a dinner, I described my friend and Eufaula's historian as "a gentleman, an intellectual, a master teacher, historian and an author."

And he was so much more. He was a valuable member of "The Greatest Generation." He risked his life at Pearl Harbor three days after the Japanese's inhumane attack in the early morning of Dec. 7, 1941.

Japanese submarines and carrier-based planes attacked the U.S. Pacific fleet. Eight American battleships and ten other naval vessels were sunk or badly damaged, almost two hundred American aircraft were destroyed and approximately three thousand naval and military personnel were killed or wounded. The attack marked the entrance of Japan into World War II on

Germany and Italy's side and of the U.S. on the Allied side.

After receiving his honorable discharge from the U.S. Army, he returned home and became an invaluable citizen. He taught Barbour County veterans in night classes under the GI Bill. Youthful Lurleen Wallace was his secretary.

Booty Flewellen passionately loved his hometown and the world of nature. He was an avid hunter and corresponded with renowned outdoors writer Nash Buckingham. His home and garden on St. Francis Point, overlooking Lake Eufaula, was a haven for wildlife. He observed the changes in the seasons and was thrilled when the purple Martins returned to their gourds hanging high above his well-tended garden that usually included a row of gloriously colorful zinnias.

I treasure his *Birds of Eufaula, Alabama* illustrated by Paul Mixon, just as I do his little books, *Golden Days and Dusty Sunsets* and *Things I Like to Remember*.

Their content reflects many facets of his sterling character. One of his scholarly lectures, "Barbour County: Home of Governors," was a highlight of the Alabama History and Heritage Festival March 4, 1983. It was included in a volume, *Clearings in the Thicket*, edited by Auburn journalism professor Jerry Brown.

Alabama's World War II governor, Chauncey Sparks, was his uncle. He and Charles Blackmon, who is also kin and connected to the governors from Barbour, researched their kinship and the governors' interconnections and presented interesting papers at the Festival. Mercer University Press later published them.

How fortunate we are in Eufaula to have his writings, yet we have lost an invaluable storehouse of knowledge in his passing at age eighty-eight. For eighty of those productive years, he was a member of First Baptist Church, where he sang in the choir for thirty-five years.

How fortunate I was to have him as a friend. How fortunate was the *Tribune* and you, Gentle Reader, to have his well written, uplifting columns and his timely, well-researched news and feature stories. What a pleasure it was to have an associate on staff that met his deadlines.

How fortunate my children and Eufaula students were to have Robert

H. Flewellen as a friend and role model. My youngest son, Bill, when he was a little boy, irreverently called him "Booty Flew," to my consternation. My wonderful father would not have been so tolerant, but times changed and our friend Booty changed with them.

Booty loved his beautiful and gracious late wife, Lenora Salter Flewellen, and his three daughters, Paula Irby, Lou Martin and Robin Flewellen and their families. Robert Flewellen was Eufaula's "unofficial" historian: following in the footsteps of "Miss Caro," (1882–1983), but his *Along Broad Street* is the definitive, accurate Eufaula history we depend upon often at the *Tribune*.

We will miss Booty. He was a priceless asset to Eufaula and a noble American.

How do you say goodbye to fishing legend, friend?

February 20, 2005

How do you say goodbye to a fishing legend and a friend? I don't rightly know, but I'm trying. I was shocked at the news of Tom Mann's untimely death from complications following heart surgery last Friday at UAB Hospital in Birmingham. How could this be?

It seemed like only a few days ago tall, genial Tom Mann, looking hale and hardy, popped his head inside my office door. It was good to see this long-time friend who meant so much to the Bluff City and to the fishing industry.

Tom was caught up in another exciting project: this time exactly six months ago, he radiated enthusiasm as he asked to borrow several file photographs to incorporate in eighteen hours of taping for a one-hour video he was filming in Eufaula, encompassing his forty-two years on Lake Eufaula.

This was exciting to me, too, because the *Tribune* and I followed the adventures of Tom Mann on Lake Eufaula even before he moved his fledgling Mann's Bait Company here from Enterprise.

Bill Roberts, the banker, and I felt sure he would change the name of his company to something besides Bait Company. That was so unimaginative, we thought.

The *Tribune* devoted full news coverage and spirited editorial commentary on the impoundment and the dedication of the Walter F. George Lock and Dam down stream at quaint Fort Gaines on June 14, 1963, while Mann, the innovative Alabama conservation officer, fished the magnificent new impoundment and designed fishing lures.

Eufaula newcomer Tom Mann became the perfect foil for the *Tribune* and me, the new editor, in my determination to promote fishing on our newly created reservoir. Add BASS originator Ray Scott and his Lake Eufaula fishing tournaments to the mix, and bass fishermen from all over the country found their way to Lake Eufaula.

While the *Tribune* and I stayed home and helped spread the word about beautiful new lunker-filled Lake Eufaula, Tom was making big waves around the country among avid anglers and outdoors writers like Homer Circle, who wanted to boat big bass. Tom's hometown newspaper began publishing scads of photographs of hog-sized bass on a stringer and touting the town and the lake as "The Big Bass Capital of the World." And surprisingly, with Tom's innovations and perseverance, the fishing world began to believe the good-natured hype.

We were all having fun, and Tom was promoting Eufaula and the lake and building a fishing empire in his backyard.

Thanks to that new project and the one before the video, Tom's book, *Think Like a Fish: The Lure & Lore of America's Legendary Bass Fisherman*, we have his life story and a memoir that tell us in depth about this American entrepreneur and award-winning bass master. The funeral service for William Thomas "Tom" Mann was held Tuesday, Feb. 15, at Calvary Baptist Church.

During visitation that morning Tom's lovely wife, Ann, and daughter, Nelda, comforted the editor, Jack Smith, and me outside the church. That hallowed ground was covered with mourners who took time from their jobs and daily routine to honor the memory of their friend and family member.

The growing church, pastored by the Rev. Alan Dodson, was filled to overflowing for the funeral at 2 PM The florists who designed the beautiful arrangements obviously had Tom's charisma and persona in mind when they chose the many cheerful and colorful flowers in the tall stands. One highlighted a fishing rod and lures among the bright flowers.

The Rev. John Emfinger, Tom's former pastor, recalled when Tom caught more fish than anybody else below the dam at Columbus; the boats were all around him. He also recalled how Tom could create a fishing lure and make it special, and how as a businessman he created jobs to feed families— from the grace of God.

Tom was a creative genius.

The preacher compared Tom's life to the actor Jimmy Stewart's in the classic Christmas film, *It's a Wonderful Life*. He wondered what life without Tom Mann would have been for many families.

The Rev. Jeff Hines, the son of Mr. and Mrs. Henry Hines, who grew up in Eufaula and attended Calvary Baptist Church, remembered the big smile on Mr. Tom's face and how he had time for young people. "Only Tom could take a fish and make it larger than life and attract hundreds [eight hundred] to attend a fish funeral. Ann hopes more turned up for Tom's funeral than Leroy Brown's."

The Fort Gaines Baptist preacher also took his text on "Buzzard Baptists" who don't come to the church unless somebody's dead.

"If you're here today," the amiable minister said, "you owe a debt of gratitude. He [Tom] loved fishermen and fisherwomen—anybody that liked to wet a hook. The greatest legacy," the Rev. Hines said, "would be if people here today give their lives to the Lord. Fishers of men are called by Jesus. Go fish for souls of men and women."

Brief graveside services were held at Fairview Cemetery Addition, near his brother Don Mann's grave and only a few steps away from my Smith family's recently acquired burial plots.

Slowly returning to my car, I spotted Tina Booker, standing forlorn under the big spreading oak tree in the cemetery. I introduced myself to

Tom's co-host of *Tom and Tina Outdoors*, on the Sportsman's Channel.

As she opened the door to her SUV, she said she had told Tom, "I'm not getting in that car until you get rid of that corn in the back: It's sprouted."

When she called Tom at UAB Hospital, he told her, "I've cleaned up the corn!"

Sharon Dixon, Tom's gracious daughter, came in the *Tribune* offices to tell us anybody and everybody is invited to come "Celebrate the Life of Tom Mann," Saturday afternoon at 2 PM at the Eufaula Community Center. Don't dress up: Wear fishin' clothes, she added.

BASS founder Ray Scott, who is no stranger to Eufaula, will conduct the celebration.

This is how we can express appreciation for the life of Tom Mann and say goodbye to our friend and legend.

REMEMBERING AMERICAN HERO, FRIEND

January 7, 2007

Our country lost another member of the "Greatest Generation" in the death of Sam LeMaistre Sr. Alabama also lost another member of the distinguished LeMaistre family.

And Eufaula lost a favorite adopted son who served the legal community well during his long professional career.

His death is as a personal loss also. Sam was my personal lawyer and represented the *Eufaula Tribune* after I acquired ownership. He represented me in the acquisition of the newspaper and continued until his retirement and I grew my own lawyer.

During my editing and publishing career, LeMaistre and I had no problems with due diligence. He was a professional who had many, many appreciative clients in our town.

It behooves me—and I believe the community—to look back over Sam

A. LeMaistre Sr.'s service to the town.

He and his beloved late wife, Jeannette LeMaistre, chose to live in Eufaula. They had been sweethearts during their college days at the University of Alabama before WWII. Sam, who was in the ROTC program, was called to enlist in the early years of the war. Throughout his time away from the campus, the couple exchanged letters.

After completing his military training, he boarded the USS *United States* in the dark of night. He was surprised to discover 5,500 soldiers were on board. When he stretched out the next morning, his arm encountered Denson Burnham, a Kappa Alpha fraternity brother from Alabama.

He helped make history when his outfit, under General George Patton, landed on Omaha Beach three days after the D-Day Invasion. LeMaistre later discovered he stormed the beaches just behind Andy Rooney. After Normandy, the company traveled throughout Europe and into Russia before ending up in Austria at the close of the war. There was little food and cold winters, but Sam survived without injury.

He once met General Patton at a military party. He told the *Tribune* during a 2002 interview for "Lest We Forget," "He was a very well educated man and a very nice person to meet." LeMaistre then chuckled, "but he was not nice to everyone."

I can understand why the general was nice to Sam, because he was polite and most enjoyable to be around. Such was the case also at the long-standing Eufaula Coffee Club where Sam was a popular mainstay along with Bobby Lockwood.

During the interview, LeMaistre also remembered how intent General Patton was in keeping a schedule. He remembered one time when suddenly Patton appeared before him as their convoy was trying to transfer.

"Patton walked right out into the middle of a sea of mud and began directing the men using traffic signals—anything to maintain progress."

We have lost an extraordinary man who personally helped make Eufaula a better community. Small town Eufaula was a perfect fit for Sam LeMaistre and today we are the beneficiaries.

Jeannette and Sam LeMaistre were a handsome, well-groomed couple who enjoyed life and were loved by many townspeople and much appreciated by his clients. He was a director on the board of the Eufaula Jaycees in 1952 when the young members promoted economic growth and had fun.

In 1954, he and Archie Grubb opened a law practice here, just in time for an economic boom following the impoundment of the Chattahoochee River. He served as a part-time district attorney and also as city attorney for the City of Eufaula. He was a founder of the Alabama Sports Hall of Fame.

Perhaps Sam's greatest contribution—besides his impeccable law practice—was his chairing and promoting the Waterfowl Refuge Association in 1959. He and others appeared before a U.S. Study Commission meeting in Dothan and argued the value of establishing a refuge along the riverway. The outcome was the development of the Eufaula National Wildlife Refuge by the U.S. Fish and Wildlife officials.

He was an influential member of the City Recreation Department board in 1968 that served 1,085 young people in Eufaula and environs.

Truly, we have lost an outstanding citizen who moved to town when Eufaula was Camelot. He helped shape the character and direction of this place apart.

This article appeared as a guest column in the Eufaula Tribune *after Mr. Smith's retirement as publisher.*

Eufaula's wealth in the era before 1860 was based on cotton. Thousands of bales, some shown in this scene on Randolph Avenue, were shipped down the Chattahoochee River to Apalachicola.

Chapter 3

Eufaula as Symbol, Old and New

'SYMBOL OF THE OLD SOUTH, CRADLE OF THE NEW'

February 8, 1962

I've heard a rumor that the Chamber of Commerce is seriously thinking about dropping its motto, "Eufaula: Symbol of the Old South, Cradle of the New," the next time they have new letterhead printed.

Now, I'm for progress, but I'm not one that thinks we're necessarily making progress simply because we're making a change. Don't get me wrong, I'm all for this modern living and like GE, I think progress is a most important product, but I do think that there are lots of things from the past that are well worth preserving for the future.

What I'm trying to say is this—while our town's progressive leaders are campaigning for our place in the sun, let's make a concerted effort to retain Eufaula's personality, while we push forward. Naturally the "Bluff City" is fast acquiring a new look as progress is made on the vast project of damming up the Chattahoochee. And like a good Chamber of Commerce, our local organization is pushing for a new industry and modern municipal facilities, just as any C. of C. worth its salt should do. This is all well and good, but at the same time let's give a little thought to the Eufaula image that our beloved old town projects for the outside world to see.

I've racked my brain trying to think up an appropriate new slogan for our Chamber's new stationery, but blamed if I can come up with anything that describes Eufaula better than that old motto. There's no getting around it, our town is indeed one of the few truly authentic symbols of the "Old South" left in Alabama, "The Heart of Dixie." I'll admit that we're not exactly a "Cradle of the New"—but we will be by the time those Army Engineers turn us loose.

Every community has a personality of its own, and I firmly believe that Eufaula is one of the South's most colorful towns. This opinion is pretty generally shared by lots of my newspaper colleagues scattered through the State.

Not long ago Fred Eiland, editor of the weekly at Heflin, in a discussion about Harper Lee's prize-winning novel, commented that *To Kill a Mockingbird* could have been even more delightful if the author had used Eufaula as a setting for her book instead of Monroeville. I hastened to explain to Fred that "Candid Comments" has already officially invited Louise Conner's sister to move on down here and start writing her next novel. I know with all our local color and scads of town characters, Eufaula could provide the setting for at least one Pulitzer-winning novel; and Harper Lee's just the gal who could write it.

Let's hold on to our lovely old antebellum homes, our tree-lined boulevards, our Confederate monuments and all of our statues and plaques that so graphically help tell the "Eufaula Story," and at the same time let's modernize our downtown stores, build more twentieth century type homes, and get hot after each new industrial prospect we hear about. And let's keep that motto—"Eufaula: Symbol of the Old South, Cradle of the New!"

Town's bachelor population grows

October 4, 1962

Eufaula's bachelor population is growing . . . darn it! If there's anything we have a shortage of, it's mature, young spinsters. As a biologist would put it, the animal kingdom in Eufaula is getting out of balance.

Last week, Dick Boyette came back home and set up a public accounting office. And only a few months ago, Albert Simpson, recent 'Bama law school grad, hung up his shingle here. Both are eligible bachelors.

Albert has suggested that we organize a Bluff City Bachelors Club if one more eligible member moves into town. Then there'll be enough bachelors to serve as officers in the club.

I don't want to sound like a Dutch uncle, but I feel it my duty to be kind to the young single fellows who move into our All-American family-type town. Since I probably qualify as a "confirmed" bachelor, I feel that I might be able to pass on some pointers to the aging young bucks that just might prove helpful.

Small towns are kinda suspicious of bachelors and young spinsters, fellows, so be on your guard. Granted, Eufaulians for the most part are unusually broadminded, but they're still curious—and interested.

You've both shown good judgment by setting up housekeeping. When you're past that college stage you're sick of roommates and, believe it or not, there are times when—like Greta Garbo—you'll want to be alone.

Hire you a good maid—one that isn't a "talker" and one that won't give out any information to the women she cleans for on the days she isn't working for you. Be kind to her. If she pours Clorox on your handkerchiefs, or hangs your pants up so that you have a new set of creases, don't complain. She's the best friend you have, so be good to her. Make arrangements for her to pick up her money at the office anytime that you rush off to work and forget to pay her.

Join all the eating organizations that you can. With careful planning, you won't have to worry about too many meals. If you don't have a religious preference, join the Baptist Church. From all I can gather, they have more covered dish suppers and more eatin' meetings than the other churches in town.

You can still eat with the Methodists at their Wednesday morning devotional, and eat with the other denominations occasionally. Your Monday night dinners will be taken care of if you join the Quarterback Club, then there are several knife and fork clubs—take your pick. Join the one that fits in with your schedule.

Make friends with Viola Mangum at the Town House and Tony Rane at The Embers. Also, you'll want to be chummy with the waitresses, especially Minnie Ruth Kay at the Town House and Gloria at the Rebel. They'll call you when they have your favorite dish on the menu or be extra nice when you take a date or friends out to eat.

Learn your limitations as far as cooking goes. Include olives, smoked oysters—if you like 'em—and crackers as staple items on your grocery list. Ask Haywood Grubbs, Tom Posey or Emory Battle for a guide the first few times you shop in one of the local supermarkets. You'll save yourself and the store lots of time and trouble. Otherwise, you'll disrupt the whole organization trying to find the olives, smoked oysters and crackers.

When you feel you've mooched off your married friends too long, and you've just gotta pay back some social obligations, put the word out that you are entertaining. Some of the married ladies you know will come through. They'll help you plan your menu—and will probably whip up the food for you. The maid'll take care of the dirty dishes.

Keep your car in good runnin' shape all the time. As much as you'll enjoy your married friends' company, you'll get to the point where you'll just have to get out of town on the weekends occasionally.

Eufaula sanctuary for 'birds'

September 19, 1963

Eufaula has been officially designated as a "bird sanctuary," and the city feathers, er, fathers, have been asked to have signs to that effect erected near the city limits.

Being a town that loves and tolerates its "birds," we should take pride in the fact that our city is a haven for a wide assortment of fine-feathered folks. The sometimes-obnoxious jay and the common sparrow, as well as the beloved mockingbird and colorful redbird, find refuge in our city. Eufaula probably has more rare birds of the five-toed species than any other locale on the Southern Flyway.

As far as the home birds are concerned, we don't need any signs to remind us that the city is a sanctuary for "birds." However, since we're fast becoming a stopping place for Yankee snowbirds, many of which are bird watchers and bird lovers, it just might be a good idea if the Chamber of Commerce can exploit the fact that we're now an official sanctuary.

It wouldn't be a bad idea either, if the Chamber's Tourism Committee could print up some sort of a bird watcher's guide for the tourists to use while "birding" around the Bluff City. In it a number of our more unusual species, and their peculiar habits, could be described. That way we wouldn't shock the visitors.

The following are a few of the "birds" that should not be left out of the "Eufaula Bird Watcher's Guide":

G-Bird (Gonzales Barrones). A rare bird indeed. Migrated from the Carolinas via Georgia. Plumage gray around tips. Voice ranges from resonant double honk to a high-pitched, sarcastic cackle. Roosts among his flock. Call: "Gee, Gee, Gee Whiz!"

Double-Breasted Hawk (Marvinus Edwardis). For years local bird watchers have studied this jovial bird that, quartered near the ground normally, soars high about every four years. This bouffant-chested hawk, in spite of numerous battles, has survived better than most birds of prey. The unusual, discontinuous distribution of this bird suggests either a decadent species of whom only a few relics survive or an aggressive species spreading and colonizing new areas. Call: "My people! My people!"

RUDDY-BIRD (Abrahamus Ruddermamus). Extremely rare. This bird has long, broad wings, a long, slightly grayish tail, and distinctive flight habits. Cocks head high while in flight, often carries a stogie in his beak, and migrates sometimes as far away as Las Vegas. An extrovert, the Ruddy-Bird can be observed at close range as he swoops up and down Wall Street or perches at Rotary. Call: "Look at me! Look at me!"

GREAT WHITE HERON (Samus LeMaistrus). The great size of this heron, frequently called the great white feather, is absolutely distinctive. The courthouse, green golf course and Broad Street café are common feeding grounds. Although this species is a slow bird in flight, his wit and good nature make him popular with the flock by day, but come nighttime, he flies to Christian Grove and perches. Call: "Fore! Fore!"

SOUTHERN MAGPIE (Martinis Daritinis). Native habitat is Georgia, but migrated to Chattahoochee Valley where he's found a home. This black-feathered bird is constantly on the move, flitting from flock to flock. This gay bird is loved by the fledglings that call him "Big Daddy." Call: "Wula! Wula!"

MYNAH or MINNIE BIRD (Minnia Kayus). One of entire flyway's most unique birds. This white-plumed bird has ability to mimic local politicians to a T. Loud yacking sound when disturbed even slightly, but when serving a flock of ladybirds at Town House, these sounds blend into a babble of noise that carries up and down North Eufaula Avenue. Truly a bird among local birds.

Dutiful patient doesn't want to be hit by truck

January 30, 2000

When, Lord, when will the Alabama DOT build an alternate U.S. 431 route through Eufaula?

I didn't look forward to the Public Involvement Meeting for the alternate route Tuesday night, but it wasn't so bad. There was no loud bickering or verbal confrontation between opposing neighborhoods or factions. Eufaulians' background, their love of community and common courtesy kept the experience from being unbearable, just as it holds down "road rage."

No formal presentation was made, and that could have been helpful but confrontational. The location engineers, traffic engineers and design experts were professional as they answered concerned property owners' questions and listened to their comments. Many took time to write their comments on forms that were distributed as they entered the building and registered.

All in all, I was impressed with beleaguered Eufaulians' civility, this despite their patience being tried far too long. And unnecessarily, I might add. They patiently, for the most part, enumerated their concerns to the Department of Transportation officials. Many also offered suggestions for changing the proposed route for the bypass. Some wanted it to be built farther west, but as one courteous, patient engineer said, if the alternate route is extended too far, the motoring public won't use it, and its purpose would be defeated.

I pored over the enlarged maps of Eufaula and environs, but it was difficult to envision the controversial plan. I couldn't believe only seven houses would have to be removed by right of eminent domain, but who wants to lose their home? Maybe some people now know how threatened we North Eufaula Avenue residents have been, I thought.

This problem should have been handled twenty-five years ago, but politics got in the way and we're paying the price today. As I drove home from the Community Center, where the public meeting was comfortably accommodated, I felt safe driving down newly four-laned Lake Drive (Old Creek Town Road) and turning into U.S. 431 under the relatively new traffic light.

Proceeding along the highway that dovetails into beautiful North Eufaula Avenue, I was forced to cautiously decide whether to detour via Randolph because traffic was backed up in the southbound lane. Two long eighteen-wheelers were stopped on the right, a City of Eufaula police car sandwiched in between.

Could they have been stopped for speeding? How odd. Maybe the city is enforcing truck regulations along clogged North Eufaula Avenue.

I realize truck drivers don't want to complicate the traffic pattern with 25,250 vehicles daily, endangering local motorists and their passengers. But some of them do fly through the Seth Lore and Irwinton Historic District, while tourists want to drive more leisurely through our beautiful and historic town.

I thought last Sunday morning as I pulled out of my North Eufaula driveway to go to church, Lord, I don't want to be wiped out by a truck traveling under Interstate speed, or by a sports car traveling so fast that if it missed me if couldn't stop in time to not crash into the rear of a stalled Mack truck.

I thought, I'm taking four pills a day: one to regulate my irregular heartbeat, an aspirin to keep my blood thin to prevent strokes, a half pill to keep my blood pressure normal and one to placate the herniated disk in my lower back. I also walk five mornings a week and do some warm-up exercises before hand.

So I'm cooperating with the government to reduce obesity, and I've never smoked. I'm not a Democrat but I support Donna Shalala who wants us Americans to "add years to our lives and health to those years."

But I don't want to be creamed pulling out of my driveway or out of the Wal-Mart parking lot on U.S. 431 South.

When, Mr. Griffin, (DOT division engineer) can we expect to make our town's streets user-friendly again?

And when can the city fathers begin planning for Eufaula's future so we might follow in the tradition of Seth Lore and the Summerville Land Co., who laid out our town's broad boulevards and sensible grid pattern?

You're a Eufaulian If...

February 24, 1966

People used to say that you were a "newcomer" if your family hadn't lived in the Bluff City for a couple of generations. With an influx of new people during the past five or six years, things have changed considerably, and the "newcomer" label applies only to folks who have moved into town within the last year.

While Eufaula has adapted very well to change and the influence of new citizens, newcomers have done a pretty good job of finding their own little niche too. In some cases, it's hard to tell a native from a newcomer.

You're a bonafide Eufaulian if you:

. . . Are a card carrying member of the Eufaula Heritage Association and if you're looking over the family's antique furnishings with the idea in mind of donating a lamp or table to help furnish the Shorter Mansion.

. . . Still refer to the Shorter Mansion as the "Upshaw house."

. . . Know the statue opposite the First Baptist Church is a likeness of the late Morton B. Wharton.

. . . Quote *Backtracking in Barbour County.*

. . . Inquire about the health of Miss Anne Kendrick Walker, who wrote *Backtracking.*

. . . Call Mrs. Caro Clayton when you need some facts about early families of Eufaula.

. . . Know that Mrs. Carrie McDowell's husband was lieutenant governor of Alabama.

. . . Recall that Moss Moulthrop was once mayor of Eufaula.

. . . Knew Rev. Joe Ellisor's brother, Thad, when he, too, served as minister at First Methodist.

. . . Get upset every time you see a crew sawing down one of the old oak trees along Broad Street.

. . . Still say Eufaula Street instead of Eufaula Avenue.

. . . Know what people mean when they refer to the old compress.

. . . Have a piece of wood in your den that came from "The Tree That Owned Itself."

. . . Take pride in showing visitors the remarkable job Tom Lewis did in restoring the old John McNab Bank building, and if you know that it is reputed to be among the oldest bank buildings in Alabama.

. . . Had Mr. Albert Dozier as a Sunday school teacher.

. . . Wonder why the men don't wear their tuxedos to the Christmas and New Year's dances anymore.

. . . Know that the Commercial Club was a forerunner of the Chamber of Commerce.

. . . Often say, "We operate our club under the old charter."

. . . Worry about whether the Methodists will build an ultra-modern sanctuary on the grounds where the old Jelks home once stood.

. . . Tell Fred Clark that you can't remember when the city's parks—not parkways—looked so good.

. . . Can name all of the five governors who hailed from Barbour County.

. . . Call Gov. Chauncey Sparks Judge Sparks instead of "Governor."

. . . Know that Mayor E. H. Graves's father was also mayor of Eufaula.

THERE IS PLENTY OF 'THERE' HERE

August 10, 1967

There is a lot of "there" here in beautiful old Eufaula, to paraphrase Gertrude Stein. That colorful, but controversial American author once described a particular American city by writing: "There is no there there."

It's a pity that Gertrude never did make it down to Eufaula, and that Paul Harvey, the big city radio commentator, has never had the pleasure of visiting in the Bluff City. Harvey, like Miss Stein, has bemoaned the fact that there is a monotonous sameness about too many cities. I agree with him—even Atlanta doesn't look like Atlanta anymore. It's more like a junior size New York or Houston or a Dallas. Those tall skyscrapers all look alike, the shops in the shopping centers all look alike, even the people in the offices and on the buses all talk alike. Atlantans don't speak with a drawl anymore.

But here in Eufaula—in spite of all the change brought about since the Chattahoochee was backed up around us—there is still a lot of "there" here. Eufaula still has that charm, that quaintness, that beauty that visitors have been commenting about for generations. Let's hope that the Bluff City will always be different from other growing little cities.

I hope that those towering elms and those spreading oaks will always shade the wide, old streets in our town. I hope that nobody will ever cut down all those ancient crepe myrtle plants that through the years have grown into twisted, but beautiful, trees that burst into full bloom during the hot summer months.

I hope that Dean-Page Hall, Kendall Manor, Fendall Hall, Shorter Mansion and all those other magnificent old mansions will always be standing here. I hope that other businessmen will follow Tom Lewis's lead and restore some of the other interesting old buildings to house their growing businesses. Someday, I hope that something will be done to enhance the beauty of that old building downtown, which has such a handsome Mansard roof.

During these times when the Confederacy and all that it stood for is under attack, I hope that Eufaulians will always fly the Stars and Bars at the courthouse and that the city fathers won't ever let a traffic engineer tell them that the Confederate monument has to come down. I also hope that Eufaulians will revive that old custom of flying the American flag along the sidewalks downtown and from their front porches on every national holiday.

I also hope that nobody will ever move the old fire bell from the parkway downtown or the old school bell from the campus on Sanford Avenue.

All of these—and many things more—are part of the "there" that is today found in lovely old Eufaula. These things are such a part of our town that they have influenced Eufaulians to be like they are. Let's hope the Bluff City of the Chattahoochee will always retain its individuality, so that future generations of Eufaulians and strangers who have not yet visited here will also enjoy our delightful, different town.

What's right with Eufaula?

July 7, 1970

I n this day of demonstrations and strife, it has become commonplace to be critical, to speak out against things. There has been too much negativism. So, it is refreshing First Baptist Church sponsored a special patriotic service Sunday night, accenting what's RIGHT with our city, our county and our country.

Ira Moore, the able young Baptist minister, gave me seven minutes on the program to tell what I think is right about Eufaula. This presented a problem, because I believe there are many, many good things about Eufaula. Newspaper editors, I suppose, are expected to point out the sensational, the corrupt, the bad and the ugly because this is news. However, to me there is much that's good about Eufaula.

First, the individual reigns supreme here. Eufaulians dare to be individuals. We may not be gaining population so fast, but we still have more characters per capita than any small city I know, and I find this delightful.

And the so-called Generation Gap isn't so wide in Eufaula. Young people are given the opportunity to be heard, to become leaders in building a better community. This isn't so in many small towns, but it is in Eufaula.

Of course, Eufaula is a Christian community. Eufaulians find time for their churches . . . they have done this traditionally. To me, it is remarkable the beautiful, historic First Presbyterian Church was built a few years after the War Between the States. Today, Eufaulians are still actively supporting their many churches.

One thing that is certainly right with Eufaula is our citizens have chosen not to abandon the public schools in light of the court order to disestablish the dual school system next fall. Then during recent years of racial strife, Eufaula handled the race problems very well. We have no racial violence as such, and we don't anticipate any when schools are totally integrated.

Eufaula will handle this tremendous problem. The city is even building new classrooms and improvements are being planned for our public schools in spite of the challenges of total integration.

Eufaula is a culturally oriented community whose citizens appreciate beauty. We have been concerned with our environment long before ecology and pollution came to the forefront. When Seth Lore and Co. laid out the streets of Old Eufaula, they had beauty in mind—our wide tree-lined boulevards resulted.

Today there is interest in preserving our parkways and our historic architecture. This is good, because a city that can't appreciate the best of its past finds it difficult to move forward in the future.

While Eufaula's needs are many, our town's citizens know how to work together for needed improvements. The annual Pilgrimage, Lake Festival and Fishing Rodeo bring literally hundreds of Eufaulians together on behalf of our community. These events help our city—not only do they provide entertainment and recreation, but they also stimulate our economy.

But the main thing that is RIGHT with Eufaula, I think, is our citizens care about their fellow man. This isn't just a trite statement. Eufaula people are actively involved; they are concerned about their neighbors. Ask any family who has known sorrow. Ask the lady who needed money to pay for a kidney transplant.

As a newspaperman, I have been in a position to learn a great deal about the "composite" Eufaula. The typical Eufaulian is proud—proud of his family, his home, his hometown and his country. He stands for the right things and can usually be counted on to do the right thing when given the opportunity. Perhaps most important, Eufaula is a wonderful place to bring up a family.

I'm glad Eufaula is my hometown—and that is by choice. I'm glad I'm from Barbour County, and I wouldn't want to live in any other country than America.

You can talk even when you misdial

June 1, 1971

There are lots of reasons why I like living in a little city and editing a hometown newspaper. I don't feel unsuccessful in the least not living up to my senior class's ridiculous prophecy that predicted that I'd be editor of the *New York Times* one day.

I like publishing a newspaper twice a week instead of every day. I like writing about people who are my friends, and I like writing about a town I know like the palms of my hands.

I like living in a town that's small enough I can . . .

Go home for lunch every day and sneak in a fifteen or twenty-minute nap on the couch after lunch.

Talk to somebody I know even if I make a mistake and dial the wrong number.

Drive at my own pace in the downtown district every day except Sunday mornings, when there's almost a traffic jam caused by good folks rushing to church.

Not get excited when I receive an overdraft from the bank, because I know all the bankers personally and they realize I don't always fill in the stubs in my checkbook.

Sit just outside the delivery room at the hospital while a good friend delivers my son.

Call the florist to send flowers to my wife who has just presented me with a fine baby boy, and she'll not only fill my order but send a bowl of flowers offering her personal congratulations, too.

In February, 1962, Smith, **Tribune** *News Editor Martha Blondheim, left, and Chamber of Commerce Secretary Betty Richards, are all smiles over the issue proclaiming that Eufaula would switch to dial telephones that Sunday.*

Excuse myself at 10:00 every morning and head for the coffee club, where I can expect to meet a dozen or two friends who'll bring me up to date on everything's that's happened in town during the last twenty-four hours.

Look for my barber or someone on the street to notice my shoes have been shined and that I am wearing my best suit during the middle of the week and quiz me about plans for going out of town.

Walk to work if I choose but find it's hard to walk a block or two because too many folks stop to give me a lift to town.

Write a poison pen editorial and make some of my friends mad, but they'll soon forgive me and keep on treating me like a friend.

Write an editorial knowing fully who'll take exception and who'll applaud my efforts.

Write about my crop failures and a reader will bring me a sack full of juicy, ripe tomatoes from his own garden.

No, I wouldn't move to Gotham if they'd make me editor of the *Times*. And I wouldn't live in Atlanta if they'd let me write a front-page column for the *Atlanta Journal*. I'm just like Brer Rabbit in that briar patch—I'm right where I belong.

Paintbrush could work magic

December 6, 1973

If I were an artist, I would enjoy painting portraits of Eufaula, like the famous artist, Richard Lewis, who recently completed a series of watercolor paintings of the Bluff City. I would take the liberty to eliminate the unsightly telephone poles and power lines, all that overhead spaghetti that detracts from so many charming places in Eufaula.

I would also paint in trees where monarch oaks once stood along our beautiful old streets or in the parkways. And if I ever painted any scenes along East Barbour, I'd either eliminate that unsightly block across the street from First United Methodist Church or I'd do a complete restoration on paper of that rag-tag block that sticks out like a sore thumb along this busy thoroughfare.

And when I painted a streetscape of College Hill, including Kendall Manor and the picturesque Holy Redeemer Catholic Church, I wouldn't paint all those chopped down trees and shrubs in the front yard of that old house that give this old neighborhood an eyesore.

And along Broad toward downtown, I'd be tempted to paint some branches and green leaves on that denuded old oak tree trunk that stands so conspicuously in the parkway in front of Eufaula's first shopping center.

In fact, I might be tempted to paint in that magnificent old magnolia tree that once stood in that asphalt parking lot across the way and the house where the mayor lived who surrendered Eufaula to General Grierson. Then, I just might paint in that old Victorian bandstand that once stood in the parkway on Broad across from the Bluff City Inn. And like that professional artist, I'd probably restore the old hotel to its former glory, cleaning the painted bricks.

Then downtown, with a few strokes of the brush I'd restore those street-level store fronts in keeping with the interesting architecture of those antebellum "storehouses" that give Broad Street a real distinction unmatched by the best designed shopping centers.

What fun I'd have removing that marine plywood off the Top Dollar store and painting in those attractive iron columns. And Cole's, the most distinctive old building downtown, would be a real challenge. I'd paint away those mirrors and other modern additions to the façade, leaving a classic building that would be the envy of other Broad Street merchants.

And MacMonnies Fountain would be spruced up a bit. To begin with, I'd paint the water on all sides as it flows from each of the three tiers. Like artist Lewis, I'd delight in capturing those red canna lilies in bloom around the fountain.

If I were painting my Eufaula scenes this week, I'd take great delight in painting the classic, early American-style Christmas decorations on the facades of the historic Pappas Building and the McNab Bank. In fact, I probably would get carried away and paint those garlands of greenery, accented with wreaths and red bows, along the storefronts of all the other buildings along Broad.

Then I would take great delight in painting the historic Vicksburg & Brunswick Depot on South Randolph. I'd paint a wooden shingle roof over the metal one and I'd repair those Victorian Venetian blinds that give such character to those tall arched windows.

If I were an artist, I'd have fun painting Eufaula's pretty face, but I'm afraid I'd take the liberty to paint over the scars and the blemishes that detract from our otherwise beautiful little city on the lake.

NUMEROUS THINGS MAKE EUFAULA DELIGHTFUL

December 16, 1976

The *New York Times Magazine* recently published a list of "100 things to love about New York City." Well, I doubt if I could begin to name all the people, places and institutions that make Eufaula and environs a delightful place to live, but just for fun, I'll try. You might make your own list, and if you come up with some different listing—and you would—I'll be glad to cover them in a future column.

1. The natural beauty of Eufaula.

2. Eufaulians generally, who by their nature are one of the most lovable bunch of characters you'd ever hope to find.

3. "Miss Caro" Clayton, the Bluff City's ninety-plus Sesquicentennial Queen who still cooks for her two sons and finds time to bake bread for folks all over town.

4. The broad parkways and little parks that make Eufaula different.

5. The Confederate monument with the Rebel soldier looking East toward the lake and not North toward Yankeeland.

6. The fried catfish at local restaurants on the nights when the cooks have just changed the grease.

7. North Eufaula Avenue and Randolph Avenue when the dogwoods

and azaleas are in bloom in the spring.

8. The way individuals here can differ yet cooperate to complete a community project.

9. The quaint MacMonnies fountain downtown when the red lilies are blooming around the pool or icicles are dripping from the fountain.

10. Coach Butch Stafford and way he motivates his basketball team and the EHS student body.

11. Mac Reeves and his always-sunny disposition.

12. The architecture of Old Eufaula.

13. Eufaula's new additions, such as Lakepoint Resort.

14. Newcomers like Jim Nason, Lakepoint's general manager.

15. Beautiful Lake Eufaula and the Chattahoochee Waterway.

16. The way Eufaula natives don't take themselves too seriously.

17. The spirit of the newcomers who pitch in and help make Eufaula better.

18. Playing tennis with my personal physician.

19. The old pews, the windows and the organ at First Presbyterian Church.

20. The delicious roast beef Robert Tasker carves for buffets at the Country Club.

21. Characters such as Yank Dean IV, who does such outrageous things as hang glide from a hot air balloon over Lake Eufaula.

22. Sipping Lake Eufaula punch when the Bluff City rolls out the red carpet for travel writers and counselors with the Fall Tour.

23. Worshipping at First United Methodist Church on Sunday mornings when the sunshine streams in through the beautiful stained glass windows.

24. Bing Eblen as he breezes into town from North Dakota with the Snow Birds who keep traveling south.

25. My Aunt Babe and Aunt Sally, who introduced me to Eufaula in the first place.

26. Fresh shrimp and oysters from Fortune's Seafood.

27. Picking up fresh, warm eggs and milling around the feeds and seeds at Eufaula Milling Co.

28. Enjoying the Columbus Symphony and sipping champagne during the annual concert under the stars at EB&T's courtyard.

29. Sitting at Rotary each Thursday with folks like Dick Boyette, Floyd Clark, Bobby Dixon, Max Arinder and Preston Clayton.

30. Enjoying dinner on the grounds at White Oak.

31. The way generous Eufaulians respond to the United Way fund drive and charitable projects.

32. The way Eufaula's great cooks shared their treasured recipes for *Eufaula's Favorite Recipes.*

33. The way Eufaulians celebrate such great events as the Sesquicentennial and the Bicentennial.

34. The Chamber of Commerce ensconced inside quaint Sheppard Cottage.

35. Sailboats on Lake Eufaula on a sunny, summer day.

36. Drinking coffee at the Holiday Inn with Herbert Satterwhite, Bobby Lockwood, Ed Richardson, Billy Dixon, Sam LeMaistre, Robert McKenzie, Ven Blinov, Ross Foy, "Pepper Jelly" Wellington, Bill Garrison, Sam Robinson, Gene Parker, etc.

37. Joking with my favorite waitress, Minnie Ruth Kay.

38. Eufaula's Tree That Owns Itself.

39. Editing the *Eufaula Tribune.*

40. Working with my friends at the *Trib.*

THERE'S LOTS TO LOVE ABOUT EUFAULA

December 23, 1976

In my list of "100 things to love about Eufaula," the Christmas season deserves special mention. In my last column, I stopped at number forty, so the list continues:

41. The Camerata Chorus' annual Christmas concert is one of the highlights of the Yuletide.

42. The beautiful music and Christmas pageants presented by various Eufaula churches.

43. Christmas caroling, an old Eufaula tradition, adds to the Yuletide spirit on Christmas Eve when carolers move about in the Seth Lore Historic District.

44. Billy Wilbourne, Eufaula High choral director, when he bursts into song, solo.

45. Charlie Vining's delicious pumpkin bread, warm from the oven, which he generously shares.

46. The helpfulness of local clerks and supermarket personnel when I have to shop.

47. Lib Logue's graciousness and concern for the less fortunate.

48. The cheerfulness of Dale Huff.

49. Sparks Tech and its genial staff including such folks as Motier Cope, Jack Powell and Bob Schaffeld.

50. The Mansard roof of the vintage building which housed Magnolia Crow, now home to Johnston Jewelry.

51. The Jaycees Sesqui gift to the city, the bandstand.

52. The old fire bell in the parkway.

53. Alexander Key, the author of children's books who has moved to the Bluff City.

54. Talented Eufaulians such as Jule Schaub, Annabel Trammell and Cathie Land.

55. Tom Posey, who greets you with "Isn't it a lovely day?" as you enter A&P, even when it's pouring down rain.

56. Earl Roberts's superb photography of local landmarks and portraits of Eufaulians of all ages.

57. The Eufaula Pilgrimage, which is really the Bluff City's spring festival.

58. The pilgrims who descend on the town to tour historic homes.

59. The friendliness of Judge George Little and the efficiency of his wife, Lois, in the Probate Office.

60. Hilda Sexton as she sits down at that great piano in Shorter Mansion and plays "The Eufaula Waltz" for tourists.

61. The way Lou Sparks and Elizabeth Upshaw keep things blooming in the yard at Shorter Mansion and Pegge Abraham keeps the mansion ready for guests inside.

62. That beautiful, but neglected part of East Broad Street on the Bluff and Broad Street as it turns into Front Street with its early landmarks, the Wellborn House and The Tavern, and the beautiful landscaped grounds, including Cowikee Park.

63. The park in front of Fairview Cemetery in the springtime when the azaleas and dogwoods make this a floral fantasyland.

64. The bronze marker at the Post Office, which marks the site of the St. Julian Hotel, which hosted Jeff Davis and his daughter, Winnie. The Daughters were able to cut red tape and erect this historical marker.

65. Postmaster Doug Nolin, who is moved by the same spirit as the Pony Express when it comes to moving the mail.

YANK AND HIS BANK SERVE EUFAULA

December 30, 1976

Rounding out my list of "100 things to love about Eufaula" are the following people, places and things:

66. Carnegie Library, ensconced in a warm and handsome old building, and its excellent staff of librarians, Mary Wallace Martin, Dorothy Ann Lockwood and Jane Hall.

67. Yank and his bank—Yank Dean and EB&T are inseparable, and they render far more service to the community than as a banker, depository and lending institution. The art exhibits and concerts are Yank's baby.

68. The collection of watercolor paintings of Eufaula landmarks, financed anonymously, now displayed at Shorter Mansion.

69. Wyndell Taylor's collection of local scenes that complement the furnishings in Central Bank's branch.

70. The Rev. Jerald Hicks's outgoing personality and his good works in the community.

71. The Rev. Marcus Smith's artistic talent and his thought-provoking sermons.

72. Tom Mann, his fishing lures and all the publicity he generates for the Bluff City on the Chattahoochee.

73. Mayor Jimmy Clark and the way he gets things done for our town.

74. Principal Dan Parker and the way he motivates the Admirals.

75. Sid Mullen's beautiful drawings of Eufaula landmarks.

76. The Chattahoochee Poochie.

77. The homemade pie Dan Leathers serves up at Chewalla Restaurant.

78. The handsome old Bluff City Inn.

79. The new-shingled roof on historic Fendall Hall and the great job contractor Harry Goggans is doing on the landmark's outside restoration.

80. The way Eufaulians ring in the New Year and have fun at the drop of a hat.

The National Bank building (third from left) was on the present-day site of BankTrust. Second stories of most Broad Street buildings housed planters' offices.

81. Chowing down at the BPW's annual Bosses' Night dinner.

82. The way volunteers coach Junior Pro, Pee Wee football and T-League baseball.

83. The crepe myrtles, the lilacs of the South, when they bloom in late summer.

84. Fishing on Lake Eufaula with one of the town's knowledgeable anglers.

85. Eating Leckie Mattox's barbecue at a church barbecue.

86. Watching the ducks fly in for a landing at Eufaula National Wildlife Refuge.

87. Watching the sun go down across Lake Eufaula.

88. Watching Eufaula's children grow up in such a delightful town.

89. The great personalities of such folks as Clara Roberts, Sarah Russell, Sam Robinson, Fonnie Strang, Nell Eppes, Solita Parker, Bobby Burtz, Mary Lou Blinov, Martha Blondheim and Mittie Griggs.

90. The Second Empire style towers that give distinction to Cowikee Mills.

91. The chimes that ring out a mini concert at noon downtown.

92. St. James's bell as it summons Episcopalians to church.

93. The picnic grounds at Lakepoint Resort.

94. The cross at Governors Park on the Bluff.

95. Watching the boat races at Old Creek Town Park.

96. The way the Street Department and the DAR fly Old Glory on special holidays downtown.

97. My three sons.

98. Broad Street's three-story storehouses, which once housed planters' offices.

99. Folks like Marvin Edwards and Lillian McKenzie, who are always such good company.

100. The 15,000 folks who proudly call themselves Eufaulians.

EUFAULA'S MANY TREASURES
SET TOWN APART

January 13, 1991

Times, they are a changing, but some things in a town are ageless and, like good wine, improve with age. They're treasures, valuables with few equals. Though historic Eufaula has lost some of its great treasures—both in its incomparable people and its notable landmarks—our town has many facets that shine like the tiny, multiple sides of a fine gem.

In composing a list of the treasures of Eufaula, we must start with the natural beauty of the place itself: The bluff rising on the west bank of the Chattahoochee, which has been impounded to create magnificent Lake Eufaula, is a treasure true, and so are the lake and its tributaries.

The Monarch oaks and graceful elms, the native dogwoods in any season and the azaleas in the spring are treasures. The sunset on Lake Eufaula is magnificent, God's living masterpiece unknown to many Eufaulians because they seldom view the lake from the Georgia side at sundown. The trees provide a beautiful setting for our treasured landmarks like Shorter Mansion, the numerous antebellum mansions and Victorian cottages and our old churches—First Presbyterian with its stained glass windows and lovely garden; First Baptist, with its fluted white columns; St. James's, with its Tiffany windows and small fountain; historic St. Luke on the bluff; First Methodist and its lovely stained glass windows; and Holy Redeemer, with its Stations of the Cross and beautiful windows.

Of course, Eufaula's people are its greatest treasure, but they wouldn't have been attracted to just any town. We have many people with class, charm and character. Fonnie Strang and Yank Dean, native daughter and son, are treasures to be sure. And so are Solita Hortman Chambers, Preston Clayton, Sam LeMaistre Sr. and retired teacher-author-historian Robert Flewellen.

The list is extensive, but they should make anybody's All Eufaula list of treasures. Organist Lillie Moorer, retired teachers Bettie Bland and Hugh

Perry, Scoutmaster John Hagood, retired librarian Mary Wallace Martin, retired teacher and columnist Annie Robinson, former basketball coach Jack Powell, Dr. Melvin Oakley, Rep. Jimmy Clark, Dr. John Jackson, Hilda Sexton, Robert Johnson, who instills a love of golf in our town's smallfry, Margaret Garrison, and Ann Smith, the editor's dedicated wife, are all town treasures.

Judd McKee, the city official who is a master violinist, is one of Eufaula's hidden treasures. There are others.

Other people treasures include the Christ Child Circle, the Camerata Chorus and Eufaula Men's Chorus, First United Methodist Choir, Eufaula Heritage Association and Eufaula Alcoholics Anonymous.

The man-made environment has enhanced the scenic bluff with its moss-shrouded oaks. The Seth Lore and Irwinton Historic District with its grid pattern and parkways is adorned with the graceful, three-tiered wrought iron MacMonnies Fountain, the Confederate Monument and the Jaycees' Bandstand commemorating Eufaula's sesquicentennial. The McNab Bank Building, the white-columned Eufaula City Auditorium, the Williamsburg-style old post office building and Eufaula Bank and Trust's early French Colonial New Orleans style building all add up to class.

The expanded Eufaula Carnegie Library, the raised Sheppard cottage and The Tavern are treasures to be sure. And so are the restored Old Eufaula Jail on the bluff, the Bluff City Inn and the concrete Richard Russell Bridge spanning sparkling Lake Eufaula.

Neither The Airport Restaurant nor the Dogwood Inn is ensconced inside an architectural treasure, but the quality of their food sets them apart from the strip of fast food franchises. Superior Pecan Company's fancy select pecan halves and Reeves Peanut Company's peanuts are treasures from the good earth.

The Eufaula National Wildlife Refuge's resident flock of Canadian geese and its forest full of flora and fauna and adjoining modern Lakepoint Lodge and Marina with its own flock of friendly geese are treasures, too.

Old Eufaula has many treasures, tried and true: The list could go on and on, but these are some of our favorite things about the Bluff City that quickly come to mind.

Things change, but in the case of our beloved Eufaula, let's hope the more they change, the more they stay the same.

Editor recalls when
sleepy Eufaula awakened

August 9, 1992

Writing a novel with a Eufaula setting would be a risky business, I wrote in last week's column. A native stopped me in passing and advised, "Don't write a novel about Eufaula. There are plenty of things that need to be forgotten." I get into too much difficulty as it is, writing editorials and a lighthearted column, to make such an audacious attempt.

Maybe, as I move along into my thirty-fifth year of editing the *Trib*, I should settle for writing a book in the style of Russell Baker's *Growing Up*, which mirrors my Depression-born Silent Generation. If it's a bestseller, then I could write a sequel centering on my trials and tribulations with the Fourth Estate in a small Southern town during the last quarter of a century: kinda like the *New York Times* columnist did when he published *The Good Times*.

Robert H. Flewellen, writing in his book *Eufaula's Gracious Lady*, about my late friend "Miss Caro" Clayton recalls:

"Joel P. Smith, who came to Eufaula in 1958 as editor and manager of the *Eufaula Tribune*, was a special friend of Miss Caro's, a friendship cherished by him and his family as long as Miss Caro lived. Joel Smith was proud of his Southern heritage, a booster of his adopted hometown. He came to know and to love Miss Caro and on countless occasions relied on her personal knowledge to fill in, for him, the gaps in Eufaula's colorful history, a history that he regularly praised in the columns of the local paper.

"Miss Caro, in turn, loved the Smith family and regularly saved articles and photos from the Eufaula bi-weekly, articles that sometimes made reference to her, directly or indirectly . . .

"Miss Caro, loyal friend that she was, wrote words of tribute to Joel P. Smith: 'Eufaula owes much to him. He has worked hard to push every new enterprise, advertised the glories of Eufaula to the four corners of our country. How he keeps up his courage I do not know, for with every booster [of Eufaula] there are two knockers. I am proud to call him my friend."

Needless to say, I was proud to call her my friend, too. She and a handful of readers understood the trials and tribulations of publishing a hometown newspaper during the George Wallace years, the integration transition and my early crusade against marijuana. Perhaps they didn't fully realize how important their support was to me.

As I reminisce about my experiences in publishing the *Trib*, I remember how easy it was for me to make the transition, moving from the Wiregrass town of Geneva, at the confluence of the Choctawhatchee and Pea rivers, to the Bluff City on the Chattahoochee.

My late friend Humphrey Foy told me my entrée into town was assured because of my local connections: my Aunt Sally, a long time school teacher with sterling character; my Aunt Babe, who loved all kinds of local characters, maybe because she was a delightful character, too; and my pretty, intelligent sister, Sarah Margaret, and ambitious youngest brother, Doug, both of whom had grown up here after our beautiful Mother's untimely death.

Times were changing; sleepy Eufaula was awakening: City attorney "Dad" Grubb and City Clerk Gene Parker had leased the Bluff City Inn to house the Corps of Engineers' land acquisition offices, as well as the engineers and construction workers who were moving here to dam up the Chattahoochee, building the second highest lift east of the Mississippi.

These were rather flush times, with new money in circulation and optimism on the rise. I relished being part of the transition that truly frustrated some aristocrats and agribusiness men. I marveled that I was publishing a newspaper in a town where character and background were more important than money. The only sacred cows, as far as the then-young editor could discern, were the Daughters—not Alabama Power, Southern Bell, the lumber barons, the merchants, or the planters whose ancestors built the white columned mansions in need of paint.

The United Daughters of the Confederacy and I hit if off, however. I took my cue from Mayor Marvin Edwards and the city fathers: What the UDC wanted, the Daughters got. This included dedication of a flagstaff in front of the courthouse to fly the Rebel flag. Yankee engineers, installing equipment at the new early-warning radar station, were puzzled.

The two Children of the Confederacy chapters sent delegates to the state convention held at the Jeff Davis Hotel in Montgomery. They also marched proudly in the Confederate Memorial Day Parade down Broad Street. "Miss" Jenny Dean directed her UDC following like a field marshal, once giving the city police chief the irrevocable order NOT to permit U.S. 431 traffic to interrupt the line of march. In her chauffeur-driven vintage black Caddie, she instructed the driver to hotfoot it from Kendall Manor on College Hill up Sanford, then Eufaula. But the rookie policeman wouldn't let them into the parade lineup, to Miss Jenny's dismay.

Celebrating the War Between the States Centennial was a festive, landmark occasion. Accepted by the Daughters, I was assigned to portray General Bulloch at the gala ball. My, what fun we had with Miss Jenny backstage directing her peers and several generations younger as we made our debut at the National Guard Armory.

Yes, those were the carefree days when convivial Eufaulians enjoyed life to the fullest. New in town, I kept confusing well-groomed Fred Clark and the new Holiness preacher. They were both Hollywood handsome, but I finally realized Dot Clark wore lipstick and the preacher's wife wore cocktail dresses in mid-afternoon, sometimes with a fresh corsage. "Spasmodic prayer is a poor substitute," I carefully typed on my trusty typewriter as a headline for the preacher's guest column. That was the minister who left town quickly after he was caught in a compromising position with a babysitter.

As time goes by, perhaps I grow a little wiser. "Flying Jenny" Dean, as the World War II crowd called my neighbor and friend, has gone to her reward. (The chandelier in Kendall Manor's great hall fell moments after her home funeral. Soon her bereaved daughter-in-law mysteriously began lighting a star nightly that was hung high inside a cupola window.)

With the Daughters long disbanded, I pay homage to no sacred cows.

Now, I am much more interested in pleasing my Redeemer, and in leaving my adopted, beloved Eufaula a little better than I found it when I moved to town that hot summer day in 1958.

WEDDING, ROAD KILL PARTY
BOTH 'ELEGANT' AFFAIRS

February 4, 1996

S aturday, after enjoying still another midday tented reception at Shorter Mansion and a Roadkill Party at Westover Plantation, I paused to marvel at the social affairs. "Ain't we got elegance?" I mused.

Eufaulians and Barbour countians have always had a touch of class.

Pioneers like Solomon Walker, who fought in the Revolutionary War and built his farmhouse on the west bank of the Chattahoochee, brought his collection of pewter to this "Last Frontier." They planted boxwoods around their homestead as they cultivated their fields.

In 1839, Dr. Thomas Levi Wellborn, who served on the staff of his brother, Gen. William Wellborn, during the Creek Indian War, built the first Greek Revival mansion in Eufaula.

They had class—and a touch of elegance. And so did Eli Sims Shorter, nephew of Gov. John Gill Shorter, who built Shorter Mansion, and Robert Walton, who developed Westover Plantation in Twin Springs.

Society reached new heights in antebellum Eufaula when Roseland Plantation was in its heyday—part of the social life of Alabama. House parties were a popular social diversion, and jubilant guests, arriving at the city wharf by riverboat, rode carriages to Roseland north of town, passing hung-over visitors who had worn out their welcome.

The social tradition continues. In recent years, Bluff City hosts and hostesses have discovered the elegance of tents. Saturday's reception was a one-tent affair, utilizing all of the flower-decked reception areas in the mansion and a white tent where a six-foot tall strawberry tree towered over the well-dressed guests, who sampled hot grits served from a tureen and shrimp stir-fried by the chef's first assistant.

The bride's cake was a work of architecture and culinary skill, towering over the Directors Room from its enormous engraved antique silver pedestal that came from venerable Charleston. It was elegance on a grand scale. Hosts and hostesses have thrown up more tents (we now rate wedding receptions by the number of tents pitched) but the catered reception couldn't have been classier, nor the food more sumptuous and spectacular.

Ben Bowden's Roadkill and Wildlife Party following in late afternoon at Westover Plantation was a study in contrast. Ben and Mary Ann Bowden carry on with aplomb Eufaula and environs' great tradition of hospitality. Three decades ago, Annabel Trammell was the "hostess with the mostest," Barbour County's Pearl Mesta. She and husband, Raymond, also knew how to entertain at their Cross Creek Plantation near Old Spring Hill.

The Westover Plantation party was no grubby affair, even though guests gathered around a run-down tenant shack, not the Big House. The menu was extensive: blackbird pie, grilled bourbon dove, barbecued pheasant, mustard glazed venison, Cajun venison and duck, deep fried catfish, barbecued bobcat, opossum and armadillo.

I didn't sample the narrow sparrow, road toad a la mode, swirl of squirrel, nor the smidgen of pigeon, but they were all on the printed menu.

Skeet shooting before dark was the diversion of the afternoon before the exotic buffet was served hot off the grill by chefs-in-training Chris Sherrill, Will Austin and Craig Koscielski. These young gentlemen, students at Johnson and Wales University in Charleston, are superb cooks.

The country ambiance—the tenant shack in the shade of a marvelous old, old oak—was perfect for the convivial hunters and their friends. The guests were invited by "Big Daddy" Ben Bowden and his congenial, Mountain Brook native son-in-law turned farmer, Charlie Speake, to bring or send their wild game and would-be delicacies.

The hatted, white uniformed young chefs grilled the exotic fare to perfection, arranging with a professional flair, delicious dove, venison, duck, etc. on platters. The Four Seasons's head chef would have been impressed.

Ain't we got elegance?

Wrong decision would haunt this old town

March 16, 2003

Eufaula is at the crossroads, at the point where the city fathers must decide whether to protect the Bluff City's identity, its renowned charm and character, or leave it to chance whether our landmarks will survive to 2020 and beyond.

The 182 property owners in the proposed locally designated Eufaula historic district—as well as other concerned citizens—must speak up in short order.

The Eufaula Historic Preservation Commission, created by the Eufaula City Council two years ago, after much research and deliberation, unanimously approved on Tuesday a handsomely illustrated, user-friendly design review manual compiled specifically for Eufaula.

Much thought and professional expertise has gone into the development of the manual, which has been needed for years to protect Eufaula's irreplaceable vintage homes and commercial buildings and to assist historic property owners in maintaining, restoring and adapting them.

LDR International, the consulting firm that designed Eufaula's Downtown Action Plan in 2000, gave its top priority the city council's approval of a locally designated historic district, after intensive input from the community. The commission has worked diligently to develop user-friendly guidelines, and I believe we have.

The Eufaula Historic District Design Review Manual is the result of considerable research and local input. The Alabama Historical Commission provided the names of several consultants qualified to survey our proposed district and draft appropriate guidelines. David Schneider of Anniston proved to be the right choice, and he worked diligently with the commission to develop the attractive manual.

Why design review? "Design review in historic districts is about enabling a community to protect and enhance the value of its historic districts," Schneider writes. "Rather than a set of rules to follow, the guidelines included in this manual should be viewed as a set of tools property owners can use to preserve the historic character of their buildings.

"They are based on generally-accepted preservation principles and practices that have been defined over more than seventy years of historic district designation in the United States."

They are indeed a proven economic development tool that, used diligently in a community, will greatly enhance the quality of life for its citizens while attracting tourists and affluent retirees.

Schneider sums up the need for design review succinctly: "Eufaula's character, identity and sense of place are largely defined by its rich historic architectural legacy. Investment in the preservation of the city's historic districts will ensure that this legacy is passed on to future generations."

A locally designated historic district and design review guidelines are in lock step with Eufaula 2020's vision statement that was the outgrowth of in-depth citizen input. The citizens' vision for the statement for the strategic plan states: "Eufaula, Ala., is a sustainable community committed to building its future while preserving its treasured assets."

One of Eufaula 2020's strategic issues is "preserving history, beauty and aesthetics," and a goal is to "protect, preserve and promote Eufaula's historic buildings, both downtown and in residential neighborhoods."

The commission followed the city council's suggestion to confine the boundaries of the proposed historic district to the original Seth Lore Historic District as listed in the National Register of Historic Places. It includes approximately two-thirds of that district that was placed on the National Register in 1973. It covers North Eufaula and Randolph avenues, Eufaula's signature historic streets, and the core of the old central business district.

This is a good choice for the initial locally designated historic district, because it includes a good sampling of Eufaula's architectural styles, including Greek Revival, Italianate, Queen Anne, Second Empire and Neo-Classical Revival.

Under chairman Doug Purcell's able and inspired leadership, the commission has done much to educate and inform the public about the importance of protecting our town's architectural treasures. The commission has followed its mandate from the city council and done a good job of formulating sensible design review guidelines.

Heritage tourism is a major component of the local economy, Purcell says. "During the Eufaula Pilgrimage and throughout the year, visitors to Eufaula spend hundreds of thousands of dollars touring our historic landmarks and enjoying the scenic beauty of our town." Preserving our historic homes and commercial buildings is also a wise investment for their owners. This has been documented in a recent study by the Alabama Historical Commission. Focusing on Montgomery, Mobile, Birmingham, Decatur, Huntsville, Selma and Talladega, it found property values inside locally protected historic districts such as we hope to designate, rise faster than property outside them. Montgomery's Garden District properties appreciated by 42.35 percent, compared to 8.30 percent for residential properties outside the historic district.

Eufaula has several historic neighborhoods and a charming downtown that should be protected, not only for future generations but also for our present population's enjoyment and profitability and our city government's coffers via sales and lodging taxes.

Watch and listen carefully as we approach the crossroads. We don't necessarily take the road less traveled; we want to choose the best course of action. The wrong decision would haunt this lovely town.

Chapter 4

War and Peace in an Old South Town

DAUGHTERS' DAY NOT WHAT IT USED TO BE

April 24, 1973

Confederate Memorial Day isn't what is used to be in heritage conscious Eufaula. Few people, other than bankers and employees of the state, observed Monday as a holiday.

There was a time—and not too many years ago—when there was much carrying on during Confederate Memorial Day. Long before the Lake Festival and the Eufaula Pilgrimage, the Daughters' April to-do was one of the biggest events of the year.

The United Daughters of the Confederacy were a real force to be reckoned with in the Bluff City. More than once that group of grand ladies would put on their hats and gloves and march on City Hall. One trip to the city council would generally do. The city fathers would always give them anything they requested—and for good reason. You just didn't cross the Real Daughters, the daughters of Confederate soldiers.

One time when the UDC was hosting an important meeting in the Bluff City, the Daughters decided things needed sprucing up a bit. They organized the city forces and even cajoled the railroad officials to paint the old depot—twice. The first time they didn't like the color, so the story goes.

And I know the Daughters erected a monument on the U.S. Post Office grounds after officials said the federal statutes wouldn't allow it. The Eufaula UDC wanted to mark the sacred spot where Jeff Davis slept, the old St. Julian Hotel. Well do I remember attending the ceremonies when the marker was dedicated. One of Jeff Davis's descendants was an honored guest and "Miss" Carrie McDowell recalled how the first and only President of the Confederacy picked her up in his arms.

But the Daughters' annual Confederate Memorial Day was a full day of activity for the delightful and gracious ladies. The spring luncheon was a real event when the UDC decorated some Eufaula veteran who in their estimation measured up to the ideals of the Confederacy. The luncheon, with a carefully chosen speaker, was followed by the parade through town and a memorial address in the cemetery and decorating of the Confederate soldiers' graves with flags and flowers.

Mrs. Jennie Dean usually was general chairman. Affectionately referred to by some impudent, young Eufaula men as "Flying Jennie," Miss Jennie ran the show. She would give explicit instructions to the Daughters on the program, the chief of police, the band director, etc. There is the delightful tale about the time she gave the police chief instructions to stop traffic on North Eufaula and Broad prior to the annual parade.

She had impressed on the chief not to let anybody break through after the appointed hour. Well, somehow, Miss Jennie was running late, and the young upstart of a policeman on duty wouldn't allow the general chairwoman's chauffer to drive to the head of the parade. The parade passed in review while delightful Miss Jennie cooled her heels as a disgruntled backseat spectator.

The Confederate Memorial Day Parade always ended at the bandstand in the park at the cemetery. Here some aspiring young lawyer would make a rousing memorial day address. Afterward, a member of the local high school band would play "Taps."

There is another delightful tale about the time the youthful trumpeter fell asleep on the job. It was a warm spring day, and the parade was behind schedule, as usual. The bugler had been dispatched down the bluff to echo "Taps." When the trumpet soloist paused for the echo—there was no echo.

The little bugler had fallen asleep on the job. A runner was dispatched, and the crowd waited until the belated echo sounded.

It is a little sad Confederate Memorial Day isn't what it used to be in Eufaula. The Confederate monument, the Stars and Bars flying from the staff of the flagpole at the courthouse and memorabilia in the Historical Museum are a few lingering reminders of the importance of the Confederate cause in the proud history of Eufaula.

EUFAULA HERITAGE ASSOCIATION BORN, NOT ORGANIZED

April 19, 1984

After purchasing Shorter Mansion, which the National Trust for Historic Preservation and the Alabama Department of Archives and History deemed worthy of preservation, an enlarged committee organized the Eufaula Heritage Association, which took on the obligation of paying off the $33,000 mortgage for Shorter Mansion.

Townspeople pledged more than $50,000 toward preserving the cultural center. The Alabama Legislature later appropriated $75,000 for improvements and for the Eufaula Historical Museum, which was moved into the mansion. The mansion was purchased and repaired with local funds at an initial cost of $57,000—and its beautiful interior was refurbished and furnished in antiques. The mortgage was burned in 1972 and more than $250,000 was invested in a major maintenance effort under Jim Murphy's presidency of the heritage association.

"The Eufaula Heritage Association was not organized—it was born," explains L. Y. Dean III, Eufaula banker and first president of the association. "As I look back, I believe that a love of our heritage has always lain dormant in the hearts of the people of Eufaula, but we just didn't realize it was there until a series of events brought this love of heritage to the surface and put it to work."

Even before the newly formed heritage association's initial restoration project was well under way, plans for the first annual Eufaula Pilgrimage were made with Florence Foy Strang as general chairman and Mrs. Gorman Houston Jr. as co-chairman. The two thousand visitors who came to the Bluff City's first tour of homes in 1966 caused a traffic jam that weekend on historic Eufaula Avenue. They came from twenty-three states and five foreign countries. The pilgrims' enthusiasm was catching. The many gracious hostesses conducting the tours inside the historic homes, the merchants and townsmen generally become aware of the importance of preserving these landmarks and sharing them with the public.

This was the beginning of a communitywide movement to preserve Eufaula's heritage of beauty. Since then, the Cowikee Mills Educational and Charitable Foundation has restored the city's first permanent building, The Tavern. The grounds around this old river inn that once served as a Confederate hospital have been beautifully landscaped.

A little farther away from the bluff, the Sheppard Cottage, built in 1837, has also been authentically restored at a cost of $45,000. Mr. and Mrs. Charles Lunsford gave the old raised cottage, located on a valuable piece of commercial property, to the heritage association with the understanding it be restored for some useful purpose. Today it houses the progressive Eufaula Chamber of Commerce.

The next historic preservation project for the association was the $28,000 purchase of the Hart-Milton House, the Capt. John Hart House, which was later sold to Jeanne Dean, who refurbished this handsome landmark.

One of five local landmarks on the Historic American Buildings Survey made during the Depression, the Greek Revival structure is also important because of its location on historic Eufaula Avenue where the residential neighborhood ends and the business district begins. It was threatened by demolition and further encroachment of the business community into this historic residential district. The preservation-minded heritage association also purchased Fendall Hall, one of the town's most noteworthy antebellum mansions, for $55,000, with the understanding the Alabama Historical Commission buy the home and its spacious grounds, restore and maintain it as a house museum and tourist attraction.

Many other treasured landmarks have been preserved by proud Eufaulians, contributing greatly to the historic preservation movement and retaining the charm and character of historic Eufaula. Today many dedicated, enlightened Eufaulians are striving to achieve a living restoration of their magnificent little city on the lake.

EUFAULIANS HELPED INAUGURATE JEFF DAVIS

February 24, 1991

When Jefferson Davis stood on the portico of the Greek Revival Alabama State Capitol to take the oath of office as president of the Confederate States of America 130 years ago Monday, Barbour Contains were active participants.

Eufaulian John Gill Shorter, Alabama's Civil War governor, was elected in 1861 while he was a member of the Provisional Congress in Richmond. He had been Alabama's representative to the secession convention in Georgia, having resigned as circuit court judge.

He continued to be embroiled in the great crises of the nation, helping later to frame the Confederate constitution.

Davis was in his rose garden at Brierfield in Mississippi when news of his election as the first and only president of the Confederacy reached him. On Feb. 18, Davis rode to his inauguration in Montgomery in a carriage "resplendent with white horses," Ann Kendrick Walker records in her *Backtracking in Barbour County.*

Edward Courtney Bullock, a member of the Eufaula Regency, a strong Southern Rights group made up mostly of lawyers from the Bluff City, accompanied Jeff Davis to Montgomery. The Eufaula Rifles, who left Eufaula on Feb. 12 following a sendoff by "a perfect crowd of men, women and children," who assembled to bid the "brave company adieux," also formed a part of the escort.

Eufaula ladies and the town's tailors had been busy making fatigue uniforms for the Eufaula Rifles, who had been drilling for months.

The Eufaula Regency has been described as a group made up of "the most consistent secessionists in the state." They refused to make any concessions to the Union: "The most advanced step looking toward secession came from the fire-eaters of Southeast Alabama under the leadership of the Eufaula Regency."

Ten thousand people who crowded the Capitol grounds cheered the newly inaugurated president. Cannons were fired, whistles blew and the secessionists were jubilant. However, a handful of people, no doubt fearful of war with the North, hung black bunting from their homes. And in Barbour County there had been "strong union sentiments." Up until 1855, the congressional district comprising Barbour had never been represented by a Democrat in Congress.

Mrs. Rhodes of Eufaula wrote in her diary, "War is impending. Our people have made a formal demand for Forts Sumter and Pickens. If not granted, they will be taken, if possible, by force."

The War Between the States, the deadliest conflict in American history, began three months later when Confederate soldiers fired on Ft. Sumter on April 12, 1861.

"Great excitement prevails," Mrs. Rhodes wrote when the news of the bombardment reached Eufaula.

The surrender of Ft. Sumter on April 13 excited Barbour Contains, who, like the Yankees, were bracing for war. Eufaula, unlike much of the South, was intact when the war ended with the Northern states victorious. That was 1865, and the Union was preserved.

Barbour Countians played big roles in the war. It's part of their rich heritage.

Eufaula saved by one day at Civil War's end

April 4, 1993

Eufaula has a proud history, and fortunately, Eufaulians since Civil War times have protected their rich heritage. They come from good stock.

Early white settlers, floating down the Chattahoochee en route to Marianna, Fla., discovered the Creek Indian village of Yufaula in 1823. They moved in with the friendly Indians, and the village grew as other frontiersmen also discovered the beauty of the place. The new villagers renamed the place Irwinton, and the Legislature chartered the town in 1832, renaming it Eufaula in 1853.

Eufaula soon became the hub of a prosperous plantation region, extending along both sides of the swift Chattahoochee. River trade thrived, and wealthy planters and merchants built many antebellum homes. They built their stately Greek Revival and Italianate mansions on wide streets with broad medians. This was a little unique, because in that era many planters built their magnificent homes on plantations.

Many of those historic houses are standing today because the War Between the States ended just before Gen. Benjamin H. Grierson, commanding 4,000 Union cavalrymen, reached Barbour County. Passing through Louisville, they arrived in Clayton on April 28, 1865. Lee had surrendered at Appomattox, Va., April 9. Grierson had not heard the news.

Masters Edward Young and Edward Stern mounted horses, and bearing flags of truce, were dispatched out the road running into Broad Street, then the direct route to Clayton, to meet Gen. Grierson. They met the Yankee general at Six-Mile Branch, delivered the message and returned.

Eufaula's intendant, or mayor, Dr. C. J. Pope and some city councilmen rode out and diplomatically greeted the federal general and cavalry, leading them into town, down near Broad Street and across the Chattahoochee to camp at Harrison's Mill near Georgetown.

Beautiful Eufaula and its mansions, churches and cotton warehouses were saved from the Union torch. By one day, Eufaula was spared.

Eufaula's homes on the hill, Eufaula and Randolph streets were like hospitals, historian Anne Kendrick Walker records. The Tavern on the bluff, "where Broad turns to Front Street," was the ward for "the blood poison cases—the gangrenous cases." The sick and wounded had been sent to Eufaula from the Armies of Tennessee and Virginia, and "those who had lived in the neighborhood before the War."

Montgomery wasn't so fortunate. There was confusion surrounding meetings between civil and military leaders on April 11. It was deemed advisable to evacuate the city. The last act of the Confederate soldiers was to burn Montgomery's cotton. Between 80–85,000 bales, worth an esti-

An historic marker in the parkway in front of towering Kendall Manor tells the story of how Eufaula's mansions were saved at the end of the Civil War. Smith believed the preservation of Eufaula's landmarks was vital for the town's future.

mated $40 million in gold, were burned. It was a miracle the city wasn't destroyed. The city surrendered.

Gov. Thomas Watts, who succeeded Gov. John Gill Shorter, a Eufaulian, left Montgomery for Columbus before going to Eufaula. Plans had been made to transfer the seat of Alabama government to Eufaula, in the likely event Montgomery was captured. Eufaula was designated the point to which Gov. Watts and the state government would flee. The state's archives were also moved to Eufaula.

Eufaula is a treasury of antebellum and Victorian architecture today because Gen. Grierson was informed, under flags of truce, that the war had ended. Folklore has it the Eufaula mayor and his wife wined and dined Gen. Grierson, "who was a gentleman," one lady wrote in her diary.

The city was saved, and so was the cotton.

INDIAN CENTER WILL FILL VOID IN OUR CULTURAL HISTORY

May 29, 1994

We have for too long neglected our cultural legacy of the Creek Indians, the first inhabitants of the Chattahoochee Valley. That changed with the breaking of ground Wednesday morning for the Chattahoochee Indian Heritage Center in nearby Ft. Mitchell in Russell County. The center will tell the story of the Chattahoochee Basin's first people, and we will learn more about the Creek Indians' contributions to the region and the nation.

The Indian Heritage Center will fill a void in our cultural history. It will "celebrate the culture and accomplishments of the Indians who inhabited the Chattahoochee River Valley until their removal west in the 1830s. It is intended as a gesture of friendship and reconciliation toward a courageous and principled people harshly treated and too long ignored in our history."

The lower Chattahoochee River Valley was once home to one of the largest concentrations of Native Americans in North America.

The Indian Heritage Center, no doubt, will become an important tourist attraction in the Valley, but more importantly it will focus our attention on the independent tribes, members of the Muscogee Nation, who were loosely bound. They were called Creeks because they lived on their ancestral lands for thousands of years along the creeks and rivers. The encroachment of the white settlers led to the Indian Wars of 1813 and 1825 and 1836.

Historian Robert Flewellen writes that the Creeks applied to the white men generally the "epithet *E-cun-naunuxulgee*: people greedily grasping after the lands of the red men."

The Red Sticks, the more warlike Indians, resented the white settlers' encroachment on their lands, and this ultimately led to the Indian Wars. "The end result was the total defeat of Indian forces and a series of treaties which would take from the Red Man his ancestral lands and would send him on a 'Trail of Tears' . . ." Flewellen writes.

Opothle-Yaholo, speaker of the Creek Nation, argued against the McIntosh Treaty of 1825, which ceded the Indian lands between the Chattahoochee and Flint rivers. He spoke eloquently:

"Leave to us what little we have. We sell no more. Let us die where our fathers died. Let us sleep where our kindred sleep. And when the last has gone, then take our lands, and with your plows tear up the mold over our graves and plant your corn above us. There will be no one to weep for the dead; none to tell the traditions of our people. Who says it is mean to love the land and keep our hearts in the grave as we keep the Great Spirit? It is noble to love the land where the corn grows, and which was given to us by the Great Spirit."

The woods around Ft. Mitchell are full of ghosts, says Billy Winn, the history-minded editorial page editor of the *Columbus Ledger-Enquirer*. It was 160 years ago, in 1833, when the hapless, beaten Creeks—once a proud people—were imprisoned at Ft. Mitchell, and they began their tragic march to Oklahoma. Some of the elder Creeks hanged themselves to escape "The Trail of Tears." One in ten died, three hundred in the sinking of a river steamer on the infamous forced march.

Winn says the "ancient ghosts hover above us . . . today we gather to celebrate . . . in a spirit of reconciliation."

Chief Eufaula's farewell speech to the Alabama Legislature meeting in Tuscaloosa touched that body of white lawmakers. In 1836, Yoholo-Micco, chief of Eufaula Town, said: "In these lands of Alabama, which have belonged to my forefathers and where their bones lie buried, I see that the Indian fires are going out. Soon they will be cold.

"New fires are lighting in the West for us, they say, and we will go there. I do not believe our Great Father means to harm his red children, but that he wishes us well.

"I leave the graves of my fathers, for the Indian fires are almost gone."

When the Chattahoochee Indian Heritage Center rises at Ft. Mitchell, the fire of the Eufaulee, the Creeks will flame again. It will be a glowing reminder of our Indian cultural heritage. As Mr. Winn says, "history lies beyond human redemption," but "we are bound to our former enemies. Bless this project for our sake and our children's sake."

WHAT WAS LIFE LIKE HERE DURING D-DAY INVASION?

June 5, 1994

What was it like on the home front during D-Day, Tuesday, June 6, 1944? Fifty years ago Monday, the *Eufaula Tribune* reported in a three-column headline: "Allied Forces Pour Across Channel into North France; Nazi Airfields Attacked."

Eufaulians were awakened at three AM by six long blasts of the siren at the fire station, signaling that the invasion on the beaches of Normandy had begun. Mayor Moss Moulthrop had announced several weeks prior the siren would give the alarm, followed by a ringing of the old fire bell.

Eufaulians rushed to turn on their radios and stood by until after daylight. "At 8:00 flags were displayed in front of business houses and at 8:30 several business firms closed and owners and employees went to church for prayer."

Gen. Dwight Eisenhower's headquarters announced that fateful day that Allied invasion forces began landing on the southern coast of France (12:30 Eastern Standard time).

The communiqué was read over a trans-Atlantic hookup directly from Eisenhower's headquarters, the *Tribune* reported. Just before taking off in the darkness, the paratroopers were wished Godspeed by "the lanky Kansas supreme commander, Gen. Eisenhower."

It was reported in the hometown newspaper the forces "thrown into operation were by far the greatest ever used in an amphibious operation. They had to be. An estimated million German troops waited in fortifications for the great onslaught."

History later recorded the rough seas were filled with 3,500 ships, seventy to each of the fifty miles of the Normandy coastline. At 6:00 AM, hundreds of landing craft were prepared and 15,000 American, British and Canadian infantrymen were on the beaches, supported by amphibious tanks, landing under fire to assault the German strongpoints.

A total of 3,000 heroic men died on the Normandy beaches on June 6, 1944.

On the home front, the *Tribune* reported the U.S. was producing a plane every five minutes, and Navy Secretary Forrestal announced there were now enough landing craft to carry the entire invasion army over the waters to Hitler's Europe.

Patriotic Barbour countians were launching a War Bond drive to reach a $624,000 quota. The Napier Field Band played for a street parade on Broad Street when the Fifth War Loan Drive was launched. Sim Thomas was Third District chairman on the War Finance Committee.

"Buy a Bond for Father's Day," Neal Logue Company's ad read. The War Loan emblems appeared in other ads, and June 6, The Telephone Employees ad wished our fighting men "Godspeed. We're backing you to the limit. The fate of humanity is now in your hands."

At the time, I was fifteen-years-old, living with my father and younger brother in Panama City, where our father worked building Liberty Ships. It was an exciting time when we gathered and a new ship was launched and pulled out to sea.

Bob, my younger brother, was a member of the Civilian Air Patrol. Nazi submarines were operating in the area, and we were accustomed to blackouts. No lights were permitted on the beaches at night, which were patrolled by Coast Guardsmen on horseback. They would sometimes frighten the wits out of teenagers caught smoking on the beach at night. We children collected tinfoil for the war effort, much as we had collected aluminum and scrap iron.

Ours was a typically patriotic Southern family: My older brother, Jack, was at Auburn University attending Naval flight training, where he soloed on April 4, 1944. Later, he sailed into Tokyo aboard the ship Pine Island the day the Japanese surrendered. Maury, who was also my senior, attended Auburn in 1944 in the Army Specialized Training Program.

We corresponded with our brothers, and with the rest of the family in Eufaula, a sister Sarah Margaret, and younger brother, Doug. With pen in hand, I'd ask how to spell a word. Bob would reply, "If you're writing Jack it doesn't matter, but if you're writing [Aunt] Sally [in Eufaula], you'd better look it up."

Those were also the days of shortages, white oleomargarine which had to be softened and color added, and rationing. Another aunt, Babe Smith, worked for the ration board in Eufaula. She knew which merchants were patriotic and which ones cheated.

At the Lee Theatre, "We are the Marines" was playing, and at the Rex, "Men on her Mind." "Uncensored" was the coming attraction. Our eyes were glued on the silver screen when the newsreels were shown before the feature.

The newsreels of that day never showed a dead American GI as did television during the Vietnam War.

Those were heart-felt, historic times. It's hard to comprehend just how tens of thousands of young men went to the shores of France to free the continent from Hitler's godless forces. There were 37,000 who never came back home.

Isn't it time Eufaula erect a World War II monument? This fiftieth anniversary of D-Day also is a time to thank those who are still in our midst. They served beyond the call of duty.

WBTS Centennial was event to remember

April 26, 1998

My southerness, my love of the Southland and Old Eufaula just won't let me ignore Confederate Memorial Day. There was a time when April 26 was a day of commemoration—if not celebration. While some think it's politically incorrect to hoist the Stars and Bars, it's part of our heritage.

Perhaps the last great Confederate Memorial Day was observed in Eufaula on April 26, 1961, during the middle of the Bluff City's memorable War Between the States Centennial. I remember the week's events well: I'd served as editor of the *Tribune* for three years, trottin' to all sorts of meetings, promoting the town and in general trying to be a good citizen.

And then I knew Old Eufaula had accepted me and I'd made the grade when "Miss" Jennie Kendall Dean, the lady of the manor at Kendall Manor, called and asked me to portray Col. Edward Courtenay Bullock in the Centennial Commemoration Pageant.

Bette Ferrell Patrick Singer, local history buff, dropped off a picture of the pageant that brought back a flood of memories. The pageant was a grand affair, and so was the Confederate Memorial Day Parade, dedication of the Confederate Museum and a barbecue.

The ball and pageant at the Old National Guard Armory kicked off the centennial events. The United Daughters of the Confederacy were in charge. "Miss" Jennie and "Miss" Carrie (Mrs. C. S.) McDowell were co-chairmen, with "Flying Jennie" as usual running the show. The local version of a Cecil B. DeMille production was directed by Martha Blondheim with young attorney Gorman Houston narrating.

The large cast in the tableau had a ball, but the production was serious business to the Daughters. Scenes depicting Eufaula in the War Between the States—never the Civil War—and the Introduction of War Personalities followed the quadrille. Governor and Mrs. John Gill Shorter, who were Eufaulians of old, were portrayed by the war governor's kin, Mr. and Mrs. Richard Comer.

Attorney Grady Cleveland, one of the UDC's favorite orators, was President Jefferson Davis. His wife, Mary, was Miss Winnie Davis. Mayor Marvin Edwards was Dr. W. H. Thornton, Eufaula's first mayor, and I reveled in portraying Mr. Bullock, leader of the Eufaula Regency and editor of *The Spirit of the South*. (The UDC knew something about public relations and how to enjoy a good press.)

Others in the auspicious tableau cast included: Hon. Preston C. and Jewel Gladys Clayton (Gen. Henry D. Clayton and Mrs. Victoria Clayton); Frankie Garrison and Caroline Cook (Capt. Hubert Dent and Mrs. Annie Young Dent); W. R. and Bette Ferrell Patrick (Capt. and Mrs. G. A. Roberts); Col. and Mrs. Ray Blackmon (Major and Mrs. Henry Shorter); Mr. and Mrs. James K. McKenzie (Capt. B. B. McKenzie and Betty Flournoy McKenzie); Mr. and Mrs. Robert H. Flewellen (Capt. Avner Flewellen and Mrs. Sarah Hardaway Flewellen).

Eufaula youths re-enacting the meeting with General Grierson, taking the urgent message that Robert E. Lee had presented his sword to General Grant at Appomattox, included Jay Jaxon and little George Little.

The orchestra played "Dixie," sung by the convivial group as the grand finale. The gala ball was followed by the parade that featured seven Real Daughters, women whose fathers actually served in the war. They were: Mrs. R. R. Moorer, Miss Rosa Moorer, Mrs. O. R. Spurlock, Mrs. R. D. Thomas, Mrs. T. G. Wilkinson, Mrs. H. R. Lee and Mrs. C. S. McDowell. Two other Real Daughters chose not to ride in the parade led by the Eufaula High Band playing "Dixie." Cub Scouts and Children of the Confederacy then placed miniature Confederate Flags on the graves of Unknown Confederate Soldiers in Old Fairview Cemetery.

Another highlight of the commemoration of "Those Eventful Years" was the dedication of the Confederate Museum on the refurbished second floor of Carnegie Library. The UDC had good-naturedly asked the ladies' club members to donate their "relics"—mementos and *not* their members—for display among artifacts moved from the crowded quarters in a corner of the library downstairs.

It was a memorable commemoration, only rivaled by the Eufaula Sesquicentennial and Eufaula's celebration of America's Bicentennial. These were some highlights of Eufaula's rich heritage your columnist observed.

Barbour County produced three Confederate generals

May 3, 1998

During the soon-to-be four decades I've edited the *Eufaula Tribune*, I've marveled at the number and the quality of leaders Barbour County has produced or fostered since the county was charted in 1833.

"Barbour County's link with eighteenth-century Virginia is inseparable, for the founders of the county, after prolonged wrangling over Indian affairs, turned to one of the great colonial families for the name that fits it like a glove," writes historian Anne Kendrick Walker.

Men debating in the Assembly at Tuscaloosa Town, then the capital of Alabama, were serious when they choose James Barbour's name for the new county bordering the fabled Chattahoochee.

Thus Barbour County, from the days of its settlement, has looked to leaders of stature who have left their mark. That our county has produced six governors and two lieutenant governors is well known.

However, many Civil War history buffs aren't aware that Barbour County contributed enormously to the Confederate military leadership. Eufaula was a booming river port prior to the beginning of the Civil War, and the town was a secessionist hotbed.

Three Barbour countians rose to the high rank of general, the most from any county, and its contribution of men in all ranks in the South was among the highest in Alabama.

Henry D. Clayton, Alpheus Baker and Cullen Andrews Battle—all natives of Georgia—were active in leading Alabama toward secession and in battle. Maj. Gen. Clayton was one of four Alabamians to reach that level in the Confederate Army. He entered as a private in a company he organized and raised, but in a few weeks he took command of Alabama troops at Pensacola with a brigadier's status.

Clayton then raised the 39th Alabama Infantry Regiment, which he led through the Kentucky campaign with Gen. Braxton Bragg. Recovering from wounds in the battle of Murfreesboro, Tenn., he was promoted to brigadier, commanding the 18th, 36th and 58th Alabama regiments, a brigade conspicuous for bravery and courage at Chickamauga.

During the Atlanta campaign, he was promoted to major general. In the last few months of the war, his division fought in the Carolinas to try to stem Gen. W. T. Sherman's movement northward from Savannah.

Clayton became circuit judge after the war and later was appointed president of the University of Alabama. He died in Tuscaloosa in 1889 and is buried in Old Fairview Cemetery in Eufaula.

Secessionist leader and Eufaula lawyer Alpheus Baker served in the 1861 secessionist convention and enlisted later as a private in the First Alabama Infantry Regiment at age thirty-two. Soon he was commissioned captain of the Eufaula Rifles and assigned to Pensacola. He rose swiftly to colonel, marching into Ft. Pillow on the Tennessee side of the Mississippi River, where he fought at New Madrid and was captured in battle.

Exchanged in September 1862, he led the 54th Alabama Infantry Regiment into the Vicksburg campaign, during which he was wounded. He commanded four Alabama regiments when he was promoted to brigadier general in March 1864, fighting from Dalton to Atlanta. His horse was shot out from under him at Resaca.

Transferring to the Gulf, his brigade was sent to the Carolinas in the spring of 1865, where he staged one of the major feats of the war: his brigade was reduced by attrition to 320 men, but Baker's brigade charged the Yankees in the Battle of Bentonville and captured 204 of the enemy.

He resumed the practice of law in Eufaula following the war, later moving to Louisville, Ky., where he became a prominent attorney. Another Eufaula lawyer, Cullen Andrews Battle, was also a militant secessionist, speaking throughout the South for the secessionist cause. He organized the Tuskegee Light Infantry and offered it to Virginia Gov. Wise on the occasion of John Brown's raid.

The veteran lieutenant colonel in the Alabama militia before the war shouldered a musket as a private but soon was promoted to major in the Third Alabama Infantry Regiment. This was a unit in the Army of Northern Virginia, under Gen. Robert E. Lee. The unit had one of the most distinguished fighting records of any Alabama unit.

He became colonel of the Third after Tenant Lomax was killed. Under battle, the Third was cited for exceptional conduct and took part in Jackson's famous march around Hooker at Chancellorsville. The Third was also distinguished at Gettysburg on July 1, when the entire brigade was repulsed except the Third Regiment, resulting in Battle's promotion to brigadier.

In a brilliant charge at Cedar Creek, Battle was severely wounded and incapacitated for the remainder of the war. He was unable to take the field and a major general's commission. After the war, he practiced law in Eufaula and was elected to Congress, however, he refused to take the ironclad oath of allegiance and was refused the seat.

So ends another chapter focusing on Barbour County leaders.

Editor's note: I am indebted to my late friend, Birmingham News *managing editor, John W. Bloomer, for his historical research.*

EUFAULA CITY SCHOOLS
DESEGREGATED PEACEFULLY

February 24, 2002

During February, the Eufaula City Schools have celebrated the outstanding system's one hundred thirtieth anniversary. Superintendent Susan L. Lockwood and the school board don't intend to rest on their laurels: Education Forums were held the first two weeks of February.

Some leaders of the community participated and gave input to the board members, the superintendent and school administrators.

Focusing on this one hundred thirtieth anniversary—1872–2002—brings back memories for me. I served on the board from 1969 to 1973, during the integration of the city schools. Along with Tuskegee, we were the first two school systems in Alabama to be integrated. It was my assignment to speak at T. V. McCoo High School's last commencement. I vividly remember giving pointers to the students who would be attending Eufaula High School in the fall.

The board and the community were pleasantly surprised at how peaceful the integration was in the old school building on Sanford Avenue.

Dating from the 1954 Supreme Court decision, the integration of Eufaula's public schools covered a period of sixteen years, as historian Robert Flewellen documents in *Along Broad Street.*

"The school year 1970–71 was the first year of city-wide, total desegregation."

The Department of Health, Education and Welfare ordered the City Board of Education to submit a plan for desegregation under a freedom of choice plan approved by the Federal government. However no black students reported to any white school for registration during the time set aside. The first year I served on the board, 1969, black students accounted for only eleven percent of the total enrollment in formerly all-white schools.

I also recall going to U.S. District Judge Frank M. Johnson Jr.'s courtroom in Montgomery. He was a tough judge who made history, but he was courteous to us. City officials were ordered by Judge Johnson to accelerate desegregation and enroll a minimum of thirty percent black students in the white schools for 1969–70.

In 1970, the Federal courts ordered total desegregation in Eufaula public schools. This was a result of the 1967 Supreme Court decision in *Lee vs. Macon.*

"The once black schools locked their doors; black students were enrolled, without incident, in the predominantly white schools; and a dual system of public education ceased to exist," Flewellen documents.

I also vividly remember when fellow school board member Jimmy Clark and I were appointed in 1970 to serve on the President's Cabinet Committee to advise President Richard Nixon during integration of Alabama's schools. My, I was in high cotton as I rode from my hotel to the White House in a long black limo to meet with other Alabamians and several members of Nixon's cabinet in the Cabinet Room.

Afterwards we met in the Oval Office, and I shook the President's hand after being introduced by Postmaster General Winton Blount, a native of Union Springs.

Those were challenging times but the Eufaula City Schools moved right along under Superintendent O. B. Carter's leadership, secure in the firm foundation earlier school leaders like Superintendent Thomas G. Wilkinson had built. Wilkinson was named principal of Alabama Breneau in 1908, and in the early 1920s he was elected superintendent of city schools. He and his wife, who organized a glee club at Eufaula High and directed a school orchestra and operettas, made monumental contributions to education and the cultural enrichment in Eufaula.

I regret that I acquiesced when the superintendent and school board were making plans to expand Sanford Street Elementary and made the decision to tear down the charming old building next door that is pictured on the Eufaula City Schools' letterhead. I feel somewhat redeemed, knowing our Super and the school board have made the decision to restore the classic old Eufaula High building on Sanford.

Congratulations, Eufaula, on the one hundred thirtieth anniversary of the first city school system in Alabama.

WWII TAIL GUNNER'S
MEMORY WILL BE HONORED

October 21, 2001

It could have been a chapter in Tom Brokaw's *Greatest Generation*.

Operations against Japan in the Pacific picked up steam in 1944. U.S. forces landed on Saipan on June 15. Our forces had possession of Saipan, Tinian and Guam by Aug. 10, giving them the key to a strategy for ending the war.

The islands could accommodate bases of the new American long-range bombers, the B-29 Super Fortresses, which could reach Tokyo at least as well from the islands as they would have been able to from bases in China.

The regular bombing of Japan began in November 1944.

Lemuel Byrd Peterson, the son of Barney and Ila Peterson of Eufaula, was promoted to sergeant prior to embarking overseas with the 897th Bomb Squadron, 497th Bomb Group, to the island of Saipan. He was assigned as tail gunner on a B-29 piloted by Capt. Dale Peterson.

By early 1945, Japan's position was hopeless, but an early end to the war was not in sight. The decimated Japanese navy wouldn't be able to come out against us again, but the bulk of the army was intact in the home islands and China. The desperate Japanese resorted to kamikaze air attacks. From Jan. 4–13, 1945, quickly trained suicide pilots flying obsolete planes had sunk seventeen U.S. ships and damaged fifty more.

On Jan. 27, 1945, on a mission over targets of Kofu and Tokyo, Japan, Sgt. Peterson's B-29, dubbed "The Ghastly Goose," was damaged severely by enemy fire. The gasoline tanks were hit, and the aircraft was ditched into the ocean just off the coast of Iwo Jima.

A second U.S. plane's crew circling the crash scene saw all eleven crew-members. They were seen safely on top of the downed bomber flashing their flashlights, indicating all were okay.

The second plane's crew accurately established the position and radioed information to rescue operations and dropped emergency equipment to the survivors before heading back to home base.

That night a storm raged. At dawn the next day, rescuers searched the sea for Sgt. Peterson and other crew members of The Ghastly Goose. They found no signs of men or aircraft. On July 16, 1945, the first atomic bomb was exploded in a test. President Harry Truman decided dropping bombs over Hiroshima and Nagasaki would save many American lives. On Aug. 14, 1945, Japan surrendered.

Byrd Peterson and the other 10 airmen were pronounced dead a year and a day after their crash, Jan. 28, 1946.

After all these years, a Veterans Administration marker will be dedicated to Sgt. Lemuel Byrd Peterson's memory and in appreciation for his supreme sacrifice. The World War II victim will be memorialized in a ceremony Saturday, Oct. 20, at four PM in Fairview Cemetery Addition.

It behooves Eufaula to remember this member of the Greatest Generation.

Well do I identify with Sgt. Peterson's family who resided off Browder Street during the war. I didn't know the brave tail gunner, but I watched his youngest brother, Billy Neil Peterson, grow up. The Petersons and my aunts, Babe and Sally Smith, and my younger brother, Doug, and sister, Sarah Margaret, were neighbors.

Barney and Ila Peterson were the salt of the earth, as my aunts would say. Byrd moved with his family from the Tumbleton/Brown's Crossroads community in Henry County in 1939 to Eufaula, where he worked in the Infant Sock Mill. He was drafted into the Army Air Corps in 1943.

His mother was beloved by Eufaulians. She was known for her delicious cakes she baked on special order. She baked the first carrot cake I ever ate, and it was just as delicious as her famous pound cake.

Barbour County lost forty-five casualties during World War II; among them was Lemuel Byrd Peterson. Let us not forget.

Battalion's return to Eufaula
yet another 'piece of history'

September 28, 2003

I n a couple of months, I will write a column celebrating my forty-fifth year of recording weekly utterances.

During almost a half-century as a columnist—I typed "Candid Comments" on my trusty Royal typewriter for over three years in my earlier life at Geneva—I've written more than 2,341 columns for the *Tribune* since 1958.

Some of these columns have been complete nonsense, a few are perhaps memorable and some have recorded pieces of history.

Commenting on Eufaula's joyous homecoming, Tuesday, Sept. 23, 2003, for the 1103rd Corps Support Battalion, will fall into that "pieces of history" category.

It was a bright and beautiful day at the red, white and blue bunting-decorated Farmers Market as the Army National Guard's families, friends and home folks waved small American flags and the Eufaula High School ROTC color guard posted the colors. The EHS band ensemble played the National Anthem, not missing a beat.

I restrained my note taking, knowing full well exemplary staff writer Susan Walworth covered this patriotic occasion. As I sat in the filled bleachers in the presence of the sharp, lean, maroon-capped column of citizen-soldiers, my patched heart beat faster. I was honored to be in their presence.

I was touched, too, by the soldiers' happy children, some with painted faces, welcoming their dads home. Mayor Jay Jaxon extended a "warm and heart-felt thanks" from the people of Eufaula. The 1103rd Corps Support Battalion mobilized 34 soldiers to Ft. Bragg on Oct. 27, 2002. He said the soldiers range in age from twenty-one to fifty-seven with an average age of forty-five.

Forty-one percent of the soldiers are veterans of Operation Desert Storm. They earned high marks and accolades for their service.

"Overall, the 1103rd supervised and managed 325 personnel from four different companies. The 1103rd contributed to the Global War on Terrorism by deploying soldiers from the four companies to Qatar, Kuwait, Okinawa and Afghanistan."

Each soldier was officially recognized and presented a medal by the battalion commander, LTC Donald B. Tatum. "It was a great day for a homecoming," he said, even as a fire truck and rescue squad sped by, and roofers on top of the courthouse continued hammering.

LTC Tatum thanked the Army National Guardsmen for putting their civilian lives on hold and for their accomplishments: Over 200 support missions resulted in over 75,000 miles driven.

He thanked Eufaula for its contribution to the global war on terrorism, and told the citizen soldiers "to never forget the history you participated in." Tatum also expressed pride in the 5,000 Alabamians from communities around the state, deployed today throughout the world. "Perhaps Eufaula is the best of the other communities."

Col. Bob Curio also expressed gratitude to the 1103rd and the City of Eufaula: "Your family is now home." He added the kind of family support the soldiers received "should be boxed and sold to every city in America. Our great Army is forever indebted to the 1103rd. They established a new standard."

The battalion supported America's front-line soldiers. They helped counter the Sept. 11 horror and helped combat the global war on terrorism.

This is an American story, a story to tell to the nation. It's an important piece of history.

'THE YANKEES ARE COMING'

April 14, 1996

If Gen. Sherman had commanded the federal troops that entered Eufaula on April 29, 1865, instead of Gen. Benjamin H. Grierson, chances are there would be no antebellum mansions standing today. Needless to say, there would be no Eufaula Pilgrimage.

Writing in *A Blockaded Family* about life in a settlement eleven miles from Eufaula during the Civil War, Parthenia Antoinette Hague describes in the schoolteacher's autobiography that day of suspense. A courier heralded from house to house the unwelcome news, "The Yankees are coming!"

"The explosion of a bomb in each one's yard could not have created greater excitement. Planters hastily fled to the swamps and the deep, unfrequented woods with their stock and valuables. At intervals throughout the day, droves of cattle and hogs were driven past my employer's residence to hiding places in the woods; and wagons and carriages, filled with whatever valuables could be quickly gotten together, were also passing by.

"It was amusing, as well as sad, to see a feather bed protruding at least a quarter of its length from a carriage window. In our great anxiety, appearances were not regarded. The single thought of the people was to protect themselves and their property as expeditiously and securely as possible.

"In the meantime we were confused and distracted by conflicting rumors. At one time that report would be, 'The army is not a mile off,' then we imagined we heard guns firing. Again it would be 'They are not coming this way at all.'"

One young woman hid her father's bag of gold and silver underneath the nest of a setting hen. Another wrapped her watch and chain, bracelets and a valuable breast pin with other jewelry in a faded rag and tossed it into the middle of a large rose bush. Yankee soldiers filled the yard but they didn't find the hidden treasure.

The writer recalled "bordering on the edge of sleep," when she was startled by a loud and hurried knock on her door. A Negro girl excitedly cried out, "Miss Antoinette, missis say come down dar quick, de Yankees coming."

She left the cottage and entered the mansion on the plantation by the back door, just in time to find "all in great confusion, caused by a false alarm. The home guards, composed of old men and young boys of the county, had that afternoon disbanded in the city of Eufaula, knowing General Grierson would arrive that night or the next morning, and that resistance would be useless. So they deemed discretion just then the better part of valor, and here they were, returning home by the road on which my employer's plantation lay, their expectation being that the Federal commander would march his column into Eufaula by a road on the other side of our settlement."

The horses' hoofs striking the bridge spanning a large nearby creek a few hundred feet away from the mansion were mistaken by lone women and children for the advance of the terrible Yankees.

Meanwhile, Masters Edward Young and Edward Stern met General Grierson at Six-Mile Branch, giving him the message that the war was over.

Eufaula never surrendered. The houses and the town were saved 131 years ago.

EUFAULA MUST PROTECT
HER FAMED SHOWPLACE

June 11, 2006

Planning and preparation for the Shorter Mansion Centennial celebration looms on the not too distant October horizon.

The Eufaula Heritage Association is launching a $500,000 capital fundraising campaign for the Neoclassical Revival cultural and social center.

My assignment is to write a history of Shorter Mansion, with input from Honorary Capital Fund Committee Chairman Florence Foy Strang. I am looking through the *Tribune's* extensive files and my personal notes made after the Eufaula Carnegie Library trustees met in 1965 and appointed me, the editor, to ask Mayor Marvin Edwards to appoint a committee to investigate the possibility of the city buying it at auction for a civic center.

I've already written a continuing history of the showplace on North Eufaula Avenue with its seventeen Corinthian columns, and many other volunteers have contributed their chapters also.

I ran across a copy of my letter to the fledgling National Trust for Historic Preservation in 1965 asking for a statement from the National Trust certifying the Shorter-Upshaw home was worthy of preservation. I also remember mailing The Trust a copy of Ralph Hammond's *Ante-Bellum Mansions of Alabama* with its inclusion of two photographs of the Shorter-Upshaw Home as an addendum: because of its "distinctive architecture. It does not fit within the time element of antebellum Alabama. Built in 1906, the mansion is Eufaula's residential showplace."

The National Trust and the Alabama Department Archives and History's executive director Milo Howard concurred that the mansion was worthy of our efforts.

A copy of my essay, "The Preservation of Something Historical," also pops up from an overloaded yellow file folder:

"A community's monuments and landmarks, such as the Shorter-Upshaw mansion in Eufaula, Ala., are constant reminders of the historical past and are significant in that they are part of the American heritage. Such landmarks help instill great local pride in one's own community and a desire to improve it is an almost universal trait of the American character.

"It is for this reason that the City of Eufaula and the Alabama Historical Commission recognize the importance of preserving the beautiful Shorter-Upshaw mansion that is important in the history and culture of Alabama."

People who made history often built great houses. Such is the case with the Eufaula "showplace." The Shorter family played important roles in the drama of antebellum Eufaula, "the Natchez of the Chattahoochee," since the days before the War Between the States. Today, the mansion and its antique furnishings are graphic reminders of the Shorter family legacy.

The Rev. Morton Bryan Wharton, whose imposing marble statue stands across from First Baptist Church at the intersection of Barbour Street and Randolph Avenue, praises the Shorters in his poem, "The View from the Bluff at Eufaula":

"A little city destined yet to rule / 'The State of Barbour' is the statesman's school. / Here dwelt the Shorters wise, and great and good."

Yes indeed, that promotional piece is equally true this centennial year as the Heritage Association pays tribute to Eli Shorter II and his wife, Wileyna

Lamar, of Macon, Ga., heiress of the SSS Tonic fortune, who completed an extensive remodeling and expansion in 1906 to give the mansion its imposing Neoclassical Revival grandeur. It was originally constructed in 1884.

Eli Sims Shorter II was the nephew of John Gill Shorter, who was governor of Alabama from 1861 to 1863 during the Civil War. When the governor died May 29, 1872, former slaves in bright regalia of their lodges marched in his funeral procession.

Governor Shorter's eulogies are most impressive, also. The *Eufaula News* editorialized, "It was sorrow too deep for words that we note the decease of Ex-Governor John Gill Shorter, and if ever we felt the real truth and beauty of the poet's thought: 'None knew him, but to love him, None named him but to praise.'"

"We cannot convey to the distant reader an idea of the loss which the city of Eufaula is called upon today to sustain. If Governor Shorter had an enemy on earth, white or black, we have yet to learn the fact. It is sad indeed to realize the mournful truth that the heart once so full of noble, manly impulses is now still forever."

The Shorter brothers, John Gill and Eli Sims, belonged to a powerful political oligarchy, the Eufaula Regency, a strong Southern rights group, principally lawyers from Eufaula.

Eli Sims Shorter was known as the silver-tongued orator of Alabama whose speeches held his audience tensely. He was "a man among men, much loved for his personality."

He and his wife, Wileyna Lamar, were the parents of Alberta, who married N. D. Eubanks, Atlanta, and Fanny, who married Herman L. Upshaw, Eufaula, and Eli Sims. Wileyna Upshaw married Robert Kennedy from Cuthbert, Ga. Their sons were Robert Kennedy Jr. now deceased, and David Kennedy, who lives in Gainesville, Ga.

Upshaw was editor, publisher and owner of the *Eufaula Tribune*. He and I became partners in July 1958. He died in January 1959. His gracious widow, Elizabeth McKeithen Upshaw (whom he married after the death of Fanny Shorter Upshaw), and I were partners in the *Tribune* until her retirement when I became sole owner. She and Col. Upshaw resided in the Shorter-Upshaw mansion until his death.

The Shorter Mansion is Eufaula's most recognizable landmark. It is also a symbol of Alabama's grandeur. It behooves the community to protect our cultural and social center.

South hasn't always celebrated July 4

July 9, 1995

Historians tell us Southern towns like Eufaula weren't so exuberant in celebrating the anniversary of the signing of the Declaration of Independence—until after the Spanish-American War and World War I.

Decades after the War Between the States, July 4 in the South was a time to remember Vicksburg, the North-South battle that split the Confederacy in half.

Vicksburg, Miss., fell to Gen. U. S. Grant on July 4, 1863, while 900 miles to the north, Southern soldiers lay dead at Gettysburg, Pa., where Gen. Robert E. Lee retreated, and his army was mortally wounded.

The Fourth of July was associated with Vicksburg, says Charles Wilson, professor of history and Southern studies at the University of Mississippi. White Southerners in Eufaula celebrated Confederate Memorial Day April 26, and Fourth of July fireworks were unheard of here until after WWI.

The Fourth was so close to Emancipation Day on June 19, the former slaves and freedmen regarded it as "their day." Neither city or county offices, nor businesses closed, but blacks frequently did not report to work.

The Spanish-American War became a symbol of reunification; Eufaulians were once again fighting with the Union in large numbers. The muster rolls of Alabama volunteers in that war of 1898 included seventy from Eufaula, Clayton and Georgetown who served with the Second Regiment of the Alabama United States Volunteer Infantry.

The war was short, and soon the South reverted to its old ways, finding July 4 distasteful, University of Alabama historian Gary Mills says.

"That attitude lingered until World War I, that being the big event when Southern boys were again fighting for the Union," Wilson says.

In my hometown of Samson, my father, a World War I veteran, and active in the American Legion post, promoted a July 4 celebration big time. Father was the ramrod, and the holiday ranked behind Christmas, of course, but before New Year's and Thanksgiving. Shooting fireworks and throwing homemade fireballs were traditions greatly enjoyed by boys and their fathers. The fireballs were made with tightly wound cotton or wool, rolled into a ball the size of a softball and soaked in kerosene.

This ritual revived by Frankie and Julia Ann Strickland at their home west of Clayton in a cleared field on New Year's Eve probably dates back to the turn of the century in Barbour County.

But, back to the Fourth of July. It was a big day when I was a boy. The downtown was blocked off for bicycle races, climbing the greased pole with a five-dollar bill attached to the top and catching the greased pig. Concession stands sold lemonade, hot dogs and hamburgers, and farm families from miles around came to enjoy the festivities.

The Fourth added color to those drab Depression days, as well as money in the cash register for participating merchants.

In Eufaula, on July 4, 1929, the *Tribune* reported: "Eufaula has Quiet Fourth: No Celebration Here, Citizens Go To Other Towns.

"Eufaula is quietly celebrating the anniversary of our more or less independence. The banks, post office and a few other places are closed, while at City Hall all is stillness. Flags are flying in front of business houses and a few residences." Many Eufaulians went to Ft. Gaines for a ball game in the afternoon.

That Fourth was marked in contrast to the town's greatest Independence Day celebration ever on July 4, 1976, the two hundredth anniversary of the signing of the Declaration of Independence.

The celebration ran for two thrill-packed days with a fabulous parade down Broad Street featuring kids dressed as Minute Men or other historical figures, and Mayor Hamp Graves and the city officials riding on the city's 1924 vintage fire truck. Tom Mann was the perfect Uncle Sam, and the Eufaula High School birthday cake float was something.

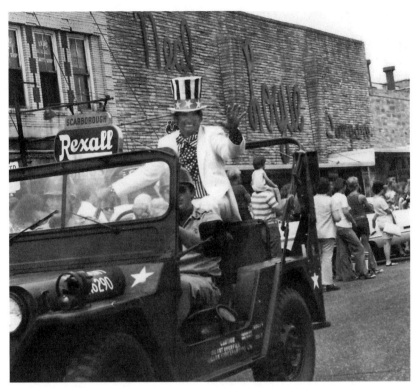

Eufaula celebrated the U.S. Bicentennial in grand style in 1976 when Tom Mann, as a striking Uncle Sam, was grand marshal for the parade down Broad Street.

An historical pageant on the bluff in front of The Tavern was one of the most outstanding Bicentennial events anywhere, as I witnessed via television. (The Tall Ships in New York Harbor were perhaps more over-powering.) Jim Scarborough was the spitting image of Ben Franklin, and Gorman Houston and Terri Porter performed like professionals as the storm broke over the "Minutes in History" tableau. Bill Quinney and Ron Beckham did the soft shoe, and Mack Price and Ben Reeves worked like fury to keep the tambourines in rhythm. The Bicentennial Ball with the Sophisticated Brass playing from a gazebo was a smashing street dance in spite of a storm that soaked the revelers, who went home, changed clothes and continued dancing for hours and hours.

As the proud editor, I vowed Eufaula must continue the Fourth of July with verve and gusto.

The two hundred and nineteenth celebration, while not as spectacular, was nonetheless memorable with the inspiring, standing-room only patriotic service Sunday night and the traditional fireworks display mirrored in placid Lake Eufaula Tuesday night.

Don't mess with our town's special character

October 14, 2001

It's suddenly dawned on me that I may be in my dotage, and I know this former editor is out of the loop. This revelation came to me while in the middle of typing my remarks I made at the Eufaula Heritage Association's annual meeting.

Shortly after keyboarding "Eufaula continues to successfully maintain its architectural integrity" and noting that "Last year *Veranda* magazine reported 'Eufaula is probably one of only a handful of communities in the United States that has successfully maintained an intact historic district without government intervention," I took a breather to attend the Eufaula Historic Preservation Commission's monthly meeting at City Hall.

I learned at that meeting Council President Jim Martin is unhappy with the size of the Seth Lore and Irwinton Historic District, which the commission has proposed the city council adopt as a local historic district with all the protection thereof.

After years of being one of only a "handful of communities" that relies either on peer pressure or civic stewardship, I thought we're finally securing our heritage and protecting a basic Eufaula industry—tourism.

This new development is more than of cultural interest—as important as that may be. We're talking about our beleaguered local and state economy.

Then I heard on the street Mayor Jay Jaxon was secretly meeting with Dr. Lee Warner, Alabama Historical Commission executive director, and a local committee to find a new use for Fendall Hall, our state-owned house museum.

I was shocked to hear Dr. Warner the next day tell the Friends of Fendall Hall board that his commission's state budget has been cut sixteen percent and that because Fendall Hall has no statewide or national historical significance, the AHC's goal is to find a good steward for the antebellum mansion built in 1859.

That shot my local preservation assessment to shreds. While we are making great strides in the Eufaula Main Street program, the city fathers are acting like politicians.

Dr. Warner says the AHC would retain ownership but seek a partner. He says their goal is to find a way for the community to support Fendall Hall. "The mayor was the logical approach," he said.

Maybe so, but why in the name of thunder didn't the executive director consult—or at least inform—his Friends of Fendall Hall board of directors first?

I'm indignant that I learned the news on the street. I was the Eufaula Heritage Association president when we finally closed the sale of Fendall Hall to the state—thanks to Yank Dean and Eufaula Bank and Trust's faith and generosity in bankrolling the Heritage Association.

How soon they forget. So I modified my State of Historic Preservation report and urged the dues-paying Heritage Association members to contact their councilmen.

I also suggest good citizens contact our district's Alabama Historical Commission representative, David Peterson, in neighboring Abbeville, and AHC chairman, Dr. Allen Cronenberg, at Auburn University's Center for the Arts and Humanities.

If I sound like one of those "Southeast Alabama fire eaters" that waged the Alabama secession effort, so be it. They're messing with our town's special character and basic industry—tourism.

Chapter 5

Barbour's 'Fighting Little Judge'

WALLACE'S HOME FOLKS WHOOP IT UP . . .

May 3, 1962

"The Little Judge" couldn't have enjoyed listening to the election returns much more than did all his friends and neighbors "down home." In Eufaula, the election caused more excitement among the grown folks than the crowning of the May Day Queen did among the kids who jam-packed the gym Tuesday night.

George's local supporters gathered in clusters to hear the returns. Tabulations were kept on large blackboards at the Wallace Headquarters on Broad Street, and interested voters crowded outside the office or sat in their cars and listened to the latest returns announced over the loud speakers at the headquarters.

Not only was there lots of excitement over "The Little Judge's" race for the governorship, but there was a great deal of interest in the various county races—some of which were nip and tuck.

While we're on the subject of politics, I'd like to suggest that our friends who edit the *Columbus Enquirer* either dust off their crystal ball or draw straws and pick out another political editor.

The bright boy who predicted in an editorial last Saturday that "The

Little Judge" would assume the role Jimmy Faulkner played in 1958 must have been spending all this time studying the problems involved in the European Common Market or exploring the effects the recent ruckus over steel prices will have on Wall Street.

He couldn't have been following politics across the river too closely to have predicted that the candidates for governor would have finished thusly; "Folsom (narrowly), deGraffenreid, Wallace, Gallion, Connor, Henderson and Wayne Jennings."

Now We Have Two Governors . . .

May 31, 1962

Governor Chauncey Sparks must be about the proudest man in town. He had predicted that his good friend, "The Little Judge," had the runoff in the bag and that George Wallace would win by approximately 50,000 votes Tuesday. Now Gov. Sparks is all smiles as he welcomes a stream of visitors to his office who come in to talk politics.

Perhaps no other man has had a greater influence over "The Little Governor" than Governor Sparks. George's father died when he was a young boy. As he grew into manhood, he solicited advice and counsel from his good friend, Chauncey Sparks. The governor recalls how young George politicked for him when he was in college and presented him with a list of pledges. It quickly became evident that George was a "natural born politician—he just loved it," Gov. Sparks says.

During the last year of Sparks's administration, young George graduated from the University of Alabama Law School, and the governor used his influence to have him appointed an assistant attorney general. The next step up the political ladder for Wallace was election to the House of Representatives. "He made quite a record up there where he sponsored progressive legislation," Governor Sparks points out. He studied the needs of the people and sponsored bills that have had far-reaching effects.

Barbour Countians were convinced that they had a leader in George C. Wallace, and they re-elected him to the legislature.

After becoming thoroughly familiar with the legislative process, Wallace decided to seek the office of Judge of the Circuit Court, and he was elected. "The way he prepared himself was remarkable," Governor Sparks says with a little smile. He recalls how "The Little Judge" fixed up a charge book—complete with an index—in which he used to charge the jury as he sat on the bench.

Wallace made a success of the judicial job, Governor Sparks says. "Then he got the big bug in his head." He ran against Patterson, and although he lost, as the Governor points out, "He ran a creditable race." The sympathy of the people was with John Patterson, whose father, the attorney general nominee, was murdered in Phenix City. Gov. Sparks gives Patterson credit for being a good attorney general, the office he filled in his father's place, and he agrees that it would have been impossible to beat him in the governor's race in 1958.

Governor Sparks commented before Tuesday's election: "I see nothing but Wallace. It's in the bag. George is a capable and courageous candidate. He will give an opportunity for the people to secure a leader such as they need at this time. He will win by approximately 50,000 votes."

Today, Governor Sparks, like all Barbour Countians, is happy over Wallace's victory. Barbour now has the distinction of being the only county in the state that can boast of both a former governor and a governor nominee.

As the fifth Barbour Countian to serve in the governor's chair, we agree with our distinguished former governor in his belief that George will make a great leader. "He's going to flood this country with speeches. The nation will know him, and I don't think he's going to give an adverse picture. In my opinion he's going to be adopted by this nation," Governor Sparks predicts.

Twisting Great Sport on Clayton Square

June 22, 1962

I haven't had so much fun since I was a kid, whooping it up at a Fourth of July celebration in Samson. That big "Wallace Day" shindig at Clayton was a barrel of fun, not only for all the Wallaces, but also for the throng of folks who crowded into the town square to greet our next governor at Clayton's big homecoming.

Everybody, just about it, got into the act, and the event turned out to be the kind of homecoming country folks love. Being somewhat of a country boy myself, I got a bang out of the day in Clayton. The town was all dressed up for the "show," and the home folks were in a festive mood, setting the stage for the very special day.

The formal part of the program was just as it should have been—very informal. In spite of Bob Ingram's ridiculous article in Sunday's *Advertiser*, George wasn't a "bust at his homecoming." He was just plain George, and the people loved him for it.

Eating the delicious barbecue, as the band played, was lots of fun. It must have been a lot like the "good old days" when communities got together for picnics and Fourth of July celebrations. It was fun talking to folks from just about everywhere, but I think the street dance was the most fun of all.

Willard Smith and I got a big kick out of watching the "Seven Sinners from Seale" as they plugged in their amplifiers and tuned up to play for the dance. We were particularly interested in hearing Louie Holmes play the drums. Charles Tigner, who really plays a mean organ, must have taught Louie a thing or two—although I rather doubt if Louie knows one note from the other—because those fellows produced some mighty danceable music.

The "Sinners," who were the official band for the evening, hadn't gotten warmed up good before a hot-shot quartet moved in, unplugged their amplifiers and plugged in the guitars. I was informed that the quartet was a really big name group—and they just might have been. They played red guitars, wore mustaches the width of a pencil mark and they had their hair slicked down like a "two dab devil."

The quartet, which incidentally brought their own piano, sang a few sacred numbers and were "unplugged" by Curly Culpepper and his "Pepper-uppers." After Curly's boys got plugged in the twisting, square dancing and jitterbugging started again.

Bitsey Hatfield, that "Big Bam" radio personality from Eufaula, played with Curl's talented band. The crowd loved the "Pepper-uppers" and their brand of music. Everybody either did the twist or joined in a round of square dancing.

I overheard one woman tell George Wallace, "Come on, let's do the twist. I want to tell my grandchildren I did the twist with the governor!" Then there was tiny, four-year-old Alice Miller who twisted like a teenager at a graceful ballet. Little Alice, I was pleased to learn, is the daughter of Mrs. Ann Martin Miller of Birmingham. Highlight of the dance was an exhibition given by the state twist champions, Helen Mostellar and Oscar Vance of Ashville.

George's inauguration might be fun, but I doubt if the "home folks" will enjoy it anymore than they did at Thursday's homecoming.

Inaugural ball an impressive affair

January 17, 1963

Gov'nor George C. has been inaugurated. His inaugural parade was the longest, his inaugural tea was the snitziest, his ball was the jazziest and his inaugural day was probably the coldest.

Our Barbour County farm boy that made good indeed is popular with "his people." Anybody that sat in the cold to watch that mammoth parade and to hear the Gov'nor's inaugural speech had to be either his kinfolk, a member of his cabinet, a staunch died-in-the-wool Wallace supporter, or from Barbour County. Or like me, although I'm for the Barbour Bantam, it took two nieces marching with one of the last bands to make me sit from the beginning of the parade almost to the end of the five-hour ordeal.

I've always wanted to show myself on television, but darned if I particularly wanted five million people to watch me, bundled up like an Eskimo, shivering so that my knees knocked and my lips quivered. So, where do I sit during the inauguration—you've guessed—right across the street from those TV cameras with the telescopic lens. My chum buddies across the state and the panhandle of northwest Florida have either concluded, that since I sat for hours in the cold, I'm either a first-class publicity hound or some other kind of nut.

Preston Clayton says he caught a cold just watching that parade on TV.

But while foot-long icicles did hang from the fountain on Dexter, the weather didn't spoil the big day for me or the other Barbour Countians who came to town. I was up, bright eyed—but no so bushy tailed—early Monday morning dialing for "my car." You see, friend Al Lingo gave me a courtesy card that entitled me to ride around in one of his patrol cars during the inaugural to do. And road ride I did . . . I spent much of the day impressing my family and friends as we crawled in and out of patrol cars, traveling to and from all the Gov'nor's inaugural festivities. Unfortunately, we had to drive up and down lots of back alleys to get places, and I didn't get to wave at lots of folks I wanted to impress.

And do you think your country editor, a friend of George C.'s, stood in that block-long line to shake his hand at the inaugural tea? No sir. Wallace cousin Charlotte Reeves's mother tipped us off about a side door entrance. "There's a highway patrolman at the door," she said, "but, Charlotte, don't you let him stare you down," Mrs. Kirke Adams advised. So that pretty gal just smiled and the door opened for Ben, my date and me. Inside at the reception, Bertie and Tom Parish, Clayton friends of the Gov'nor's, were having a grand time. Bertie played the organ and Tom stood on the landing of the grand staircase while all their hometown friends sashayed around the mansion.

The ball was an impressive affair for the spectators, if not for the gov'nor, his cabinet and the legislators. It was fun to watch them promenade back

Smith was on hand in 1963 for the first inaugural of Gov. George C. Wallace, shown here being sworn in by his brother, Jack Wallace, who succeeded George as circuit judge. Future Gov. Lurleen Wallace looked on as her husband began his first of four terms.

and forth during the grand march. There was ol' Seymore Trammell and his wife, Sim Thomas and daughter, Virginia, Al Lingo and daughter-in-law, Faye, Senator Jimmy Clark and wife, Marie, and of course, the Gov'nor and Lurleen. As if the day hadn't been a big enough ordeal for them, they walked back and forth, up and down that floor—the length of a football field—until I thought some of the ladies would split their tight skirts or that some of those overweight would pass out.

Yep, Gov'nor George C. has been inaugurated.

Keep your eyes on Lurleen Wallace

January 12, 1967

It might sound a little incongruous to say it, but Alabama's new Governor is a real honey.

While she did a splendid job as a "stand-in" candidate for her famous husband during the gubernatorial campaigns, Lurleen Wallace has proven to Alabamians that she is quite a remarkable and capable individual herself.

Well do I remember the ribbing that one of my "refined and cultured" friends gave me way back when the *Tribune* editorially endorsed Mrs. Wallace's candidacy. We pointed out that she suited us better than any of her male opponents and were so bold as to say that she was capable and qualified.

I haven't taken any ribbing lately. Alabamians and Americans in general are discovering that Mrs. Wallace is not a retiring young woman who will be content to serve as hostess at the mansion and a "stand-in" governor at the capitol. Granted, she is a charming hostess, poised, attractive and not at all over-shadowed by her nationally known, greatly admired, but controversial husband.

Those of us who packed the State Capitol Building almost to the rafters to hear Lurleen announce to Alabama and the nation that she would be a candidate in the election were tremendously impressed—and I suppose surprised—at the splendid manner in which she handled herself. Not only did she appear more radiant that I can remember, but her voice was strong, and she spoke with authority.

As Bob Ingram told me, "She was chomping at the bits to run," so I'm convinced that she WANTED to campaign on her own behalf. As she campaigned with the governor, it was evident to the thousands who heard her that this was a woman who could stand on her own two feet and command respect.

As one of her women friends in Clayton told me the other day, "The national press is going to find out that Lurleen is not a patsy." Perhaps this best describes Mrs. Wallace. She is plenty capable, and the Alabama newspapers are fast acknowledging the fact.

Unlike Ma Ferguson of Texas, Lurleen didn't campaign by telling the voters that they could have "two governors for the price of one." However, she has made it quite clear from the beginning that Governor George Wallace will be her "number one advisor." In essence, we will be getting two Wallaces for the price of one—and I hasten to add they'll both be a good bargain.

No, the national press won't be able to get too much mileage out of a Ma and Pa Ferguson-type approach. The big-time newsboys, if they're very objective, will learn pretty soon that Lurleen Wallace is a fine lady who not only has learned a great deal during her years as Alabama's First Lady, but that she is a warm, good-natured individual who is certainly capable of making some mighty good decisions as a real chief executive.

You Need Agile Elbows At Lurleen's Inauguration

January 19, 1967

When I go to Washington to cover George Wallace's inauguration, I am going to get an over-sized nametag, which says "OFFICIAL"—and I'm going to get both Lurleen and George to sign my press pass.

I'm learning how to go about covering a big event like an inauguration. Aware that the major networks and the daily press would scoop me on Gov. Lurleen's inauguration, I resigned myself to looking for some feature angles that might be of interest to our readers, even though they are a couple or three days late.

I learned from the first Wallace inauguration that the best way to get up close to where the action is taking place is to be aggressive—using both elbows when necessary—and to act like I was a member of the official party.

This technique worked fine Monday, when I worked my way through the jammed, mass of humanity that engulfed the Capitol to see the first lady governor sworn into office. Holding the camera over my head, I squeezed through the crowd, past the long, double line of Guardsmen in green berets and took my stand on the top step just outside the portico.

When the dozens of TV cameramen, photographers and reporters surged forward—all competing for a choice place in front of the lectern—officers ordered them to move back. I explained that I was from George Wallace's home newspaper and darned if a kindly, gentleman officer didn't introduce me to another officer, who informed several Guardsmen that I was to have a choice perch for the historic swearing in ceremony.

When I spied Judge Jack Wallace and his pretty wife, Betty, the Gerald Wallaces, and Judge Chauncey Sparks on the portico behind the spot where Lurleen was to stand on the Jeff Davis star, I stepped over to take an informal shot or two before the Governor-elect walked up the steps.

In the excitement of watching Lurleen make her dramatic move past the Guardsmen and highway patrolmen, I lost my place and couldn't out-elbow the battery of newsmen. I decided to stand on a windowsill behind the lectern and photograph the small lady Governor. Big and impressive Sgt. Mack Brown from Eufaula announced to those around that I could stay up there and make all the pictures I needed. I did, thanks to good old Mack.

Rather than fight the mob any longer, I teamed up with Ben Reeves, Eufaula's DA who knows his way around the Capitol, and we walked past several dozen policemen and guards and right into the Governor's office. Charlotte Reeves, the Governor's pretty cousin, and my wife, Ann, my pretty official film pack holder, joined us to wait for the brand new Governor.

Judge Chauncey Sparks, looking dapper in a new narrow brimmed hat, his private nurse, Mrs. Annie Morgan, and Rodger Daniel Jr. hospital administrator, were already in the Governor's suite watching Mrs. Wallace give her inaugural speech.

Immediately after her splendid speech, Lurleen was escorted into the office. Seymore Trammell arranged for me to make the first pictures of the sincere, gracious, but tired new governor after she walked into her office. I asked both Governors Wallace to pose for pictures with their dear friend

Chauncey Sparks, who sat by the governor's desk in a wheel chair. Judge Sparks pushed out his chest and stood up to be photographed with the Wallaces.

When I told Gov. Sparks that I was focusing my camera on his glasses, he said focus on Lurleen. She is the center of attention. Indeed she was.

Receiving "home folks" treatment from the prettiest governor Alabama ever had, I was given time to make several pictures before the waiting hoard of photographers outside in the hall were allowed to come inside for Gov. Lurleen's first pictures behind the big, mahogany desk, which had been occupied for four years by her famous husband. The thoughtful lady thanked the *Tribune* for publishing the special inaugural edition, adding that she hadn't had time to read all of it but that she intended to.

Pleased that I had been fortunate in coming up with some exclusive pictures, I tucked my camera under my arm and climbed into an "official" car with Ben, Charlotte, Ann and Gerald, the Governor's brother. We were chauffeured to the Gold Room to join in a festive Barbour County inaugural celebration.

It was a big day for Barbour Countians and for the Bluff City "Fishwrapper's" number one reporter. Yep, when George takes office in Washington, I'm going to do like several of his staff members did—I'm going to pin a big "OFFICIAL" sign across my chest and elbow my way up to the podium.

CAMERAS FOCUS ON WALLACE'S CLAYTON

November 7, 1968

Eufaula High's colorful band set the tempo for Presidential Candidate George C. Wallace's rousing homecoming in Clayton Tuesday. The famous Barbour Countian was late getting down to the courthouse to vote, but the large crowd that gathered didn't seem to mind. In a festive mood, the crowd gathered on the courthouse steps and on the sidewalk below, clapped their hands and kept time as the band played "Way Down

Upon the Suwannee River."

The kids had a field day, too. They played on the lawn, and students from Wallace High carried a banner that read, "Wallace High Welcomes Pre. George." In a prominent place, a huge sign proclaimed "Dixie Academy salutes Hon. George C. Wallace." The Civitan Club erected a sign on the lawn, too.

As the crowd gathered, James Teal, clerk of the Circuit Court, answered a call from the *New York Times*. They wanted to know how many people had gathered to welcome Wallace home. Cigar-smoking Teal told the reporter about 5,000 were gathered around the Clayton Town square. "That's more people than both of the other candidates drew when they went to vote!" the reporter exclaimed.

Scattered among the crowd were several photographers and reporters, and shortly two chartered busloads of representatives of the news media arrived. Such nationally known newsmen as Peter Jennings, ABC commentator, and Marvin Scot, Mutual newscaster, converged on the Barbour County Courthouse. Around seventy-five newsmen and photographers from the nation's major dailies, the three TV networks and several foreign correspondents were there to cover Gov. Wallace when he came home to cast his ballot.

The visiting photographers almost stole the show from Wallace. Sporting long sideburns and even beards, with every conceivable type of camera and light meters hanging from their necks, some of the photographers were something to watch as they went about recording the historic event on film for the major newspapers and TV networks.

The dapper Jennings, who looked like he needed a haircut, was very pleasant. He "liked this part of the country," recalling the time he came to Eufaula to cover, "Al Lingo Day." Mr. Jennings told us he would be ABC's anchorman for the network's coverage at Garrett Coliseum Tuesday night. He explained he likes to travel with candidates so he can see how they affect people. No doubt he was impressed with the warmth Barbour Countians showed their favorite son that day.

When the former Governor arrived, the friendly throngs engulfed him. Security men tried to shield him, but the Secret Service men, all wearing small ID pins in their lapels, hadn't counted on Wallace shaking hands with the home folks. Finally, the Third Party Candidate made it through the crowd in front of the courthouse and into the small auditorium where the voting machines stand.

Dozens of cameramen were set up and ready when he signed his name and stepped inside the voting booth. It took him a little while inside, prompting one newsman to ask, "Did you vote a split ticket?"

"I voted under the rooster," the former Governor answered. "The switch got locked!"

Exuding confidence, Wallace spoke as a dozen microphones were shoved practically into his face. He remarked his success has shown a Southerner can be nominated. People do not care whether you're from Clayton, Ala., or Long Beach, if they agree with your philosophy, he stated for the news media.

As he emerged from the modern, marble façade of the courthouse, the Eufaula High band struck up "Are You From Dixie," one of Wallace's campaign songs. Nearby, a Secret Service man shook his head as Wallace shook hands and hugged several "home folks."

Several in the crowd yelled, "Speech! Speech!" and the popular Barbour native obliged. He said, "It's good to be back home," like he meant it. He thanked everyone for turning out. Thanking the Eufaula High band, "one of the finest in the country," he shook hands with Director Clarence Tapley and several members of the band.

The band played "Stars Fell on Alabama" as the candidate walked out into the street, in front of the Confederate monument, still shaking hands as nervous Secret Service men shook their heads.

It was almost typical Wallace homecoming

April 23, 1970

It had all the markings of a typical Wallace homecoming.

Two pretty girls pinned big pink roses in each of the former governor's lapels.

A small boy, wearing a "Dixie Academy" T-shirt, carried a printing-shop-printed placard, which read, "Win with Wallace."

Two older youths held a big, homemade banner which proudly proclaimed, "Dixie Academy supports Wallace."

And it was a beautiful day for a political rally. The throngs, which gathered early at the Eufaula courthouse in front of the bandwagon, enjoyed the music of Johnny Dollar and Benny Williams, high-priced Nashville entertainers.

In short it was a festive crowd, until a small group of militant Negro youths began shouting in unison and waving an opposing candidate's bumper stickers.

But for a while the crowd and the large Wallace entourage ignored the hecklers. One of the Wallace workers on the platform remarked, good naturedly, "One thing I like about America—we have freedom of choice."

The Wallace partisans cheered.

Several attractive Eufaula women, wives of staunch Wallace supporters, passed suds buckets and asked for campaign contributions from the home folks. Bobby Bowick, a full-time Wallace campaign employee from Eufaula, obviously enjoyed greeting old friends as he mingled with the crowd.

As the crowd grew bigger and bigger, courthouse regulars looked down from the second-story windows.

"This is Wallace County, isn't it?" somebody yelled out.

"Yea!" the enthusiastic crowd roared.

The youthful Negro hecklers countered with a vocal "No!"

The string band played a stirring rendition of "Dixie" and George Wallace in person stepped up to the microphones. The predominately youthful crowd greeted the Barbour County native with an enthusiastic reception.

George Wallace addressed a raucous crowd in Eufaula during his 1970 campaign for governor against Lt. Gov. Albert Brewer. Only minutes after Wallace began to speak, police had to escort him from the platform as hecklers shouted him down.

It was almost like an old-fashion political rally—complete with banners red, white and blue bunting and all the trimmings. But it was more. The press corps covering the small city political rally included political reporters from the *Washington Star* and the *Christian Science Monitor*.

What had all the markings of an enjoyable homecoming for the former presidential candidate almost turned into a nightmare. The fun ended when the Negro youths succeeded in shouting down Gov. Wallace's speech.

Editor's note: The Democratic primary race between Wallace and Gov. Albert Brewer in 1970 was perhaps Wallace's most contentious race in Alabama. Only three or four minutes into this speech, police had to escort Wallace from the platform, and the campaign took an ugly, bitter turn.

Gov. Wallace shouldn't run in '72

May 12, 1971

It's now a proven fact Gov. George Wallace hasn't lost his touch. A number of writers have had much to say about the "new" George Wallace since he began serving his second term as governor. The Barbour native has been described as more subdued and less forceful in his oratory.

While we do see some indications Gov. Wallace has changed, his speech to the opening session of the Alabama Legislature and his address to a large group of Texas supporters proved he can still excite an audience. The Governor spoke to a cheering, applauding, foot-stamping crowd of some one thousand partisans who paid from twenty-five to fifty dollars to hear him.

During the Dallas speech, the Governor also hinted he may be a third party candidate for president again in 1972. Last Saturday night he told Texans he may take the school busing issue to the people of the United States in a second bid for the presidency.

There is increasing speculation as to whether "The Fighting Little Judge" will indeed run again. Columnist Marianne Means says the White House is now virtually convinced Wallace will not mount a national campaign for President again in '72. She contends President Nixon's political strategists base their judgment primarily upon the fact Wallace is not enlarging his staff, contacting supporters, raising money or in any other visible way expanding his extra-territorial activities.

The Washington columnist may be correct—and we hope she is.

We think it is fine for Wallace to speak out on national issues. He should. Gov. Wallace is in a unique position and is a national figure who can be heard when he chooses to speak.

We hope he will continue to speak from time to time and will continue to appear on national television. In short, we hope he will continue to be a critic of the two national parties. Certainly, both the Republicans and the Democrats need raking over the coals from time to time. Gov. Wallace can serve his country well by speaking up as the "loyal opposition."

We also hope Gov. Wallace will continue to devote most of his time to the job at hand—serving first and foremost the people of Alabama. Our state needs a full-time governor.

The special session of the legislature was proof positive Gov. Wallace has his work cut out. Much needs to be done if Alabama is to realize only a small portion of its tremendous potential. Our state has abundant resources—and yes, people who are "just as refined, just as cultured" as people anywhere—but we are lacking in leadership. That's where Gov. Wallace comes in. He has a tremendous capacity for leadership. He can excite people, he can move lawmakers to do the things they should do for their constituents, their state.

So we hope the Governor won't seriously entertain any thoughts for running for president again. We are convinced it would be another loosing cause for him personally and for Alabamians collectively.

Alabama needs George Wallace on the job in Montgomery. He can move our state forward and become one of the most dynamic governors in the nation. He can also continue to speak out on the issues and be heard all the way from Goat Hill to the White House—without running for president.

WALLACE HELPED BUT IT'S TIME FOR CHANGE

January 11, 1979

I t's about time for that promised, and highly publicized, "new begin-
ning" in state politics. This was dramatized Saturday when Gov. George
Wallace said so long to his many longtime supporters, and Lt. Gov.
Jere Beasley bid farewell to the Alabama State Senate Tuesday.

While it may be a little difficult for some Barbour Countians who
have been spoiled because two native sons have held the two top jobs in
Montgomery for the past eight years, I believe many of us actually feel,
deep down inside, it is time for a new beginning.

No doubt about it, Barbour has benefitted because a Wallace from Barbour County has been in office for almost two decades, and during the past
two terms, native sons have served as governor and lieutenant governor.

While Barbour is the Home of Governors, it's about time we pass and
let Lee County enjoy the honor. In many ways, the Wallace years have been
good years, but it will be good for state government and good for Alabama
to have a new chief executive.

Political dynasties aren't usually too good for the general welfare of a
county, a state or a nation. A Kennedy shouldn't be elected to high office
because of his charismatic name, and neither should a Wallace occupy a
political office because his name is Wallace. Nepotism comes too easily
when such is the case.

Don't get me wrong. George Wallace hasn't forgotten from whence he
came, and he did do many things for Barbour County. He appreciates the
fact the people of his home county gave him the opportunity to serve in
state government.

He is aware the home folks made it possible for him to evolve into
the celebrated "Fighting Little Judge from Barbour County" and become
another Barbour Countian to be elected governor of Alabama.

And Wallace has done more concrete things during his tenure as governor for Barbour County than any of the several other men to serve as
chief executive of Alabama. However, don't forget the contributions his

Although the Tribune *ceased to endorse George Wallace in his later campaigns, he and Smith remained friends throughout. Pictured with Gov. Wallace during one of his many visits to Eufaula, Smith covered the Barbour County native's story from his first election as governor through his tearful retirement and his funeral in Montgomery.*

beloved late wife, Gov. Lurleen Wallace, made during her abbreviated term of office. The state parks program was passed through the legislature during her tenure and developed while George Wallace served.

Remember it was George Wallace who gave the nod to building Sparks State Technical College in Eufaula. While local leadership pushed for a junior college, Wallace compromised by locating the trade school here.

Eufaula would have been a very desirable place for a liberal arts school, but the trade school has proved extremely beneficial to this area of East Alabama. Lakepoint Resort is now a reality, but the area hasn't begun to realize how important this magnificent vacation park really will be to the economy and the local quality of living. And we have both Gov. Wallaces to thank.

The state trooper post was located here, too, during the Wallace administration, because the late Al Lingo, public safety director during Gov. Wallace's first administration, saw the need and favored his and the governor's home county.

The Eufaula Adolescent Adjustment Center was also established under the Wallace administration. And the Alabama Highway Department located a district engineer's operation on the Clayton Highway.

The Historic Chattahoochee Commission, based in Eufaula, was created by a legislative act during the Wallace years when Senator Jimmy Clark was such a powerful Wallace ally on Goat Hill, and Bill Neville Jr. was an imaginative member of the House.

The Water Patrol Post was built on the lakefront within the city limits of Eufaula, too.

Of course it didn't hurt the local Chamber's quest for new industries, because a Barbour native was governor and later another native son held the gavel ever so tightly in the Alabama Senate. Such plants as American Buildings and Dixie Shoe were built here under the Wallace Act.

There were some good years under the Wallace leadership, no doubt about it. But I still believe it is time for "a new beginning."

NIXON, WALLACE CENTRAL FIGURES
OF A GENERATION

May 1, 1994

Now at an age when my sense of mortality is keen, I feel the death of Richard M. Nixon personally. Sixteen years my senior, President Nixon was a central figure of my generation, much as George C. Wallace has been the dominant personality in recent Alabama history.

Well I do recall when Vice President Nixon was nominated for president by acclamation in 1960 and lost to John F. Kennedy by a narrow margin.

Born in the Depression and bred a Democrat, I found the handsome Ivy Leaguer Kennedy much more appealing than the jowled, bottom-heavy face of the stern Quaker. Their televised debate was won handily by the articulate Bostonian. Nixon's perennial five o'clock shadow and foreboding brows and reticent personality were no match for JFK's made-for-television charisma.

In 1968, when Nixon defeated Vice President Hubert H. Humphrey and third party candidate Gov. Wallace, I along with 99.4 percent of Barbour countians supported our native son from Clio.

I can close my eyes and almost see the "Barbour Bantam" strutting on the Birmingham City Auditorium stage, to the delight of the enthusiastic crowd as he repeatedly demeaned his chief opponent, "Richard MILHOUS Nixon." Every time he mockingly said "Milhous," the crowd roared.

As the partisan home county editor, sitting with a busload of Barbour countians, I duly recorded the rousing speech and photographed local supporters.

During the Dog Days of summer 1970, John Henry Williams was cutting my hair as I sat in the Bluff City Inn Barber Shop when someone from the *Tribune* came to tell me to call Vincent Townsend, the *Birmingham News's* erudite executive editor. When I didn't respond immediately, the runner returned with my mentor's message that what he had to tell me was far more important than getting a haircut. He asked me to serve on President Nixon's Cabinet Committee on Public Education for Alabama.

No good American would refuse to serve his President. Then Sen. Jimmy Clark, contacted by Attorney General John Mitchell, and I flew to Washington to meet with the Cabinet committee in the White House and to meet with President Nixon in the Oval Office.

I felt important riding alone in a black limousine to the White House, where we met with Cabinet members George Schultz, Elliot Richardson and Winton Blount, the postmaster general from Union Springs, in the Roosevelt Room, just outside Nixon's office. We served in an advisory capacity "in respect to the problems of changing from a dual to a unitary school system in Alabama."

Chairman J. Craig Smith, vice president of Eufaula's Cowikee Mills, said, "the state has no choice but to work for quality education for black and white students." Chris McNair, the black photographer from Birmingham who lost his little daughter in the bombing of the Sixteenth Street Church, was vice chairman.

We were frank in our discussions with the Cabinet members. The press was not invited, and since I was the only journalist sitting at the long oval table, I felt a little uncomfortable. While all committeemen took notes, I took extensive notes, almost as a natural reflex, as the postmaster general, the secretary of HEW and the attorney general answered our pointed questions.

It was an honor to meet the President inside the Oval Office, where I put away my pen and notebook, as protocol dictates. Besides, Nixon loathed the press. On this occasion, I found the normally ill-at-ease president gracious. When Red Blount introduced me as being from Eufaula, I told the President I was from Admiral Thomas H. Moorer's hometown. He said his next appointment was with Adm. Moorer and the Joint Chiefs of Staff.

"This is Alabama Day," the warm and friendly chief executive told our group of twenty as we stood around his imposing office. As tokens of appreciation, the president presented each one of us with an autographed tie clasp and a gold pin for our wives. A White House photographer took my picture as Mr. Nixon shook my hand.

I stood around, hoping to catch a glimpse of Billy Moorer's brother, the chairman of the Joint Chiefs, but when our session reconvened, I took my seat at the conference table and had my turn speaking my piece. So did Sen. Clark.

A fleet of chauffer-driven black limousines whisked us away to the Hotel Washington for a luncheon. After the Washington crowd excused themselves, our committee prepared a statement—which I was asked to help write and edit—calling on all Alabamians to support public education in the coming months.

Returning home, I wrote in this column on Aug. 20, 1970: "The briefing and discussion were beneficial. I am now convinced the president is concerned about quality education for Southerners, both black and white. He has chosen to form these advisory committees even though he had no part in the court's ordering the disestablishment of the dual system. Of course, it would be good politics for him if there is a smooth, violence-free transition this fall, but I am convinced he is genuinely concerned about the need for quality education when schools are completely desegregated."

The Sept. 10, 1970 edition of the *Tribune* reported Eufaula's schools were integrated and "off to a good start." I firmly believe President Nixon's effort made a difference in the Bluff City, where Jimmy Clark and I served on the city school board. There was no violence and few real problems in eliminating the dual system. (The board superintendent O. B. Carter and I had earlier met in Judge Frank Johnson's federal court on July 22, 1969, to present our plans for desegregation, which were accepted by the judge on July 31, 1969.)

President Nixon ended American fighting in Vietnam and opened the door he once shut to China and improved relations with the USSR. Reconciliation was his first goal, but the Watergate cover-up led ultimately to his resignation.

I remember vividly his great triumph televised in the People's Great Hall in Peking and the influence he had on me to work for peaceful integration of the Eufaula City Schools. I've forgotten calling him "Tricky Dick."

I am saddened by his death.

EDITOR RECALLS FOUR DECADES COVERING WALLACE

September 20, 1988

During the last four decades—and a few years before—I have covered George Wallace as a newspaperman. Perhaps because I wasn't born in Barbour County, I didn't support the "Fighting Little Judge" in 1958, when he ran in a field that included my newspaper friend, Jimmy Faulkner, and John Patterson.

Perhaps as the youthful editor of the *Geneva County Reaper,* I had visions of a New South governor. I still had vivid images of Big Jim Folsom campaigning when I went to work for the *Birmingham News.*

I had moved from Florida, having graduated from Florida State University during my sojourn in The Sunshine State. I was turned off when Big Jim told an outdoor rally that sure he stole during his first administration (1947–1951) but "I stole for you, and you and you," he said as he pointed to people in the crowd.

I was so turned off, I wondered if perhaps I'd made a mistake in moving back home to Alabama. However, after moving to Eufaula to edit the *Tribune,* I helped promote John Patterson Day to help Eufaula and Barbour County get back in the newly inaugurated governor's good graces.

Not long thereafter, George Wallace and I got well acquainted. I remember running into him at the Bluff City Barber Shop, where he sprung his newly coined slogan, "Stand Up for Alabama," on me. Frankly, I wasn't impressed. That shows how much I know about appealing to the masses. He was practicing law again in Clayton, and he had never stopped running. He drove all over the state speaking at every opportunity.

The *Tribune* and I personally supported him when he beat Folsom four years later in the primary of 1962. In the run-off, he defeated the rising young politician Ryan DeGraffenreid, whom I admired. The *Tribune* staff and I got caught up in the general election when Wallace polled the largest vote ever given a gubernatorial candidate in Alabama.

Those were heady times for me, a young editor dedicated to rebuilding the Eufaula-Barbour economy, along with the struggling *Tribune.* I latched onto covering George C. Wallace and his political exploits.

It was a great day for Barbour countians. While older Eufaulians had experienced the inauguration of Chauncey Sparks, I was wrapped up in Wallace's 1963 inauguration. I served on Barbour County's inaugural parade committee and arranged with my brother for a Smith Craft boat he manufactured to pull our float promoting Lake Eufaula.

The inauguration was a festive time for the large Eufaula contingent that gathered in Montgomery. My friend Al Lingo, Wallace's appointee as public safety director, assigned a patrol car and a trooper driver to chauffeur me around during the cold weather.

Sitting in the VIP stand for the inaugural ceremony, I was in high cotton, dating my beautiful, future wife, Ann. We nearly froze. But then I couldn't believe my ears when GCW threw down the gauntlet and said: "Segregation now! Segregation tomorrow! Segregation forever!"

Of course, like many Anglo-Saxon Alabamians in my generation, I grew up with segregated schools and restaurants. But I thought now that we'd elected George Wallace governor, we'd move on in peace and harmony building a progressive Alabama.

Gov. Wallace didn't forget from whence he came: He was good to his Barbour County friends. But then after the novelty wore off, I got tired of him running in the presidential primaries. I thought we had too many things in Alabama that Wallace needed to devote his time to. I was amazed, however, at the strength he showed and the impact he made, first on Richard Nixon and then on Ronald Reagan.

When the *Tribune* quietly stopped endorsing George Wallace, the Governor couldn't understand. He would call late at night, after I'd gone to bed, and tell me that he coveted my endorsement.

Somehow, though, we remained friends, and I again admired him when he renounced segregation—I also appreciated the impact on the new social conservatism that helped shape America's politics in the '70s and '80s.

My thoughts go back to those big Wallace rallies in Clayton and Birmingham. Wallace could strut, and salute the applauding and adoring crowd, making his colorful jabs at the Supreme Court and the pointy-head Washington bureaucrats. I have vivid memories too, of his tearful farewell to politics in the historic House chambers. Photographer Walt O'Neal and I worked overtime to get our historic coverage into print for the next edition.

Clayton was favorite in race against Wallace

July 14, 1996

There is a postscript to Preston C. Clayton's obituary that should interest history buffs and provide more biographical information on this Southern gentleman, who was an able public servant as well as a distinguished attorney.

Rep. George C. Wallace took his first big political gamble in 1952 when he opposed Sen. Clayton, his legislative colleague, for judge of the Third Judicial Circuit Court.

Historian Dan C. Carter, author of *The Politics of Rage: George Wallace, the Origins of the New Conservatism*, and *The Transformation of American Politics*, writes that most observers said Clayton was the favorite.

"When state senator Preston C. Clayton—a wealthy breeder of Arabian horses, decorated World War II veteran [a lieutenant colonel, no less], distinguished lawyer and legislative floor leader for Gov. Persons—announced for the post, most observers gave him the edge," Carter says.

He adds that while Clayton made a few "dignified forays through Barbour and Bullock counties," thirty-two-year-old Wallace "sallied forth every day at dawn," promising voters a "fair and equitable enforcement of the laws," reminding World Ward II veterans that he had been a sergeant. He quipped that all the officers could vote for Clayton and all the enlisted men could vote for him.

Carter's book says that fifteen years after the election, there was some bitterness on Clayton's part. After all, he had served well in the Alabama Senate for sixteen years. Wallace, serving his sixth year in the House, had a reputation as a man of the people.

Even then, he had his eye on the Governor's office. His bill to provide free college tuition to widows and orphans of Alabamians killed in WWII, as well as to disabled Alabama GIs, easily passed in the House of Representatives. Sen. Clayton successfully sponsored the bill in the Senate.

Clayton and Wallace "represented mirror images of Southern leadership of the time," Stephen Lesher observed in *George Wallace: American Populist* (1994). "Clayton's family was considered Southern aristocracy; Wallace's people were farmers and professionals. Clayton's grandfather, Gen. Henry Clayton, was a Civil War hero who himself had been a probate judge.

"Clayton lived in a small but gracious home that had been occupied by Claytons for more than a century; Wallace, whose family home had been sold years earlier, was paying twenty-five dollars a month to rent a garage apartment."

Clayton had been a member of the "relatively genteel Alabama Senate," while Wallace had been active in the "more raucously political House."

Lesher says it was a contest between the Southern Bourbons and the neopopulists.

As it turned out, it was a big victory for young George Wallace, and with the loss, Preston Clayton became more immersed in his successful law practice, years later associating his son as a partner.

Lesher quotes Clayton as saying during the campaign that Wallace would tell those country men that he was living in a mansion while he (Wallace) was living in a small house and paying twenty-five dollars a month rent. He'd tell the voters that the successful attorney didn't need to be circuit judge.

Wallace won the race handily, garnering 6,700 votes to less than 2,400 for Clayton. Wallace later said that Clayton told him, "a year or so after I defeated him that I had done him the best favor in the world because he made more money practicing law in a month than a judge did all year."

George Wallace's successful campaign gave him valuable experience in how to politic. The rest is history.

This is an important footnote to Barbour County and Alabama's colorful history. We have lost a noble man in the death of Preston Copeland Clayton, ninety-two, whose useful, dedicated life spanned many challenging, eventful decades.

Chapter 6

Family: The Ties that Bind

It's not a good idea to forget your anniversary

June 9, 1996

Woe be unto the man who forgets his anniversary. Since June is a popular time for weddings, it's also a time of many anniversaries. So husbands beware.

I learned my lesson early in my married life. My wife's first birthday after we married caught me completely unaware. I have trouble with clocks, and calendars are an even bigger problem. I work a lot like the dirt farmer, not from sun up until sun down, but from paper to paper, unaware of the date. Somebody so deadline-oriented shouldn't operate that way, but I do.

June 4 was our thirtieth wedding anniversary. It brought back memories. I was a bachelor who was saved by family and friends who were afraid they had a serious hanger-on problem. My Aunt Sally found me a wife in an alumni newsletter—The Huntingdon College newsletter.

This lovely young scholar had joined the faculty, and the college published her pretty photograph. Aunt Sally liked what she saw and what she read about the new history teacher, Ann Moxley Sutton. She showed everybody in the family her picture, and she told me that was the kind of young lady I should get serious about. My dutiful brother-in-law, John, exclaimed, "Why, that's Ann Sutton. I know her." He and my sister promptly arranged an introduction, and it turned out that Charlotte Adams Reeves was her former roommate.

The rest is history, as they say. After three years of courtship, including many fancy-dress balls in Montgomery and dozens of candlelight dinners at my newlywed sister's apartment, I popped the question on New Year's Eve in 1966. Six months later, we were married in a little Methodist church in Springville.

My single aunt's advice—after meeting Ann and thoroughly approving of her—was to decline invitations to the "secret dances" and to take Ann out in the moonlight.

That was some of the best advice I ever received.

The nuptials thirty years ago included a wedding overrun with Smiths. Each of my four brothers and my sister were attendants. When our wedding party arrived at the Birmingham Country Club for the rehearsal dinner, the brother-in-law confided there was a small problem. The club manager had booked the dinner for the following Friday night. Not to worry, though, the cooks rustled up some filets, and in no time we sat down to a delicious dinner, sans a floral centerpiece. Frankly, I don't believe anybody noticed.

In my will, I should leave money to the Springville United Methodist Church to buy a new piano. I must have greatly impaired the church piano. The proverbial nervous bridegroom, I had been cautioned by the minister to open the door into the front of the sanctuary carefully, because the piano stood only inches away, nevertheless, I slammed the door into the piano with a bang, calling attention to my poor physical state.

Aunt Sally confessed after the ceremony that she seriously considered stopping the proceedings when the preacher asked, "If anyone knows any reason this man and this woman should not be joined in holy matrimony, let him speak now or forever hold his peace." I looked that bad.

But there was joy in Springville. The old-fashioned drug store, with lazy paddle-armed ceiling fans and a marble soda fountain that still served milkshakes, closed for the wedding. The owner posted a sign on the door: "Gone to the wedding," to the delight of my Eufaula friends.

My future in-laws, W. E. G. and Evelyn Beck Sutton, hosted a lovely reception in the church's fellowship hall. I recovered from the ceremony, and the color returned to my cheeks.

Following a honeymoon in Acapulco, courtesy of my eldest brother, Ann and I settled down briefly in one of "Dad" Grubbs's apartments on Malone Alley. At that time, the rundown Couric Homestead on North Eufaula Avenue was for sale. I loved its classic white columns and could picture in my mind a happy home.

Ann bought my idea, and we bought the low-rent apartment house and moved in days before Christmas.

Life is still full of surprises. A couple of weeks ago when family friends gathered to celebrate my third son's college graduation, the dinner was held, through his arrangements, at the Café Dupont, a fine restaurant in tiny Springville.

We were shocked to discover the French-style café was ensconced inside the former church fellowship hall where our reception was held thirty years ago. (The quaint white-framed church burned years ago.)

The story has a happy ending. It's been a wonderful life. I have three sons and a faithful, devoted wife, and we're not your customary "help-mates." I have a great wife and hard working business partner, all rolled into one.

No, I didn't forget our anniversary. I planned a small dinner and gift-wrapped a little surprise.

Hard to say goodbye
to a wonderful friend

February 26, 1988

It's hard to say goodbye to a lifelong friend. It's heartbreaking to watch an elderly loved one fight for her life against insurmountable odds. In my grief over the loss of my Aunt Babe, only days following her ninety-first birthday, my thoughts keep reminding me of happier times.

She wasn't what one might call a generic aunt. She was more than a typical aunt, if Southern folks have such. She was in a class by herself. Babe Smith was an original. The fourth daughter of Saul Pierce and Sarah Mixon Rawlinson Smith, she grew up in the thriving, new Wiregrass town of Coffee Springs, down home in the pineland country. Her father, a building contractor-businessman who also operated a small hotel when the town named for General Coffee was a summer resort, nicknamed her "Babe" when she was a baby.

Her numerous namesakes are named Lydia, her proper name, but none of them are nicknamed Babe, and properly so, because there will never be another Babe Smith. The sophisticated fragrance, "Babe," couldn't have been named for her, because no perfume could have ever captured the essence of her unique personality in so small a bottle. She was effervescent, bubbling, dramatic and entertaining. She could also give a keen nephew his comeuppance, if need be.

Most of all, Aunt Babe was my warm and wonderful friend.

And she was all that and more to her brother Abb's five sons and his daughter, whose beautiful mother died when the youngest son was nine months old. Babe and her younger sister, Sally, reared their nephew, Douglas, and their niece, Sarah Margaret. Their Eufaula home became our home away from home—a place to visit on weekends and during the holidays after the death of our devoted father.

Aunt Babe believed in me. As a child, growing up in a farm town during the Depression, she gave me confidence and boundless love. Her pride in her family was contagious. Money never was really important in her estimation; the more enduring qualities were all important.

She insisted on teaching her wild young nephews and her tomboy niece good manners. Aunt Babe had a dash of "Auntie Mame" in her, or better still the Broadway play character possessed a bit of her flair, her wonderful, unique personality.

She had traveled, and she shared her exciting adventures with her wide-eyed young nephews. She taught us how to "register" at a hotel, years before I ever remember checking into the Battle House or The Tutwiler. Aunt Babe knew style, and she communicated to us at an early age that indeed the Smiths had class, as well as character.

She gave me confidence when I chose to leave the *Birmingham News* to edit and manage our former home county newspaper, the *Geneva County Reaper*, and when I announced I'd marry Ann. We would talk things over, just like good friends do.

Now, I've lost that wonderful friend. I've lost my Aunt Babe, but I can't continue to mourn that great loss. She's at peace now. She suffered two heart attacks and broke her hip when she fell from her bed in the nursing home. She was like "The Unsinkable Molly Brown," my sister mused after Aunt Babe made still another amazing comeback recently.

God let her go mercifully, just as she had asked, "God, God, let me go, let me go," she had whispered quietly after coming home to Eufaula, not knowing one of her devoted nephews was sitting in her room.

Her loving heart just finally stopped quietly.

*

'HEY, LOOK ME OVER!'

February 10, 1966

It's the truth. It's actual. Yes, it's official. I'm now a fiancé. After a rather lengthy courtship–over three years–my ladylove has accepted my rather modest engagement ring. Her parents have looked me over, and barring some unforeseen difficulty, we'll be married June 4.

Ann Sutton is her name. She's a perfectly delightful young lady. She's pretty, smart, charming and a good companion. And she can make sand tarts and brownies.

Best of all—she really loves me!

And she isn't buying a pig in a poke, either. She's seen me under all sorts of conditions. She's seen me sitting on top of the world, she's been around when I act up, and she knows how involved this small-town newspaper publishing can become, like the time the radio station lambasted me with a recorded editorial every hour on the hour for a full weekend.

You think she's dumb? You were never more mistaken. Why man, she's a Phi Beta Kappa! But you're still wondering why such a lovely, intelligent creature has agreed to marry the likes of me. Well, maybe she LIKES aging balding men who are set in their ways.

Don't take my word for it. Read today's society page. It's there in black and white. We've been announced!

Indeed, Ann's parents have followed through and officially announced that we'll be married. We've motored up to her hometown of Springville, and they looked me over. It wasn't the first trip; I'd stopped by on my way to Gatlinburg on a skiing outing.

But this time it was decidedly different. I was on exhibit. No sooner had her parents looked me over with a jaundiced eye and her father discussed some new theories in mathematics—I even had trouble with my multiplication tables—than did the neighbors start dropping in to take a look.

This was it. If ever I'd done a selling job, I thought to myself, now was the time to use every trick in the book . . . but then I remembered that one friend had suggested that I not try to charm the ladies, lest they get the idea that I am an insincere show-off.

First, a group of neighborhood ladies called. They were nice enough, but they sure did stay a long time and make a lot of small talk. I almost got coffee nerves from gulping down so much coffee. After supper and a quick shave, it was no time before another group arrived. This time, some of the community leaders and their ladies called.

Just when I began relaxing and started feeling a little confident, I was introduced to the banker and his wife. That good lady took me by the arm and announced that she wanted to "really look you over." And she did. She looked me straight in the eyes, and after a pause that seemed like an eternity, said she thought I'd do.

The next day was church day. I met everybody else in the community who hadn't called the evening before. I felt like a revival preacher after preaching his first sermon in a strange, new town. But I must admit, my intended's mother, the lovely lady that she is, arranged things so that we missed the Sunday school crowd and arrived just in time to take our seats.

Then it was home for Sunday dinner. No sooner had we gotten out of the car and members of the family started arriving. They were all friendly enough, and I even managed to laugh out loud when an aunt inquired politely if we'd set the date. Ann told them we had—that it was June 4. Then her little nephew spoke up and quizzed, "Why don't ya'll get married on the Fourth of July?!!"

ONE DAY IS NOT ENOUGH
TO PAY TRIBUTE TO MOTHERS

May 14, 1995

"Mother" is the most beautiful word in the English language to me. I can't conceive of "an unfit mother," because it was my fate to have been born to a lovely mother. I was also blessed to have a wonderful paternal grandmother—my maternal grandmother died before I was born—and a marvelous step-grandmother. I have also been fortunate to have a lovely mother-in-law, all joking aside. My wife, Ann, is a marvelous mother to our three sons.

Therefore, Mother's Day is not just another Sunday. I'm sure I speak for legions of others, too.

As a little tow-headed boy growing up during the Great Depression, I must have emulated my mother. She was the society editor and writer for the weekly *Samson Ledger*. She also was a correspondent for two or three daily newspapers.

On my way to school, I'd drop off her copy to the *Ledger* office. I can't remember when I wasn't aware of newspapers. My mother laughed when I looked up from the paper and asked what was a "RE-sent" bride. In my childlike mind, I thought those recent brides my mother wrote about so profusely must have been retreads or divorcees marrying again.

I also remember an irate reader chewing my mother out about an error in fact or typography that appeared in one of her stories. And I won't forget how angry my father was with that small-town social climber who dealt my mother woe. My mother's name was Rose. Like her name, she was beautiful. Her sisters-in-law said she looked like she stepped out of the "bandbox" when she dressed up. I didn't know that a bandbox held hats, but I did know my mother was beautiful.

She was also talented. She had a "trained voice" and like her Drane kinsmen before, she shared her talent generously.

However, her greatest talent was motherhood, next to being a wonderful wife to our adoring father. How she kept her sanity with five sons and a tough little daughter with pigtails, I'll never know.

The Depression years must have been a trying time for a mother, whose husband's fortunes were severely tested. Yet, we never knew just how tough times were for our family. My brothers and I were rather enterprising boys, always encouraged by our father.

One of our uncles joked that our mother could shop in Montgomery— where her prosperous kin lived—spend five dollars and buy each child an outfit and bring home a surprise or two.

I remember our father helping the children in the neighborhood build a clay tennis court. A young aunt gave my older brother her steel string racket. Bobby and I wrote our "rich" bachelor uncle in Montgomery to inquire if he had any old tennis rackets in his locker at the country club that he didn't need. I contemplated asking our very religious great aunt, whose late husband was a Methodist preacher, to pray for me a tennis racket.

Sure enough, I wound up with two identical white junior-size rackets. It was enough to make me believe in prayer, reinforced by wealth.

Even in the worst of times, we had a family cook. Our mother could teach Emma Poon how to prepare a dish to her specifications. The household help also loved her. She didn't demand respect; she earned it by her delightful manner.

Mother was almost a fanatic about cleanliness. The kitchen floor was scrubbed, and the big front porch and the white outside walls were washed. She also inspected our ears to make sure we washed inside as well as behind them.

In the spring, she gave us doses of calomel, and in the winter she gave us spoonfuls of castor oil saturated in orange juice. She also prescribed soaking our feet in hot Epsom salt baths when we stepped on a nail. Epsom salt was also one of her country physician father's favorite remedies.

I remember log truckers stopping to give her a lift as she walked along Main Street to town. She wrote her newspaper articles at the Tip Top Café, my aunt's restaurant that served the best hamburgers in South Alabama, or at City Hall, where she could type in peace.

I don't recall ever seeing her type an article on her father's old upright L. C. Smith. There must have been too many distractions at our house. Maybe she depended on using the city's telephone since we didn't have one at home.

I was eleven years old when our lovely mother died. It was years before I could even talk about her. My heart was broken. It didn't help when a well-meaning aunt said we should act like "brave little soldiers." No one should ever mourn as long as I did.

As a boy, I remember wearing a rose on my shirt for Mother's Day services at the church. Half a century later, I still miss her. Even with so many other wonderful family members to love, no one ever filled the void she left in my life.

Mothers and motherhood are almost sacred to me. There is no way we can sufficiently pay tribute to our mothers on one special day in the year.

MR. SUTTON HELPED SHAPE STUDENTS' LIVES

January 28, 1990

William Ewart Gladstone Sutton was truly one of the most remarkable people I've ever known. He was my father-in-law. His life touched so many Alabamians. Until hospitalized with pneumonia some three weeks ago, he hadn't been to a doctor in two years. He was ninety-seven-years-old.

He cared for his ill wife, who was several years his junior, the past three or four years. For the past thirty-five years, he religiously taught his Sunday

School class, the W. E. G. Sutton Sunday School Class of elderly friends.

He was one of the most intelligent men I've ever known. Not only was he a Phi Beta Kappa—the first to earn this academic distinction at the University of Alabama while completing his undergraduate studies in summers—but he possessed good common sense, too. He received a sheepskin diploma when he graduated from Jackson Agricultural Institute at age fifteen or sixteen. He earned a master's degree at Vanderbilt.

He served in the Army in France during World War I, advancing from private to second lieutenant. While abroad, he became friends with an aristocratic family with which he continued to correspond until a few years ago. He entrusted his collections of letters to his daughter, Ann, and me. With some editing, they would make an excellent historical paper that details interesting things that happened on both sides of the Atlantic during the Post WWI era.

I've often marveled at the knowledge he possessed. He continued to read books dealing with mathematical theory and history. Just about any area of study interested him.

Truly, W. E. G. Sutton was a gentleman and a scholar. His impeccable character, along with his great intellect, drive and courage, made him an ideal educator. For fifty-two years, he helped shape the lives of students in several school systems, the last being Springville, where he served as principal, and Ashville, where he taught algebra.

His father-in-law, M. L. Beck, as chairman of the Glenwood school board, was responsible for his teaching in that Crenshaw County town. He fell in love with the chairman's daughter, Evelyn, but the successful businessman, a sawmill owner, didn't want his daughter to marry a teacher. When Gladstone Sutton called his daughter, he would hit the telephone lines with a fishing pole so they couldn't carry on a conversation.

Their marriage, however, must have been made in heaven. They lived through good times and bad times and were an effective team, whether running a school or their home. While Mrs. Sutton was in the hospital in Anniston with their first-born baby, he was taken aback to hear President Roosevelt announce over the radio that the banks would not be open the next day.

Mr. Sutton was a distant cousin of President Harry Truman. And he and Truman had much in common. There was a strong family resemblance, and while Mr. Sutton was always a gentleman, his personality was spirited, too.

He was a craftsman, a master gardener and an excellent fisherman. At age eighty-two, he made a cabinet for the grandfather clock he gave our family. The beautiful walnut lumber was grown on his wife's land in Crenshaw County. He also made his son a similar clock and a smaller version for his wife, Evelyn.

Only weeks before he became ill, he was planning his vegetable garden. Until a few years ago, he plowed his own garden with a Roto-Tiller that would just about shake the operator's liver loose. He knew the best varieties of everything to plant, and in the summer the Suttons kept busy freezing fruits and vegetables from his garden. He also supplied the family with plenty of bass and bream.

His death is a real loss. He taught and inspired countless numbers of Alabamians, many of whom have excelled. In 1984, some of the former students surprised Mr. and Mrs. Sutton with a marvelous *This is Your Life* program at Springville High School. The former students, many of them retired, the school janitor and others presented a lively tableau depicting their successful careers.

While I am sad, I am grateful to have known and loved this wonderful man for over two decades. I cherish the fact that my three sons were privileged enough to know their outstanding grandfather for so many years. He leaves them a legacy of pride, hope, character, intellect and love.

W. E. G. Sutton was one of the finest Southern gentlemen and greatest educators I've ever known. His contributions to society were truly monumental. Few have ever left such a legacy.

New in-laws pay first visit after nuptials

October 20, 1966

I n case you've forgotten, that first visit your in-laws paid you was a big event. I've just gone through that experience, and I think I came through with flying colors.

The Suttons from Springville had been most patient. Only days after our wedding, they both were involved in running a summer camp and couldn't get away. But soon the summer was over, and it was past time for their first visit in our humble home.

My father-in-law, whose initials W. E. G. sound like a radio station's call letters, is an avid outdoorsman. Naturally, during visits in his home, I bragged about all the big bass in Lake Eufaula.

So, he served notice he was loading his fly rods and his five-horse-power motor and intended to check out our little lake. Not being much of a fisherman, I quickly accepted Tom Culpepper's offer to show him where the big ones are.

Up and at 'em early Saturday morning, we drove over to the Culpeppers, and I suggested that the two fishermen might want to dock the boat at Chewalla Motel and meet Ann, my mother-in-law and me for lunch. I learned that my newly acquired father-in-law often forgets to eat when he's out fishing—but I kept wondering how po' ole Tom was making out with an apple and a handful of cookies.

Late in the afternoon, the fishermen returned. Tom looked bushed, and Mr. Sutton probably would have been for taking a hike around the lake—if anybody had suggested it. As luck would have it, their catch consisted of a couple of skinny catfish, an anemic bass and an assortment of several other dwarf species. Anxious to learn his opinion of our lake, I foolishly quizzed, "What do you think about Lake Eufaula?" "The lake's fine—ya'll just need to get the government to stock it with fish!" Tom muttered something about never catching so few so fast.

Some days you can't win for losing.

Like his daughter, my new in-law's a Phi Beta Kappa—interested in engineering, mathematics, politics and you name it. Being one of those less fortunate souls who has trouble making his checkbook balance, I tried to get my Phi Kappa Phi brother, Bob, to talk some algebra to him before the nuptials so that he might be sufficiently impressed with my family's intelligence.

I also welcomed my Malone Alley neighbor's visit during the weekend; barrister Albert Simpson is an excellent conversationalist, and he sounds smart when he talks. Professor Sutton was impressed.

My Aunt Babe is one of those few people who think I'm the kitten's toenail. She gave moral support. Aunt Babe told me that I was smart, too, and that besides, I knew more about newspapers than my new Pa-in-law. She didn't have a comeback when I said, "Oh no. His family owned a newspaper—and he knows all about them, too."

My new mother-in-law is a jewel. She likes our jam-packed tiny apartment. She even liked the furniture I'd collected during my bachelor days, she loved Eufaula's old homes and wide boulevards and she thought the people she met were delightful. While the father-in-law was obviously disappointed in the size of fish in the lake, he concurred with his wife, Evelyn, on all other points.

I'm hitting it off so well with my in-laws that I won't have a thing to contribute when the conversation at the coffee club gets around to talking about mothers-in-law.

Ann was pleased with my conduct and that's important, as all veteran married men know. The reason why I know that my wife was pleased was because I overheard her tell the betrothed city clerk, Dick Boyette, "When in-laws come to visit, ask Joel to tell you how to act." I grinned from ear to ear. I'd cleared another hurdle.

OLD TIME EVANGELIST RODE
BUS, NOT MERCEDES

June 5, 1987

During the depths of the Great Depression, my great Aunt Mamie, a dedicated evangelist, proclaimed the gospel of Jesus Christ to the poor, the downtrodden and to our proud, middle class family.

As an impressionable child of the '30s, I held Aunt Mamie in awe, just as I did my rich, bachelor Uncle Bob. And let me hasten to explain, Uncle Bob, who drank demonic bourbon at Beauvoir Country Club and dated glamorous women, also listened when my lovely mother's aunt opened her big, black Bible and preached the family a sermon during her extended summer visits down in rural Geneva County.

Once, my younger brother Bob, Uncle Bob's bright and spirited namesake, and I were discussing who we had rather pay us a visit, Aunt Mamie or Uncle Bob. I opined Aunt Mamie would be the more welcomed houseguest since she could "pray you well" if you were sick. I vividly recall her laying her wrinkled right hand on my hot forehead, praying to the Lord for my fever to abate. And it did.

Aunt Mamie became a revival preacher after her well-educated Methodist minister husband died. Back then, Methodists didn't allow their womenfolk in the pulpit. I remember accompanying her when she preached to a black congregation, as well as other Pentecostal churches in the poorer part of Samson. She also composed beautiful religious songs and accompanied herself on the guitar. (Some excellent songs were plagiarized from her and published.)

When Aunt Mamie up and married a younger man, she explained to her bewildered kin "the Lord told me to marry Hubert." Daddy, who gave Hubert a job driving a rolling store concluded, "The Lord played the devil," too.

No wonder I don't have any sympathy for Tammy and Jim Bakker, the PTL, nor that group of contributors to the Praise The Lord network, which is organizing a campaign of lawsuits and public pressure to oust the

Rev. Jerry Falwell as PTL's president.

I learned first-hand, at an early age, the power of prayer when prayed in earnest by a devout Christian. But I see no plausible reason why humble followers should continue to contribute their "cold cash" to those televangelists who have been putting them on for years.

It's ironic. Tammy Fay Bakker's navy blue Mercedes station wagon and her sleek, mascara black 580 SL—with tan leather interior—are now for sale on the Ward Motor Co.'s lot in Geneva. I hope my friends, John and Levy Ward, don't get stuck with them, or the $59,000 silver Mercedes sedan, also fresh from the PTL.

Aunt Mamie walked, or maybe Hubert drove her in the old Chevrolet rolling-store when she preached. She rode the Greyhound bus to Samson from her modest home in Wrens, Ga. To save money, she wrote on both the front and backside of penny postcards, to spread the gospel or to inform my mother, Rose, she'd be paying a visit.

No wonder I'm turned off by glamorous television evangelists of today who prey on the poor, the downtrodden, the well-heeled and the well-intended, gullible TV viewers who funneled money to the PTL so Tammy and Jim could enjoy their extravagant, go-go lifestyle more akin to *Dynasty* than Christian ministry.

TYPEWRITER PORTRAIT SHOWS LOVING, CARING FATHER

June 19, 1994

If I were an artist, I would paint a portrait or make a drawing of my late father, Abb Jackson Smith, and submit it to the *Montgomery Advertiser*. A number of drawings will be featured in the newspaper on Father's Day. Since I can't draw "My Reflection of Dad," I'll try to "paint" a typewriter portrait of a remarkable father called Abb.

I'd paint a kind, smiling face, because he was more than kind—he was a loving father. By precept and example, he taught, perhaps unknowingly, his five sons to be good fathers. He taught us what real love is all about.

He married our beautiful, talented mother, Rose Drane Sellers, in 1921. Theirs was a blissful marriage. A bachelor businessman, he was considered "a good catch," but so was mother. Together they weathered the depths of the Great Depression. Somehow, during the toughest of times, they provided well for my five siblings and me.

In the good old summertime, he often took us swimming in one of several beautiful creeks. And what a treat it was to travel with him out of town on business. One-on-one, he was wonderful, attentive company. A real treat was riding with his driver on his rolling store. I liked meeting the country folks who would barter with eggs or a chicken. Thinking back, I marvel at the innovative ways he made a good living for us during some tough times prior to World War II.

Long before supermarkets, he designed and built a meat wagon, which was screened and included a big chopping block and tub back chairs. He supervised his helpers in butchering beef cattle, which were hung in quarters inside the meat market. Sales were cut to order. The wagon was parked in the front of his general mercantile store on Saturdays, the big trade day for farm families in Samson.

Father was also a marvelous cook. Late Sunday morning breakfasts were his specialty. He cooked delicious steaks, sometimes directly on top of the eye of the wood-burning stove. Salt fish and fish roe and brains and eggs were often on his menu. He made delicious fried toast so light you would eat several slices.

His culinary skills served us in good stead. Our lovely mother died in 1940, as war clouds gathered over Europe. Soon the family would move to Panama City, where our father worked in the J. J. Jones-managed shipyard building Liberty Ships.

He was an exemplary single parent. He was always home at night to see that his children had things they needed. He kept well informed on public affairs and was an inveterate newspaper reader. He also loved politics, a love he shared with his marvelous mother, Sally Rawlinson Smith. They took great interest in local elections down home in Geneva County. Once to

Daddy's dismay, he learned Grandmother was politicking for a candidate who was running against his man. Since both had minds of their own, I don't know how their difference was resolved.

One of the things I appreciate most about my father is how he never compared his six children to each other. How I don't know, because we were all alike and yet different. The brothers younger and older than I were excellent mathematicians—and so was father—but math was my undoing. I never saw the need for algebra, except perhaps it was character building. My father would console me by saying, "You can hire a bookkeeper."

I was a very special son in a family of five sons and a daughter. I'm sure each sibling feels the same. This is a quality I hope to emulate with my three sons, all individuals, yet bound closely by family ties.

"My Reflection of Dad" couldn't be captured in a portrait. He had such depth, such love that an amateur artist couldn't begin to paint. On this Father's Day, my one wish is that I have become half the father to my three sons that my daddy was to my four brothers, a sister and me. He shaped my life as no one else. It was a sad time when he died in 1950, just a decade following my lovely mother's death. While three of us were in college at the time, we continued our studies, and two younger siblings also finished college.

My most painful memory of father is the summer he died. I had finished my sophomore year at Florida State University and contemplated serving an internship in Ft. Lauderdale, continuing work with the Florida State Department of Education or spending the summer in Montgomery with my father. I've often thought it was divine intervention that led me to Montgomery. Daddy became hospitalized, and I was there to visit him in the evening before his untimely death.

Fatherless, going back to college that fall was a sad experience. I had lost my best friend. However, our close-knit loving family gave assurance somebody still cared.

Quoting from the privately published Smith family history: "His mother was often heard to say, 'He [my father] was a wonderful son, husband and father.' He did not live to see his dream come true but five of the six children finished college with honors."

50 YEARS AFTER MOTHER'S DEATH,
TEARS STILL IN HIS EYES

May 12, 1991

I have a friend whose family never celebrates Mother's Day or Father's Day because they're artificial. Well, maybe they have become greatly commercialized, like Christmas. Even so, those days are important to me.

One of my four brothers recently reminded me the fiftieth anniversary of our lovely mother's death had passed, and April 15, 1991, was the hundredth anniversary of our father's birth.

This touched me.

While many wonderful people have influenced my life, there have been none who influenced my formative years as did my loving parents.

The great tragedy in my life was the death of my mother, Rose Drane Sellers Smith, on June 12, 1940, in Samson. I was a skinny, blond-headed eleven-year-old. Those were the Depression days, but life had been wonderful in that little farm town.

Our mother, daughter of a country doctor whose brothers were very successful as a doctor and businessmen, was a beautiful, talented lady. She sang at club programs and when radio was big, I remember listening to her sing over a Dothan radio station. She attended Alabama College at Montevallo and a business college in Montgomery before marrying Abb Jackson Smith in 1921. Their life together was a marvelous love story with a tragic ending. She contracted Bright's Disease, a liver ailment, and died on that fateful summer night.

It was a tragedy: Our father loved her so much he never dated another woman. He became the best single parent imaginable to me and my brothers and sister: Jack who was sixteen at the time of our mother's death; Maury, thirteen; me, eleven; Bob, nine; Sarah, six; and Doug, seven months old.

There is a strong breakdown in the family structure, I heard a college dean say just this morning: "Students don't come from *Leave It to Beaver* families," he says. They come from single parent families. "Parents are frustrated; students coming from that environment are frustrated themselves," he says.

What's happened in these last five decades?

What could have been more challenging than for a father of six to lose his devoted wife during the depths of the Great Depression? Yet, our father, with tremendous support from his widowed mother and maiden sisters, managed to lift our spirits. He also instilled in us high principles and the desire for an education. Some way, somehow, we all made it to college. Education has been the great equalizer, and with those early principles instilled in us by our lovely mother and courageous father, we have all lived productive lives.

With a father such as I knew and loved, it's hard to comprehend fully the profound single parent problem plaguing society today.

So, Mother's Day—and Father's Day, too—are very meaningful to me. After fifty years, I still have tears in my eyes when I think about my lovely mother. Life is rushing on so quickly that I scarcely can believe last month was the one hundredth anniversary of my wonderful father's birth. He was a single parent who made a real difference. No wonder I also think of him on Mother's Day.

How fortunate I am today to have a lovely wife who is a wonderful mother to our three sons. That puts the joy back in Mother's Day for me.

Chapter 7

Reflections
of a Lifetime

EVERY BACHELOR NEEDS A MAID LIKE MITTIE

December 2, 1965

Every bachelor should have a maid like Mittie. Not only is Mittie a good cook and a right fair housekeeper who cleans up my office, but she's delightfully entertaining as well.

Mittie is a part of old Eufaula, and she prides herself on knowing all the old families in town. Through the years, she has worked for a number of different families, and she counts among her friends many from the white community.

Mittie lives in her own little house on the Bluff, which has a breathtaking view of Lake Eufaula below. Her dog, Slugger, Mr. Slugger Griggs, is her constant companion. Sometimes, she refers to him as Slugger, and then again, she might call him Mr. Griggs. This used to confuse me in our conversations until she explained that she is a widow and that faithful dog was "nozzilated" Slugger.

One of the good things about Mittie is that, being naturally a little on the bossy side, she'll just take over and get things done around my apartment. She plans the meals as well as does the shopping. This is a real service to a bachelor type. And Mittie's not extravagant with my money.

She'll walk all over town checking out the bargains. Actually, I think she likes to shop. "I like for folks to see me buying things in the stores," Mittie explains, "They think I've got lots of money." Then she adds, "It's all right to fool other folks—but don't fool yourself!"

And Mittie doesn't mind coming back at night occasionally when I invite a few in for a little dinner party. She likes serving my "high hat friends" and putting on the dog. Once when she was serving turkey at a dinner party, she brought her own gravy boat from her home because my limited china set didn't include one—and she made apologies for forgetting to bring her turkey platter.

Mittie usually stops by the office to confer with me about plans for lunch three days out of the week, but if I should happen to be out of pocket, she just might spend her own money for groceries or dig out something she has tucked away in the freezer unit. On Labor Day, Mittie didn't come by the office, and I decided to call home before taking off for lunch. Mittie answered the phone with, "Get yo' rich self home!"

Mittie's good help, except when it comes to moving. When the two aunts, their maid Ola, and Mittie moved me into a new apartment not long ago, Mittie wasn't a bit happy about the situation. She ran around like a confused chicken, scratching her head. Aunt Babe and Mittie on that occasion reminded me of Scarlett O'Hara and Prissy in *Gone With the Wind*. Mittie, like Prissy, got excited but Aunt Babe held her feet to the fire until the ordeal was over.

Mittie, in the habit of going to work at my little cottage in the shadow of Kendall Manor, forgot and walked up the hill a couple of times before it soaked in that I'd made a change of address. She got lost the first day, but identified the apartment because she placed the charcoal scuttle on the front porch. Since "Dad" Grubb's apartment building is equipped with a range, I was stuck with two stoves. But when anybody makes a comment about two stoves in the kitchen, Mittie explains that "one's for everyday cooking and the other's for Sunday."

Yep, every bachelor should have a maid like Mittie.

1950S WAS DECADE TO REMEMBER
FONDLY IN EUFAULA

May 5, 1996

Were the 1950s a decade to remember fondly?

A recent poll conducted by Knight-Ridder Newspapers and Princeton Survey Research Associates found that the 1950s were a decade that continues to exert an almost mythical hold on the American psyche. To be sure, those were some happy, yet sad times for me.

The pollsters found it was a time that lingers memorably for practically all types of Americans except blacks, which is surely understandable.

The early '50s were wonderful years—my college years. It was a marvelous time to be a student on the beautiful pine-shaded campus of Florida State University in Tallahassee. After graduating from Bay County High School in Panama City, I was one of many in my class choosing to attend the former Florida State College for Women, which had only been coeducational a couple of years. Those were the best of times. Women students outnumbered men. I didn't follow my big brothers to Auburn and Alabama. It was a great life, though. I remember packing my footlocker with favorite personal possessions: It was like leaving home for good. I found a home in Tallahassee.

I loved the newfound freedom and independence. I lucked into a great job with the State Department of Education. The historic state capitol became like just another building on "my campus." The state superintendent of education's secretary would even type a term paper for me when I got in a tight.

It was a great life. The minimum hourly wage was only seventy-five cents, but money went a long way, and I enjoyed buying my own clothes, a sporty watch and other things I wanted. No, I didn't have a car, and would you believe, I turned down my father's offer to buy me a car? (There were two other brothers in college, too.)

It was a good life. My younger brother and I pledged our older brother's fraternity. I've often said I majored in Sigma Nu. The FSU Interfraternity Council passed a rule that a chapter couldn't be entertained more than three times a week. The sororities were ensconced in big houses, and the newly chartered fraternities lived in makeshift quarters. But that didn't matter. It was a great life. Dressing up in a white dinner jacket for sorority dances was a regular weekend outing.

The good times of the '50s were tinged with sadness after the summer of 1950, though. I had loved college so much I went to summer school after completing my freshman year. After my sophomore year—another great year in the classroom and on the job—I was torn between interning with a small Florida newspaper and spending the summer with my father and brothers in Montgomery. My guardian angel had nudged me, and I spent that fateful summer with my wonderful father. He died that September. Thus began one of the saddest times in my short life.

Friends and fraternity brothers, my former high school principal, J. T. Kelley, and fellow employees and family helped me through that difficult time.

Editing the college magazine, writing a column for the *Florida Flambeau*, a trip to New York and serving as fraternity president were highlights of my junior and senior years. More good times were to come, including a delightful year as a classroom teacher (to help pay back a State of Florida scholarship). I was soon doing what I wanted to do—working for a newspaper—at the *Birmingham News*.

That marvelous decade found me enjoying life in the city on a small salary. The Magic City was great, but I had a desire to be a small-town editor. My wish came true when Howard Scott hired me to be editor of the *Geneva County Reaper*, where I quickly learned that I love most things about a small newspaper. Surprisingly, I enjoyed small town life, made more appealing because I built a beach house near Panama City.

The decade's latter years are memorable: I become editor of the *Tribune* in the late '50s. The U.S. Corps of Engineers was headquartered in the Bluff City Inn, acquiring land along the Chattahoochee that would soon be inundated by the river's muddy, swift waters.

During the '50s, Eufaulians took time to have a good time. They formed flotillas and cruised downriver to Bainbridge, and hosted the Bainbridge Boat Club, which lodged at the Bluff City Inn. They dined at Solita Hortman's Town House and later at Tony Rane's Embers Restaurant. Lee's Drive-In was a favorite spot for teenagers who loved Lee and Elizabeth Smith's steak sandwiches.

The UDC still observed Confederate Memorial Day, and some stalwart youths were active in the Children of the Confederacy. Eufaula High School football was big. We lined Broad Street for a parade before every home game.

The Peckerwood Club at Pittsview often invited Eufaulians as guests, and the Longfellow Literary Society (a front) met on Wednesday afternoons when it rained and the golfers couldn't play. The Birdwatchers boarded the George Taylor bus—when the schoolchildren weren't on a field trip—and toured the mile-long earth dam site at Ft. Gaines and the Corps of Engineers' construction site at Columbia.

Ladies wore hats to teas, and men didn't wear ties to work until young attorney Gorman Houston hung up his shingle.

That recent poll found the most nostalgic tend to be people most comfortable in the 1950s stereotype: "Those who make a good living, closely follow news about their government, vote Republican and participate in civic organizations."

I can't say I'd like to return to the decade of the 1950s, but those were nostalgic years. I didn't hit my stride until I married, had three sons and bought the *Eufaula Tribune*.

Maybe Oliver Wendell Homes was on target when he penned: "What lies behind us and what lies before us are tiny matters, compared to what lies within us."

I hope so.

GREAT PHYSICIAN WILL HEAL
EUFAULA'S BROKEN HEART

November 12, 1995

My open-heart surgery has been put to the test. Minutes before my B. W. and I checked out of the University of Alabama Hospital, we received the tragic news from Eufaula that our friend had been found murdered in her home. Two months later, on a Saturday afternoon, another friend called bearing more terrible news: The victim's husband had been found dead of a gunshot wound.

My surgery was put to the test before I left the hospital. It was shocking to learn one of my wife's closest friends had been shot dead. This was the friend who called every day during my wife's prolonged bout with pneumonia several years ago. We had thrown out the "live" Christmas tree and put her to bed at home, because I couldn't find a doctor on Christmas Day to admit her to Barbour County Hospital.

My friend, Dr. Rufus Lee, a Dothan allergist, prescribed for Ann via long distance, and a local pharmacist filled his prescriptions and offered me encouragement. So did Ann's dear friend—every day during her home-bound illness.

I'll never forget her encouraging telephone calls daily—nor those of other friends and family. Those were tough times.

It was a long ride home from Birmingham to Eufaula this past Sept. 12. Lesser women would have called for help, but my able, dutiful wife took the tragic news in stride and drove the recovering patient home—with a rest stop and lunch with kinfolk in Montgomery.

The patient did fine. My aortic valve had been replaced with a pig's valve. But both our hearts were broken over the tragic news.

My recovery has been nothing short of miraculous, and I have measured up to every medical test. Dr. Al Pacifico and his renowned cardiovascular team have repaired yet another faulty heart. Their handiwork has passed the stress test several times since my discharge from University Hospital.

My life has already been enriched. God answered my prayers and the prayers of my family and friends—and the prayers of some who don't even know me.

This morning, as I continued my home physical conditioning program, I felt like my old self again. Except that my heart was almost broken again. I tried not to dwell on the double tragedy that struck beautiful Eufaula as I walked my old, routine early morning walk—the same route I was plodding when I suffered my heart attack.

The good news is that I completed the three-mile jaunt feeling great, except my heart was sad. (And, yes, I miss my faithful walking companion, the family dog "Ace" who now rests in peace.)

Dr. Pacifico has done a marvelous job repairing my aortic valve and performing open-heart surgery on other Eufaulians, too.

Now, this town needs a specialist to mend our broken hearts grieving over our tragic news. Modern medicine, cardiologists, surgeons and our local doctors have saved and enhanced many Eufaulians' lives, and we are thankful.

Mending those many broken hearts can only be done by the Great Physician. Prayer is the only effective prescription.

HE'S HAD ENOUGH PIG PUNS AND GRIZZARD BOOKS

October 15, 1995

Enough. I've had enough of pig puns and Lewis Grizzard. It's been five weeks since I had open-heart surgery at the University of Alabama Hospital, and, yes, the patient's fine. It did take a spell to recuperate from the big dose of anesthesia, but now that I'm enjoying reading once again, I want you generous readers to know I now have a full set of Lewis Grizzard books.

However, keep those funny letters coming. I do have a sense of humor even though I must admit I don't think the pig's valve is quite the joke the late *Atlanta Journal* humor columnist did. Oh well, maybe "Jowl" is a funny new nickname suggested by one gentle reader.

My irreverent coffee club wants to know if I drink a toast to the generous pig that donated me his valve every time I eat barbecue. Well, would you believe that my last meal before cardiovascular surgery was an early evening barbecue repast? The last meal and the body shave and prep reminded me of John Grisham's novel, *The Chamber*, and prepping a prisoner for "the chair" at Parchman Prison in Mississippi. It was my last tasty morsel before experiencing a "prudent diet." I am enjoying a reprieve, though. Dr. Melvin Oakley, my hometown doctor, has temporarily waived the prudent diet so that I may regain some of those pounds I lost following cardiovascular surgery.

I knew it was time for the countdown when the male nurses shaved my skin from my bony neck to my skinny ankles, removing every stray hair that might hide a sneaky bit of bacteria.

The surgical team that opened my sternum so the surgeon could reach my malformed aortic valve must have thrown out several fatty spare parts before they sewed up my chest, because the next day when the nurses weighed me, I'd lost several pounds.

The fringe benefit is a relatively unrestricted diet. For my first dining out, would you believe, my best girl and I enjoyed dining alfresco at Sam's Barbecue? It wasn't exactly the same sensation as lunch at a sidewalk café on Paris's Champs-Élysées but it was a delight for this patient to sit on the porch and watch the passersby in downtown Georgetown as I enjoyed my barbecue chicken. I didn't have the heart to order ribs. How could I do that to a pig?

Now, folks, you are most kind. I really do appreciate the paperback, *I Took a Lickin' and Kept on Tickin',* and *They Tore Out My Heart and Stomped That Sucker Flat*, and the collected *Wit and Wisdom of Lewis Grizzard*. They're crammed full of chuckles and a few poignant truths about his trials and tribulations with his leaky aortic valve. Grizzard checked into Emory Hospital in Atlanta in 1993 for his third heart surgery in eleven years. Like me, the funny man from Moreland, Ga., was born with an imperfect aortic valve. In 1982, he had his first porcine (hog) valve implanted. That valve became infected in 1985 and was replaced by another pig valve, "which was worn out and ineffectual by March of '93." His doctors decided it was time to switch to a mechanical valve.

My surgeon, Dr. Al Pacifico, UAB's world-renowned heart surgeon, laid the facts out for me, and I changed my mind and took his recommendation to implant a pig's valve. He says my pig's valve will last between eleven and fourteen years. Hopefully, it'll be that long before having my sternum split open again and unwired so they can repair my heart.

The best years of my life are on the bright blue October horizon. Now that I better understand my own mortality, I plan to be more discerning with the way I spend each day that God gives me. Even before my heart attack that occurred while getting in my regular constitutional, I tried to thank Him for the new day I was experiencing.

A heart attack has an uncanny way of getting your undivided attention. It also opens the door so you know the power of prayer and experience the goodness and thoughtfulness of friends as well as strangers.

NURSING DUTIES MIGHT QUALIFY HIM AS LPN

October 6, 2002

"An old dog is never too old to learn new tricks," goes that old adage.

I've thought about that old saying lately as I've taken on new kitchen and laundry room responsibilities.

The B. W. is laid up in bed with a bad case of the epizootics and three compressed fractures.

I have been pressed into service. The kitchen stove, the microwave, the dishwasher and the washer and dryer are all high technology I've never taken the time to master.

Well, why should I? The B. W. is perfectly capable of such domestic responsibilities. All these years, we've been a great team: We've restored an old house, educated three sons, paid for a business and started a retirement kitty.

All the while—even after I promoted her to associate editor—she's performed on the domestic front like a trooper.

Two of my sons weren't married any time before they discovered their old man is spoiled rotten when it comes to household chores. (I do do the gardening, and the B. W. hardly sets foot in the yard except to get to the car. And years ago she had the audacity to accept the coveted Brenau Cup for maintaining the Most Improved Yard in town.)

I grew up with a devoted father who cooked: Sunday morning breakfasts of steak and eggs, salt fish and fish roe were his specialties. When I was a tike, he would sear a fresh-butchered steak directly on the iron eyes of our old wood stove, and it was delicious. My older brother learned to make donuts, oatmeal cookies and chocolate fudge, but I never did feel cooking was my calling until now.

Now, I'm here to tell you I cooked a chicken pie for lunch, along with a pot of peas accompanied by yeast rolls. Well, I heated all those menu items that gracious family friends dropped off.

Timing is everything when it comes to getting a meal together—and I'm about as uncoordinated on the kitchen Linoleum as I am on the ballroom floor. I am making progress with breakfast, though.

I'm about to catch on to cooking toast without burning the bread, while brewing the wife's fresh-ground coffee, heating water in the microwave for my hot tea, pouring the orange juice and two glasses of ice water while peeling peaches, slicing cantaloupe or whatever fruit is in season.

And mind you, all these are placed on TV trays and served in the B. W.'s sick room.

Breakfast was coming together rather well until yesterday. Sleepy-eyed and running late for breakfast, I quickly measured out four little scoops full of roasted coffee beans and tossed them in to the top of the coffee bean grinder.

I mashed the little white button and all hell broke loose in the kitchen. Coarse ground coffee was slung into the room out of the grinder at ninety miles an hour. It was like running through a Columbian coffee storm as I frantically tried to stop the coffee grinder as it speeded up and slung coffee grounds into my face, down my pajamas and all over the kitchen.

I'm beginning to feel like a combination Chinese houseboy and an LPN. If my luck and our friends hold out, I won't have to do too much cooking, but I do need to devise a system for storing containers of delicious food prepared by wonderful friends. Locating items stashed away inside our refrigerator, in a hurry, is trying.

A few more weeks of kitchen and nursing duty, and I believe I could qualify for a coveted LPN pin.

PARENTS DIDN'T BURDEN CHILDREN
WITH PROBLEMS

September 22, 2002

Editor's Note: This is a continuation of last week's column, written for my granddaughter, Sutton, age three. She loves to hear stories about her parents or grandparents, when they "were little."

As a little boy, I loved to ride with the driver in my father's rolling store. One time I picked a citron from a farmer's field and played a trick on my mother. A citron looks like a watermelon but has no taste—unless you are a cow. Cows loved them.

Well, our mother loved watermelon. She insisted we store the green melon in the bottom of our oak icebox that stood on the back porch, because it needed a hole in the floor for the melting ice to run out.

She let the "watermelon" stay in the icebox for a couple of days so it would be real cold when we cut it. I couldn't wait for the watermelon cutting, usually a treat in the summertime. The rind was so hard and cold when my brother Maury tried to cut slices that he broke the knife's blade. My how my brothers and I laughed.

I loved to be at the store when the rolling stores came in after a day traveling through the countryside. I would check the wire cages under the truck's body and claim any bantam (little) chickens. I also looked for bantam eggs that must have been worth half as much as a Rhode Island red or white leghorn's eggs.

When I was a little older, I joined the Four-H Club and raising biddies (baby chicks) was my club project. The County Agent's staff worked with us, and I loved attending Four-H rallies in Geneva at the theater where we sang songs like, "The More We Get Together, the Happier are We." We had field day at the golf course, and that was fun.

I remember vividly the time my sister Sarah's cat ate some of my biddies. It was a Sunday morning, and I caught the darned cat and tried to chop his head off with the ax. The cat squirmed and clawed me, so I decided to dump him in the country. I asked Maury, who was probably an under-aged driver, to take me out in the country to dispose of the cat. A mile or two out of town, we passed a wagon loaded with bales of peanut hay. I slung that cat on top of the hay.

We stopped downtown where Maury got a shoeshine. When we got home, the cat was there.

When I was a little boy living on Johnson Street, the street where I was born, we had billy goats that pulled homemade carts. Goats were lots of fun but they would eat anything, including the glue on tin can labels. Some mean goats would butt you with their horns.

The earliest traumatic experience in my life was the time my billy goat disappeared from the neighborhood. I searched everywhere, and then walked down to Emma and Henry Poons's house.

Emma was our family cook, and she was also our washwoman. When I asked the crowd at the Poons's if they had seen my goat, they laughed and pointed to a slaughtered goat strung up in a tree. It made me so mad I read them all the riot act.

Another favorite toy was a homemade log truck. We loved pulling them around, hauling small sticks. Slingshots were favorite toys too. Some boys could kill birds with their stock, sawed from a piece of wood and tied with strips from an inner tube.

They didn't appeal to me too much because I loved birds. I loved to trap the wild canaries in a pear orchard near our house and to bait traps with chicken feed and catch sparrows in the alley at our Grandmother Sellers's in Montgomery.

This childhood story is too long, Sutton, but my early childhood was an ideal time in my life. It must have been a challenging time for my wonderful parents, who didn't burden their five boys and one girl with their problems.

V-J Day brings memories of loss, responsibility

August 20, 1995

It's been half a century ago, but how could I ever forget V-J Day and the end of World War II? No, I wasn't in Eufaula on Aug. 14, 1945, to celebrate the end of the war. I didn't mingle with the crowd gathered at the old bandstand on Broad Street, but in my mind I can hear youthful new congressman George Andrews rising to the occasion after the Cowikee Mills Band played "triumphant strains of music" and Eufaulians sang "America."

I was only a lad of sixteen at the time, a student at Bay County High School in Panama City who frequently visited my Bluff City kin. However, I later became friends with the U.S. Representative from Union Springs, and my brother, Doug Smith, who grew up in Eufaula, became his administrative assistant.

The Congressman told the crowd that for three years, eight months and seven days he had looked for, hoped for and prayed for a day of peace following one of the blackest wars in history.

In my youthful mind, World War II lasted much longer. It was the worst of times, yet the war afforded opportunity. My lovely mother had died in the summer of 1940, crushing my spirit and devastating my very being. The following summer of 1941, the United States was in a state of undeclared war with Germany. It was shocking to hear over the radio that Japanese airplanes made a deadly, surprise attack on Pearl Harbor on Dec. 7, 1941.

My Aunt Babe had often taken her text on the importance of Congress fortifying the Philippine Islands, just as her hero, President Franklin D. Roosevelt, advocated. (She later worked in the Office of Price Administration in Eufaula issuing ration books and checking businesses to make sure they complied with regulations.)

Things changed rapidly. Men who had been without real jobs during the languishing days of the Great Depression were hired to build Camp Rucker. Others, including my widowed father, Abb J. Smith, moved to Panama City to build Liberty Ships at Wainwright Shipyard overlooking beautiful St. Andrew Bay. We learned quickly about "blackouts" during practice alerts when lights were turned out. And we feared German U-boats would torpedo the shipyard.

The war years quickly changed my life. I leaned to hate Emperor Hirohito and the Japanese. As a fourth grader, I'd written a theme about Japan with her flowering cherry trees and magnificent Mt. Fuji. As a class project, a couple of other pupils and I devised at "Depression-Era TV" from a cardboard box, two sawed-off broom handles and a long roll of butcher paper, on which we pasted cut-out pictures depicting the Japanese people and their culture. One kid would slowly turn the broom handle and roll the pictures onto the "screen," and I would give my spiel about beautiful, far away Japan.

My dreams of visiting that country in Asia were forever shattered. Watching newsreels before the Friday night Westerns in the Royal Theatre in Samson had a devastating impact. I hated Hitler, the Germans and the Japs. Yes, we quickly forgot our history lessons and called the Nipponese "Japs."

My first trip abroad years later was to Germany, but during my travels since I've never wanted to visit Japan, although I financed a college interim trip to Tokyo for my son.

My oldest brother Jack, a pre-med student at the University of Alabama, left school to enroll in the U.S. Navy Air Cadet V program and later soloed in the spring of 1944 during flight training at Auburn. After gunner school and flight training at Pensacola, he was transferred to the ship "Pine Island." As a boy, I worried about his safety and wrote him short letters. The atomic bomb may have saved his life, along with thousands of others. He was in Tokyo Bay on the day of surrender.

During my boyhood, I witnessed a vast change of America emerging from the Depression into a changing order which catapulted our country into prosperity and into a world power. I marveled at farmers, shop owners, teachers and housewives who quickly learned to build Liberty Ships. We all purchased War Bonds with our excess cash, which became surprisingly easy to accumulate, what with rationing and the scarcity of goods and services.

Fortunately, my two older brothers returned unscathed from military duty, and so did my cousin, Abb Smith, who served in Dutch Harbor, Alaska. But other families I knew weren't so fortunate. We all displayed small red banners in a window with a blue star for each member of the family who had joined the service. A gold star was substituted when someone in a family was killed in action.

So, I have a flood of memories on this fiftieth anniversary of V-J Day and the end of WWII. I learned that America is the greatest nation in the world, and I learned never again could we as a people let our guard down, nor could we be so isolated from the rest of the world.

To keep the "peace," we also must learn and appreciate the many diverse cultures.

Truck has become the way
to travel in Alabama

October 1, 1995

I never thought I'd see the day when a truck became my favorite mode of transportation. In fact, I want to be one of the first Alabama rednecks to drive a Mercedes-Benz sports utility vehicle to my garden at the Fourth Estate and to the college campus for football games.

Driving my low-mileage Jeep Cherokee, at first, seemed about as out of character as wearing a leather jacket I bought at a Lakeside auction. That Country edition of the classic has evolved from the WWII Jeep and its forerunner, the pickup truck.

Being a child of the Great Depression when few could afford to buy new vehicles and a youth during WWII when Detroit manufactured GI-issue Jeeps, I had a fixation about cars and trucks. In fact, building tiny roads and playing under the house with toy vehicles was a favorite pastime during a summer shower.

However, I couldn't understand my father's logic in assigning a light tan Chevrolet roadster to his best salesman, nor why Daddy drove a pickup truck. In fact, I didn't understand pickups any more than I do now. Since we were in the mercantile business, complemented by a network of rolling stores and salesmen pushing textile products, I don't know why we needed the pickup, unless it was to haul a sack of cottonseed meal for Daisey, the family milk cow.

I was a farm-town kid with some city ideas I picked up from time to time while visiting my mother's family in Montgomery. The grown-ups used to chuckle when I'd exclaim, "I want a car with a back seat in it!" That precluded a T-Model Ford with a rumble seat, likely the flashy one my bachelor Uncle Bob's girlfriend drove.

I'll never forget how jealous I was during the Depression when our next-door neighbors, the Dowlings, bought about the biggest Buick touring car I'd ever seen. And to add insult to injury, the Segrests also bought a Lincoln Zephyr the same week my father brought home the fanciest

Ford pickup I'd ever seen. The handsome wooden panels were removable, creating a flatbed, but it was still a pickup, and little boys were expected to ride in the "air-conditioned" back end.

No, I've never quite understood we Southerners' love affair with the pickup truck. They're not really that useful. Load up something you need to move across town or across state and it's sure to rain. Better anchor your cargo, or like Hansel and Gretel, you'll mark your trail with items blown from the flatbed. Of course, most cabs offer little storage space, but then there are those monster pickups with back seats that are so long they can hardly turn off South Eufaula without blocking four lanes.

Pickup truck sales have grown the last three decades, along with the economy. About half the new vehicles sold in the South are pickups. Families "keeping up with the Joneses" seem to choose flashy pickup trucks as their second or recreational vehicle.

". . . The pickup has become a status symbol for many. In historical and literary context, a 'good old boy' without a pickup is like a cowboy without a horse," according to the *Encyclopedia of Southern Culture*. As the delightful encyclopedia notes, "In a more modern vein, the rising number of fancy pickups, the 'showboats,' in suburban driveways, represents a curious phenomenon in America's love affair with motorized vehicles."

Most of us urban truck drivers won't drive "no ugly truck." The color combinations are so enticing it must be more difficult to pick just the right truck than to select an automobile.

Now, I look forward to the day when Mercedes sells "program" sports utility vehicles manufactured near Tuscaloosa by Alabamians for Alabamians: Wouldn't that make a great bumper sticker? And wouldn't it be great to celebrate Alabama's good fortune at the annual Weindorf festival in Tuscaloosa?

Just think—we roaring rednecks could become the envy of all other road riders.

WE'LL PROTECT OUR FREEDOM
AND BUILD GREATER COUNTRY

September 16, 2001

The B. W. and I were enjoying our breakfast while watching Katie and Matt on the *Today Show* Tuesday morning. I couldn't believe what I was seeing on the TV screen. We watched in disbelief as a commercial airliner crashed into the World Trade Center in New York City at 8:42.

Was this some joke? Was this real? That's what I thought as we watched the television camera capture the second of two hijacked airliners crash into the south tower of the World Trade Center.

"These pictures are beyond belief," Katie Couric commented.

There was more to come in this "Declaration of war by terrorists" and coordinated terrorist attack, as Tom Brokaw informed the *Today Show* regulars.

At 9:43 AM, an American Airlines jet with sixty-four passengers and crew aboard crashed into the Pentagon. This heightened my emotions as I frantically tried to call our son, Bill, a political consultant who just moved from Arlington, Va., to the District of Columbia. His cell phone didn't respond, however, a short time later he called the *Tribune* to let us know he was okay.

My thoughts turned to my nephew, David, who is employed by Deutsche Bank in their NYC operations. A call to his father in Huntsville revealed he is in Madrid, Spain.

That reminded me of the tight security that European country employed during the World's Fair hosted in Seville several years ago. When Ann and I traveled from Madrid to Seville on a new fast train, the security along the tracks by military personnel armed with machine guns was a little disconcerting. So were the armed guards at museums. And when we departed from the Madrid airport, we and another couple were detained by security guards because we had checked our luggage through from the smaller, less secure airport in Granada. We were thoroughly grilled about our plans and our luggage and were detained in the airport until take-off time.

This type security may be in our future following the terrorists' attack on America. "We are at war with terrorists," President Bush told the world. "Freedom and democracy are under attack."

Speaking the next day to our son who was in his Washington apartment, I learned the capital was "very locked down and the police are everywhere," and that "all buildings downtown have sharpshooters."

"It could have been a whole lot worse," he adds.

This reign of terror shut down the nation's airports, but it won't shut down the country. There is a resolve to get back to business and identify the terrorists and their support. Our President and our leaders are determined to make no mistakes in their conclusions and their response.

Sen. Richard Shelby calls it "a war without boundaries, but it's total war." Our senator, who is the ranking Republican on the Senate Intelligence Committee, calls the strikes a "wakeup call for America."

Sen. Jeff Sessions, former prosecutor and state attorney general, says military force—not courts and laws—should be used to battle terror. "These are not normal rules in play here," the Armed Services Committee member says.

Closer at home, two Alabama National Guard units in Barbour County remain on an increased state of alert.

Mayor Jay Jaxon says, "As a community, we offer our ongoing prayers and support for victims and families of the terrorists' attacks on New York's Twin Trade Towers, the Pentagon and the airline flight . . . In the meantime, let's join hands and hearts, confident in our ability to focus on our future."

Barbour countians were also interested to learn that Charoen Pokphand USA, which operates a multi-million dollar integrated chicken industry in Barbour and surrounding area, didn't have employees at work at its twenty-first floor offices in the Trade Center at the time of the attack.

Eufaulians responded to the terrorist attacks by participating in a community prayer service at St. James's Episcopal Church Tuesday afternoon. The Chamber and Lakeview Community Hospital are organizing a blood drive to help the surviving victims. A Chamber "After Hours" reception and a Rails to Trails organizational meeting were also postponed. Flag sales picked up at the *Tribune* office and stores in town.

Rest assured, though, the Attack on America will result in greater resolve to protect our freedoms and to work for a greater country.

God bless America.

PREACHER WORE HIP BOOTS AT BAPTISM

July 5, 1973

My four-year-old little boy is full of questions. And sometimes his Mama gets impatient with his inquisitive nature—and so does his papa. But not our patient, long-suffering maid.

Lottie could hardly eat her lunch the other day—the Friday before her three children were to join the church—because Joel Jr. had so many things to ask her about the forthcoming baptism scheduled that Saturday night. The maid patiently explained about the baptistery in the church, and how the visiting preacher would baptize Trish, "Bubber" and "Buck Wheat."

Patiently, as she tried to eat her lunch, she answered such questions as, "Do they have a diving board in the church?" and "Do you have to have a swimming suit?" While stretched out in the adjoining den, I overheard Joel's cross-examining Lottie about what sort of thing the preacher would have on, if her children would be wearing pajamas. And she went into details about how there would be a white sheet handy to wrap around each of the forty-odd children and an adult or two after they were ducked into the pool.

Further questioning, my little boy wanted to know, "Do you wear shoes?" (The preacher wore hip boots.) Lottie, who's intelligent as well as patient, even tried to relate the real significance of being baptized. A good Baptist, she also explained to him how our church (Methodist) sprinkles instead of immerses new members, and reminded Joel how little brother Jack was "sprinkled" by the preacher when he was christened.

Oh, to have such patience—and to be kind enough to treat a little one as an adult when he asks such serious, searching questions.

And Lottie talked at length about this business of joining the church. She recalled how in the good ole days her mother was baptized in the river. But when Trish, "Bubber" and "Buck Wheat" join the church, they'll step down into the refurbished sanctuary's pool and prepare to be immersed. Since the church is carpeted, Lottie says they'll have to put plastic down to take care of any dripping.

My little boy was indeed keenly interested in the highly successful protracted meeting held at Georgetown, conducted by the visiting preacher from Albany. He was all ears when the maid told us about the new converts who saw the light or committed themselves because others were planning to join at the climax of the revival.

Now if Lottie is half as patient with her three smallfry as she is with my four-year-old, Trish, "Bubber" and "Buck Wheat" will understand the real significance of joining the church even if they are just kids.

Oh, to have the patience to answer my little boy's every question . . . but thank goodness for the likes of Lottie. She's worth her weight in gold.

Chapter 8
Presidents, Politicians & Other Notables

ADMIRAL THOMAS H. MOORER MADE US PROUD

February 22, 2004

I t would be appropriate for the City of Eufaula to fly the American flag at half-staff Tuesday, Feb. 24, at 1 PM EST during the funeral for Adm. Thomas H. Moorer.

The great American hero and Pearl Harbor veteran will be buried that afternoon at Arlington National Cemetery in Arlington, Va., with full military honors.

As his brother, Dr. W. D. Moorer, says, "He had a great love for Eufaula and the people here."

I am moved to join others in the print media and on the Internet to pay tribute to the forty-one-year U.S. Navy veteran. On Tuesday, America will pay tribute to a great hero and the nation's former top military leader who became chairman of the Joint Chiefs during the divisive days of the Vietnam War.

It was my honor as chairman of the Eufaula City Schools Board to preside at the dedication of Admiral Moorer Middle School, named in his honor, in April 1971. That was a great day for Eufaula when Adm. Moorer's hometown honored the native of Mount Willing, who moved

Dignitaries in Eufaula for Admiral Thomas Moorer Day in April, 1971, included Postmaster General Winton Blount, Gov. George Wallace and his wife, Cornelia Wallace, U.S. Sen. John Sparkman and U. S. Sen. Jim Allen, reviewing the parade down Broad Street.

here with his family in 1927 after graduating from Cloverdale High School in Montgomery at age fifteen.

He formed a strong attachment to Eufaula while waiting until he was 17 to enter the Naval Academy in Annapolis, where he played football. He was commissioned an ensign in 1933. Tom Moorer joined one of the early generations of naval aviators.

The *Eufaula Tribune* and its readers followed his career. In 1941, as a member of the Pacific Fleet 10, he survived the attack on Pearl Harbor. His plane was one of the first U.S. planes in the air.

Reading about his heroic actions during World War II in the bound volumes of the *Tribune* made me proud of this hero who called our town his home. During visits home with his wife, the former Carrie Ellen Foy of Eufaula, the Admiral graciously granted exclusive interviews to the *Tribune.*

My wife, Ann, a former associate history professor, reported those timely interviews. She also introduced Adm. Moorer after he retired and addressed the National Newspaper Association's Governmental Affairs Conference in Washington in 1992. That year, I chaired the conference and took hometown pride in his addressing concerns in the military after his retirement.

This wasn't the first time he addressed the NNA. When he spoke in 1971 in Rochester, N.Y., unfortunately I was not present, but the Admiral mailed me a copy of his remarks from the Office of the Assistant Secretary of Defense, with the attached message: "Joel, I'm running a publicity campaign for the *Eufaula Tribune.*"

"As you know, I'm a native born son of Mount Willing, Ala., and as such I believe I have some hometown familiarity with and understanding of the operation of a small town newspaper," he told the editors and publishers. "The fact is, I know a great deal more about the *Eufaula Tribune,* which my close friend Joel Smith now publishes, than I do about some mass circulation metropolitan dailies I could mention . . . but won't.

"My initial exposure to a newspaper was with the *Eufaula Tribune.* I soon learned, as a boy, that what I read in the *Tribune* was factual, because if it wasn't the editor heard about it . . . by telephone call more often than by letter. I also learned that the *Tribune* printed all the news that was fit to print. And lastly, I learned that everybody in Eufaula read the *Tribune . . .* not just nearly everybody."

My, how that boosted my spirits and made me sorry I wasn't there in person to also hear him say, "America must not lose sight of the fact that the Armed Forces of the United States are a reflection of American society. In fact, I know of no other organization that comprises more of a cross-section of the American community."

Like many proud Eufaulians, I have vivid memories of Adm. Moorer and his lovely wife, Carrie. As one tribute to his memory on the Military Families & Couples website says, "Hardly a retirement wallflower, Admiral Moorer combined forces with several politically powerful retired officers to continue addressing concerns in the military. He used his retirement to assist in educating Americans about military policy and political policy commenting on everything from the Tailgate to the Carter Administration's kowtowing to Castro. Moorer maintained an outspoken advocacy against giving away the Panama Canal and vigilantly fought to keep the Soviet Union in check during the Cold War."

Jennifer Harper writes in the *Washington Times*—headlined Adm. Moorer set standard in Navy—"A stalwart believer in traditional Navy codes and devotion to duty and country, Adm. Moorer remained true to his values during a sterling career punctuated by civil and cultural upheaval here and abroad.

"The soft-spoken Alabama native was a strategic thinker with sound judgment who steadfastly called for the modernization of naval forces to counter a growing Soviet threat and the challenges of the Vietnam era. But Adm. Moorer never forgot the true strength of the American military."

The *Times* also quotes Secretary of the Navy Gordon England, who credited the admiral with guiding the Armed Forces through turbulent times. "No matter how complex and how awesome you build the weapons of war, man is still the vital element of our defense. Men make decisions, men fight battles and men win wars," he adds.

Christopher Ruddy writes, "It is a sad day for America when a national giant passes. Adm. Thomas Moorer of Eufaula, Ala., was such a giant!" Writing for NewsMax.com, Ruddy maintains "His plan ended Vietnam.

"Moorer told me that Nixon was at Camp David, in one of the retreat's rooms, with a longtime friend. Nixon asked what Moorer thought they should do. He told them bluntly: Bomb North Vietnam as they had never done before. Nixon nervously gave Moorer the O. K.

"So, when we honor and remember this great warrior, we should remember his last warning: Beware of China. To the very end, this heroic American was looking out for his country with his certain clarity of thinking."

Let's lower the American flag Tuesday at City Hall and at Admiral Moorer Middle School. Let's also remember our country and Adm. Moorer and his devoted family in our prayers.

We have lost a great American and a great friend.

Ann Lowe: Couturier to rich and famous

August 29, 1998

Barbour County, known for its famous people and historic landmarks, has one more native to add to its bragging list. Ann Lowe, an extremely talented black woman born in Clayton in 1898, designed and made Jacqueline Bouvier Kennedy's wedding gown.

Her intriguing success story by *Tribune* associate editor Ann Smith is the cover story in the current summer edition of Alabama Heritage magazine. This is the second time the prestigious quarterly magazine published by the University of Alabama and the University of Alabama at Birmingham has focused on Barbour County this year. The winter edition featured "Fendall Hall's Murals" by Elizabeth Via Brown in a beautifully illustrated story that helped boost attendance at the Italianate mansion in Eufaula during the Pilgrimage.

Now, Alabama Heritage subscribers are reading about Lowe's true story, "Aspects of it bear a strong resemblance to a fairy tale . . . a little black girl from a rural county in a poor state makes it, by dint of her own skill and talent and hard work, to the world of haute couture in New York City."

Ann (Smith')s sister-in-law, Cile Smith, a Clayton native, suggested the idea of a feature on Ann Lowe to *Alabama Heritage's* editor. She researched articles on Lowe that appeared in the *Saturday Evening Post* (1954), *Ebony* (December 1966), *Flair Holiday* (1982), *American Legacy* (Winter 1999) and the *Clayton Record*. The magazine's editors borrowed historic wedding photographs from the John Fitzgerald Kennedy Library and individuals to illustrate the article.

At the height of Lowe's career as a couturier to the rich and famous, in the 1960s, she designed and produced hundreds of gowns each year. Ann Lowe Originals was her famous design studio.

She was also listed in the national *Social Directory*, along with her "famous, wealthy clients, and was occasionally referred to in magazine articles of the day as the 'Dean of American Designers.'"

Ann Lowe's crowning achievement, no doubt, was designing Jacqueline

Bouvier's wedding dress for her 1953 marriage to "the handsome senator from Massachusetts, John Fitzgerald Kennedy."

"Lowe's story is especially remarkable considering that she climbed her career ladder during an era when opportunities for blacks were scarce at best, and opportunities for young black female artists were all but nonexistent," Ann Smith writes.

"Barbour County at the turn of the century was populated primarily by tenant farmers and sharecroppers who eked out a subsistence living. Ann Lowe's forebears on her mother's side, however, lived in better circumstances than the vast majority of Alabama blacks, and—according to Lewis Cole, Ann's first cousin, who still lives in Clayton—better than a lot of poor whites."

Her maternal grandfather, "General" Cole, a free black carpenter, worked for the contractor who built the Greek Revival courthouse in Clayton. He arrived in the county seat in 1853 and fell in love with a young female slave, Georgia, a seamstress, whom he purchased from her owner and married. Their daughter, Janey, married Jack Lowe and they were Ann's parents.

Janey Cole Lowe made fashionable dresses for Barbour County's wealthy women. Her little daughter, Ann, watched her talented mother sew, and she learned the skill at an early age.

Her mother died in 1914, leaving the sixteen-year-old Ann with four ball gowns to finish for Alabama's first lady, Mrs. Emmet O'Neal. She rose to the challenge and her phenomenally successful career as a dress designer was launched.

It's a fascinating story; one Barbour Countians can indeed be proud to retell.

EDITOR MISSES CHANCE FOR 15 MINUTES OF FAME WITH PRESIDENT

March 5, 2005

Pussy Cat, Pussy Cat
   Where have you been?
   I've been to London
   To look at the Queen
   — Mother Goose Nursery Rhymes

I can identify with this oft-read short poem printed on the cardboard thick pages in my granddaughter Sealy's Mother Goose book. I've been to Montgomery to look at the president, and to listen to George W. Bush's "Conversation on Strengthening Social Security."

The nursery rhymes, first published in the 1780s, were used to educate and to entertain small children. W.'s conversation with his legions of friends in Alabama on Feb. 10 was used to drum up support for his plan to strengthen Social Security for the twenty-first century.

I trust I'm not being too familiar with the Commander in Chief of the United States. The president and I are friends, even though I've never met him personally.

Our friendship began soon after his first inauguration in 2001. I liked our friendly young President from the very beginning of his first campaign. That cliché, "The apple doesn't fall far from the tree," comes to mind. I supported his father, George H. W. Bush, one of America's most qualified candidates for president.

I personally chatted with him at the White House during a reception for the National Newspaper Association. I talked with him about bass fishing, and I invited him to come fish in Lake Eufaula with Tom Mann. (I believe he would have come if my contact at Techsonic, makers of the Humminbird depth sounder, had followed through. Dolly Parton has plenty up front and she loved fishing Lake Eufaula, but wouldn't it have been a coup to have hosted the president?)

So it was with a great deal of enthusiasm that I greeted George W.'s first inauguration. I didn't contact my other friend in the White House, Karl Rove, and seek press credentials. I acquiesced and encouraged my son the editor to attend our forty-third president's inauguration.

I stayed home and watched every scrap of CNN's and NBC's coverage, and I cheered out loud when this decent young man took the oath of office.

In my March 4, 2001, column, "Publisher squarely behind Bush tax cut plan," I wrote that I hoped the President and Congress would also repeal the death tax and help the Smith family keep publishing our seventy-two-year-old twice-weekly newspaper.

"Mr. President," I concluded, "the *Eufaula (Ala.) Tribune* and I stand squarely behind your ideas on spending and on your tax cut package."

Now, don't believe that individuals in small towns in America are never heard at the White House. I sent Karl Rove a copy of my column and a copy to Publishers Auxiliary. Would you believe President Bush quoted my comment about small family-owned businesses in his first speech to a trade association? When he addressed the National Newspaper Association's Fortieth Governmental Affairs Conference March 22, 2001, in Washington, he said, "I want to quote from one of your own—publisher from Eufaula, Ala., the *Tribune*—Joel Smith.

"I'm hope I'm—if Joel is here, I hope I'm not embarrassing you. But sometimes, when we say things, words come back to haunt us. (Laughter.) Well, not exactly haunt us in this case. (Laughter.) Here's what he wrote: 'I hope the President and Congress will repeal the death tax and help my family keep publishing our seventy-two-year-old, twice-weekly newspaper.'

"That's what he said. He represents the sentiments of hundreds of Americans who work hard to build up their asset base, with the dream of being able to pass it on to a family member."

Unfortunately, I often attend NNA's conference, but I missed my chance for fifteen minutes of fame that year. Remembering that, I don't feel so bad about not shaking President Bush's hand during his visit to AUM. I was close enough to step down a couple of rows and shake his hand, but I looked down at my "White House Press Pool" tag and reminded myself that I was in the jam-packed, friendly confines of the gymnasium to gather information about his visit to Alabama for this column. (I've been kicking myself in the seat of my pants ever since.)

I also received a letter from President Bush, dated Dec. 17, 2004, thanking me for my column on winning reelection: "Karl Rove forwarded to me a copy of your column from the *Eufaula Tribune*. Thank you for your strong support."

Our personable, smart, quick-witted president held the 5,000 Alabamians present for his conversation in the palm of his hand. He thanked AUM for setting up his trip, and he fondly recalled the Elite Café during his stay with the National Guard in Montgomery. "My old friend [former Mayor] Emory Folmar, is he here?" He was, and so were hundreds of his staunch supporters.

Sensing the friendly crowd wanted to know about his bright and beautiful wife Laura, he said, "She's doing great," and "Laura is a good First Lady."

He noticed, "Patsy Riley brought her husband." He thanked Attorney General Troy King, Treasurer Kay Ivey and other state and local officials for coming.

"If you want to serve our country, be like one of those soldiers in the army of compassion in Iraq where millions went to the polls. The desire for freedom is universal—it is powerful. We will win this war, long term. Freedom is on the march."

Bush talked about the economy, too.

"More people are working now than ever. We have overcome the recession. Unemployment is only 5.3 percent in Alabama. The credit goes to the entrepreneurs and the growth of the new technologies."

He touched on Congress's medical liability bill, as well as his plan for Social Security. "Don't run the doctors out of business," Bush said.

"Social Security is used in a lot of campaigns to frighten people. It is a job for the president. We've got a problem . . . if you're near retirement, the government will pay you what we said we would pay you."

He said there is too much politics in Washington, D.C. "People from both political parties should come together and fix this for the American people. I've got some good ideas myself. I ask Congress for their ideas. "

The cheering crowd loved him when he said, "I'm saying to members of the United States Congress; let's fix this system permanently—no Band-Aids."

When Dr. Jeff Brown, a professor of economics, said Social Security requires action soon and that we must "think about ways to save the system," Bush confided, "I was a C student. What does that tell you? All you C students don't give up!"

There was much applause, as with several other remarks. It was all too obvious to the students and townspeople alike that our president is plenty sharp. He didn't refer to notes when he talked simply about the Social Security plight.

Following his hour-long informal remarks and comments from six guests on the stage, the president concluded, "It's going to be an interesting debate in Washington, D.C."

"God bless you!" he told the adoring crowd, as "Stars and Stripes Forever" rang out and they reverently recited the Pledge of Allegiance.

"We love you, Mr. President," a group of coeds cheered as he waved goodbye. The doors remained closed until Air Force One and the president were in the air.

I loved it. It was a highlight in my fifty-year newspaper career.

EUFAULA PROUD OF HARPER LEE, ACADEMY INDUCTEE

September 2, 2001

I had neglected to write down the date for the induction of Nelle Harper Lee into the Alabama Academy of Honor on Monday. It was my intention to be present when Eufaulian Louise Conner's sister was honored by her home state.

While I could kick myself for neglecting to note the date on my calendar, I have fond memories of highlights in her literary career. Eufaula claims the Monroeville native, too. We shared Louise Conner's excitement when Lippincott published her novel, *To Kill a Mockingbird*, in 1960.

The *Tribune* followed her literary career, including *Mockingbird's* selection by four book clubs and winning the Pulitzer Prize on May 1, 1961. That made the front page, complete with a photograph of the youthful looking novelist of international acclaim. In one edition, we published so many articles about Harper Lee we referred to that issue as "The Mockingbird Edition."

"Dody's" friends—that's what we called her before she became famous—in the Bluff City have followed her literary career with enthusiasm.

There haven't been interviews when she came to town to visit her sister, like when Admiral Thomas H. Moorer, the retired chairman of the Joint Chiefs of Staff, visits his brother, Dr. Billy Moorer.

I once wrote a column inviting Harper Lee to come to Eufaula and write a second novel with a Bluff City locale. Needless to say, that didn't happen. The next best thing happened, though, when our steering committee worked with Auburn University professors to stage the Eufaula History and Heritage Festival in 1983. Alabama's best-known fiction writer accepted our invitation to participate in this marvelous undertaking.

The author of *To Kill a Mockingbird* made a rare public appearance.

Not only did she visit with Eufaulians and autograph her book, but she also presented a paper, "Romance and High Adventure," on Albert Pickett's "History of Alabama" that was first published in 1851, after he gathered material for seventeen years.

It was a splendid, scholarly presentation. Dr. Jerry E. Brown, an Auburn professor coordinating the Festival, later wrote: "Her ability to define characters such as Scout and Jem against the backdrop of Alabama history may be one reason why twelve million copies of her novel have been sold. With swift authority, Harper Lee does more in this essay than simply present to us a quaint and forgotten fragment of our past.

"She pricks our conscience and reminds us—yet again—that history is a living creature, waiting to be noticed."

While Harper Lee never published another novel, she did permit publication of that splendid essay in "Clearings in the Thicket: An Alabama

Pulitzer Prize winner Harper Lee was the main attraction at a History and Heritage Festival in Eufaula in 1983, where she signed copies of To Kill a Mockingbird.

Humanities Reader." Other papers presented to the Eufaula History and Heritage Festival included a paper, "Barbour County: Home of Governors," by Robert Flewellen and Charles Blackmon.

I pulled down a bound volume of the 1961 editions of the *Tribune* to read coverage of Harper Lee's winning the Pulitzer:

"When Dody's book was so well received by the public," Louise Conner is quoted, "we were most grateful when it made four book clubs and we were overwhelmed. Now the Pulitzer—there's no adjective left to describe the way we feel."

At that time, Universal had been signed to film *To Kill a Mockingbird*, and Gregory Peck was picked to play Atticus Finch.

Of course, the movie brought on more coverage in the *Tribune*. Both the novel and the movie have become American classics. The moving story set in Alabama in the 1930s became an international bestseller.

Delightful Louise Conner has some health problems and wasn't able to attend the induction of her beloved sister into the Alabama Academy of Honor. Alice Lee, their much loved older sister, is still practicing law in Monroeville on the square near the well-preserved courthouse where their father tried cases and which Universal Studios recreated for *Mockingbird's* dramatic trial scene. She will be ninety next month.

Down in Mobile, "they think they own her," says Louise Conner. The *Mobile Register* had a field day covering Harper Lee's induction. If your intrepid columnist had been on the ball, there would be a timely photograph of "Dody" in Wednesday's edition.

Jimmy Clark was great 20th century Barbour County leader

April 11, 2000

The death of retired Speaker Jimmy Clark is cause for me to reflect on my own mortality.

It was a time of new beginnings for the successful farmer and for me, the young editor and general manager of the *Eufaula Tribune*, when I moved to town in the summer of 1958. The pending impoundment of the murky waters of the Chattahoochee prompted us both to look at new opportunities.

Jimmy had returned home from WWII to find his parents in poor health, and he changed his plans to enroll at Auburn and took over the family farm north of town on U.S. 431.

He raised cattle, peanuts and cotton on some 5,000 acres he eventually amassed, expanding the family farm from seven hundred acres including a country store his father ran.

The 1940 Eufaula High School valedictorian again demonstrated his flexibility when the Corps of Engineers moved into town and acquired land along the river that would be flooded when they built the dam at Ft. Gaines. He ran successfully for the Alabama Senate in 1958 and was waiting for the Legislature to convene in 1959 when I became editor.

We each had a vision for Old Eufaula, an aristocratic town that had slept for the previous twenty-five years. Jimmy had moved in from the farm after selling his cattle and farming equipment.

He invested the money in a savings and loan association, along with his brother, Fred. After selling his land to the government, he and several others, who also sold farmland for the lake's bottom, later chartered Citizen's Bank, which later became Compass Bank.

He and banker Young Johnston also organized a successful insurance and real estate business. They built some five hundred houses for the growing town.

I jokingly dubbed the new bank "Goose National" because some money to incorporate the venture came from the sale of land for the Eufaula National Wildlife Refuge. Those were exciting times for Eufaula.

The new Senator had vision, it was soon apparent. As editor, I articulated my dreams on the editorial pages.

I covered James S. Clark's legislative career from its exciting beginning in 1959 to its triumphant ending in 1998. In between, I also reported on his dynamic actions as mayor of Eufaula (1976–78).

So in a real sense, Jimmy's death is a personal loss. While there was the customary professional relationship—as it should have been—between a public officeholder and a newspaperman, we managed to remain friends nevertheless.

As a youthful newcomer to Barbour politics, I learned quickly to be my own man with such powerful politicians as Probate Judge George Little, Rep. Sim Thomas, Sen. Jimmy Clark and Gov. George Wallace in the thick of things.

I also learned that Jimmy Clark had the vision for Eufaula, Barbour and Alabama that would make a difference. I learned he had the will and the power to make good things happen.

His farm background made him aware the Tree Farms and the backwaters covering rich farmland would necessitate drastic changes in the local economy, if we were to prosper as a community. He fostered industrial development, luring American Buildings to the new State Docks Road Industrial Park, followed by a succession of other plants that industrialized Eufaula.

Of course, Sen. Clark didn't do this alone, but he inspired others to become leaders. And he inspired Eufaula's many sons and daughters who had completed college and moved to the cities to come back home to seek their fortunes.

While working for his constituents back home, he was also working to help Alabama overcome racial strife during the Civil Rights era.

"He's very well liked and he tries to serve his community, both black and white," the Rev. G. H. Cossey, an African American preacher, said in 1994.

Jimmy Clark, the powerful legislator and three-time Speaker of the House of Representatives, should have been the seventh Barbour countian elected governor. However, he served as Gov. George Wallace's, Gov. Lurleen Wallace's and Gov. Albert Brewer's floor leader.

He adjusted to new administrations like he adjusted to the times—and Barbour County and Alabama benefited. He had the political courage to keep a safe distance from the governors: They needed him as much as he needed them to push tax incentives for roads and schools and state parks and airports and historic sites.

It was a great day for Eufaula when the rising waters of the Chattahoochee River forced the youngest of the six Clark children to move to town.

It was also a blessing for the struggling hometown newspaper and its aspiring young editor that Jimmy Clark had chosen to run for the Legislature. He gave us much to write about, and he inspired us to dream big dreams.

As I wrote in January 2000, James S. Clark was one of Barbour County's twenty great leaders of the twentieth century. He was also a friend. I can't imagine Eufaula and Alabama without him.

Justice Houston keeps Barbour's rich
TRADITION ALIVE

October 10, 1985

B arbour County, home of six governors and two lieutenant governors, continues to produce outstanding public officials. J. Gorman Houston Jr., a native Eufaulian who has practiced law in the county for twenty-five years, now takes rank with other distinguished Barbour Countians to hold high office. His investiture as associate justice of the Alabama Supreme Court Monday in Montgomery brought honor again to historic Barbour, home of six Alabama governors from John Gill Shorter to George Wallace.

Two other distinguished Barbour Countians, Preston C. Clayton, himself a former justice of the Alabama Supreme Court, and Gen. Henry B. Gray III, former commander of the Alabama National Guard and present director of the Alabama Alcoholic Beverage Control Board, made some outstanding remarks about Justice Houston during the formal investiture. It was another red-letter day for Barbour County with hundreds of citizens on hand to witness Chief Justice Clement C. Tolbert Jr. administering the oath of office to an outstanding Barbour Countian.

"The old, historic county of Barbour is happy to present to the court its brilliant native son, J. Gorman Houston Jr., of whom it is justly proud," Former Justice Clayton said so eloquently.

"Barbour County has a long and rich history of distinguished sons who have made outstanding contributions to state government." Gen. Gray said. "Gorman Houston will add a new chapter to that history."

"Having been reared in the same city with him—part of the time just across the street—and having known him and his family all his life, no one has had better opportunity than I to know his qualities and qualifications to serve as a justice of this great court," Clayton told the court and some six hundred plus guests present for the investiture.

Reflecting on his junior colleague's twenty-five years of practice in Barbour, the distinguished Eufaula attorney said Houston successfully handled cases in all courts of the state, in federal district courts in both Alabama and Georgia and in the U.S. Courts of Appeals at New Orleans and Atlanta, and he has been admitted to practice before the Supreme Court of the United States.

Clayton also paid tribute to Houston's family. "Gorman's beautiful and charming wife, Martha," he said, "is certainly entitled to some credit for the many attainments of her distinguished husband." Quoting from the book of Matthew, he said, "'The tree is known by its fruits.' Gorman's children are living witnesses to the fact that his is the right kind of tree." His daughter, Mildred Houston Sasser, a graduate of Duke University and the University of Alabama Law School, is trust officer of First Alabama Bank of Montgomery, and his son, Gorman III, a graduate of Yale University School of Divinity, is the minister of First United Methodist Church of Loxley, Clayton said.

And I must add, his lovely gracious mother, Mildred Vance Houston, is one of Eufaula's finest ladies.

Clayton said in conclusion, "On behalf of the Bar Association of Barbour County, the people of the county generally and for myself personally, we are exceedingly proud of this occasion and of the man whom I am honored to speak of today."

Gray, a close personal friend, said while Houston's "entire life has been one of achievement and accomplishment," he wanted to talk about "Gorman, the person, and share with you the kind of person he is and why he is so particularly well-suited for this appointment."

He said Houston would add an extra dimension to the high court. "He brings a high intellect with a unique aptitude for research, and he even enjoys research. Gorman is a man of honor with absolute and unquestionable honesty and integrity. He has the courage to take a stand for what is right regardless of the pressures or consequences. Gorman is a person with intensive dedication and will give this job everything he has; he will give it his very best.

"And above all, Gorman is a caring person, one who constantly gives of himself and reaches out to help others, to help his church, to help his community and to help his fellow man. Gorman cares deeply about justice for his fellow man."

Justice J. Gorman Houston Jr., continuing that long line of distinguished officials who hail from Barbour, has brought honor to his hometown of Eufaula and the county of Barbour. And an extraordinary number of Eufaulians and Barbour Countians honored our county's newest high official by their attendance at his investiture at the Montgomery Civic Center Monday afternoon.

KATIE COURIC'S ROOTS ARE DEEPLY IMPLANTED

February 21, 1999

It will take more than a long weekend to trace Katie Couric's roots and to hear all the stories about her Eufaula ancestors.

Probate Judge Anne Adams and a small band of volunteers have found the original abstract from minutes of the Barbour County Circuit Court whereby Charles Maturon Couric, Katie's great-great grandfather, "made his solemn declaration that it is his bona fide intention to become a citizen of the United States and renounce forever all allegiance and fidelity to Louis Philippe, King of France."

Court was held in a log courthouse at Clayton when a twenty-two-year-old Charles Couric applied for his American citizenship. The late attorney Preston C. Clayton found the old record book in 1937 in the courthouse basement and made a copy of the extract from court minutes. When *Today* segment producer Terry Schaefer saw Ann's and my copy, which Clayton sent us after we bought the Couric Homestead, she wanted to film the original.

Volunteers Ed and Margaret Slade, Margaret Russell, Margaret Garrison and Frances Askew spent hours pulling down and thumbing through old minute books and other legal documents to no avail. But alas, after finding Charles Couric's will, they found the original 1840 document in which he states he "intends to reside in the state of Alabama," that he emigrated from

Katie Couric's 1999 visit to Eufaula brought out hundreds of fans, including Eufaulians Barbara Lee, Martha Ann Porter, Virginia Ransom and Angie Bowman.

"said Kingdom in the month of August in the year 1837, having landed at Pensacola in the Territory of Florida."

Gracious and meticulous Judge Adams has arranged to temporarily move the original documents to the Eufaula courthouse and open her office Saturday so the NBC camera crew can scan them for the *Today* segment on tracing co-anchor Katie Couric's roots.

It's the personal touch, like this, that endears Katie and co-anchor Matt Lauer to their six million plus viewers. Her Eufaula fans were happy when her youngest daughter, Caroline Couric Monahan, was born (Mayor Jay Jaxon extended congratulations and sent baby Caroline a key to the City of Eufaula) and they mourned when her husband, Jay Monahan, died a year ago.

Katie's visit has taken on a life of its own: Bertha Smith has written and the *Tribune's* Nancy Hancock has printed her a lovely poem. An artist has painted a picture for her. The patients at the Dialysis Clinic have called to ask Katie to stop by; they watch her *Today Show* every morning, and the ALAGA Antique Car Club wants her to stop by their show Saturday at Old Creek Town Park.

She'll graciously greet Eufaulians at the bandstand downtown Saturday morning at 11:30 and at Shorter Mansion at the Eufaula Heritage Association and the *Tribune's* reception Saturday evening. But when will she find time to hear all those marvelous stories about her colorful Couric kin?

Old-timers have endless stories about the *Tribune's* inimitable society editor Willie Copeland Couric and her cantankerous husband, Lex, one of the town's all time great characters. Gwen Conner can regale Katie with tales she heard growing up in the Hortman house next door to Lex and Willie Couric and their sons, Cope, Charles and William. Ester Wilson vividly remembers sisters Molly and Pauline Couric, the last family to live in the Couric Homestead (Couric-Smith Home).

I love the one about the time the Lex Couric family drove down College Hill in their car with a rumble seat. The boys were jabbering as their father drove toward town. Mother Willie kept telling Lex, "Stop the car!" in her lady-like manner. Cope kept begging "Papa! Papa!"

When the car came to a complete stop on Broad Street downtown, Lex counted heads and quizzed, "Where's William?"

"That's what we wanted to tell you, Lex. He fell out when you hit the bump in front of the Catholic Church." But that was mild. Lex let out a yell of profanity that could be heard next door the time modest Miss Willie painted the commode seat and didn't tell Lex before he took his seat.

Who knows, Miss Willie's popular column, "Here, There & Everywhere," and her long and productive newspaper career just may have influenced John Couric and his famous daughter, Katie, to pursue journalism careers. Miss Willie, bless her, wrote about many a hostess "pouring tea in the hall" and about Eufaula guests being "greeted by the Christmas tree in the hall." She diligently reported on the United Daughters of the Confederacy, Barbour County Chapter, the Daughters of the American Revolution, all the garden clubs and the literary clubs, too, but it was decades later—after Elizabeth Upshaw was family editor—before cocktail parties made print.

Happily, they'll probably pour cocktails in the hall at Shorter Mansion Saturday evening and drink a toast to Eufaula's favorite ancestral daughter, Katie Couric.

McCoo Family Visit was all about love

May 6, 1988

Marilyn McCoo is a superstar, but her father, Eufaula native Dr. Waymon McCoo, likes to keep things in perspective. That was evident during "The McCoo Family Visit" to the Bluff City last Saturday.

There are three outstanding McCoo sisters, whom Frances D. Jones, family friend and Golden Owlettes board member, brought back to their roots.

When arrangements were made for the descendants of the late, beloved Dr. T. V. McCoo, Eufaula's first black doctor, to visit, the Eufaula Chamber of Commerce's planning committee was informed the event couldn't be publicized and that Dr. McCoo wanted it to be a family affair.

It isn't every day a celebrity visits Eufaula—although we do have more than our share of distinguished visitors. The fortunate few invited to the luncheon honoring the McCoos were clearly excited. Chamber President Ed Garrison, presiding, confessed he hadn't been so excited since he got married twelve years ago.

Minutes before leaving for the luncheon, a member of the library expansion committee called to suggest I get in a plug for the fund drive. I pondered on the way to Lakepoint Lodge just how to handle the last-minute request. I didn't want our town to come across as another Mayberry, as delightful as Andy Griffith and townspeople made the mythical town on his TV series. Eufaula's too sophisticated, I thought, and so is Marilyn McCoo.

Dr. McCoo graciously presented an excellent portrait of his late father to Librarian Jo Boyer. The portrait will hang quite appropriately in the library's branch, the McCoo Memorial Children's Library, presently housed in the City Housing Authority boardroom in Chattahoochee Courts.

"The McCoo Family Visit," as the day was billed on the carefully scheduled program, was a heart warming experience—both for the accomplished and gracious McCoos and the Eufaulians invited to participate.

My memories of Dr. McCoo were tinged with sadness, yet a feeling of gratitude for the towering, slightly stooped giant of a man who had served our town so well—as a wonderful physician and humanitarian and as leader of the black community. I recalled Dr. McCoo's appearance before the Eufaula City Council during the height of racial unrest in the South. This peace-loving gentleman, then in his twilight years, was troubled. He didn't understand all the undercurrent, but he wanted peace in his beloved hometown. As a young editor-reporter, I was touched by his approach.

Dr. Billy Moorer, school board member, commented that Dr. McCoo's name isn't on the records "down at City Hall as an official member of the school board, but I can assure you that from a practical and functional standpoint, he was very much a member. Dr. McCoo's good judgment, common sense, integrity and the respect in which he was held by the entire community made his help and advice invaluable."

Six years after his death, Dr. Moorer added, his qualities of leadership were still felt when the Eufaula schools made a smooth transition from a segregated school system to an integrated one.

Dr. Phillip Woodbury, who practiced medicine with Dr. McCoo, is a talented actor with the Little Theater, but he was so touched with emotion he found it difficult to deliver his prepared remarks. Twenty-five years ago, the two were on the five-member physicians staff of the Barbour County Hospital. Dr. Woodbury, a McCoo family associate recalled, was responsible for Dr. McCoo's being invited to join the Barbour County Medical Society, even though he had spent years providing health care to the community.

"He was respected by the entire hospital staff, doctors, nurses and aides," Dr. Woodbury recalled. "Although he was nearly eighty-five, and had long since closed his office, he was continually and frequently called on by his many loyal patients, who seemed to want him to go on practicing forever."

"We need more occasions like this when we are able to feel and express love," Dr. Waymon McCoo said. Marilyn McCoo and her sisters, Glenda and Mildred, did just that, too.

And that's what "The McCoo Family Visit to Eufaula" was all about—love—love of family, love of community, love between the races. It was a day to remember.

QUITMAN COUNTY CARTER'S
TURNING POINT 40 YEARS AGO

October 20, 2002

F ormer President Jimmy Carter wouldn't have won the 2002 Nobel Peace Prize if Quitman County's political boss hadn't stuffed the ballot box forty years ago.

Jimmy Carter, the peanut farmer and peanut warehouseman from Plains, announced his candidacy for Georgia state senator on Oct. 1, 1962—the day James Meredith attempted to enroll as the first black student at the University of Mississippi.

While the press reported this historic event on the front page, Carter's announcement was buried even in his local newspaper, the *Americus Times Recorder*.

This was the harbinger, however, the forerunner of a series of events, which would change things all the way from Georgetown (pop. 860) to Washington, D.C., via Atlanta.

Things have never been the same since Election Day, Oct. 16, 1962, when only 333 people came to the courthouse in Georgetown to vote for Homer Moore of Lumpkin or Carter. But officials took 420 ballots from the box and counted them. There were about one hundred ballots in the box for which the voting officials could not account.

When the B. W. and I heard the news on television that Jimmy Carter had won the prestigious Nobel Prize, my thoughts raced back to that day in Georgetown in 1962, when I was standing in front of Gary's Store, across from the courthouse, and Jimmy Carter's Cadillac kicked up dust as it came to a halt. The mad, youthful, redheaded candidate stepped out of his car and "read the riot act" to the bystanders.

Rep. Joe Hurst, one of Georgia's most powerful political bosses, had cheated him wholesale at the polls.

The brash young newcomer to politics faced a turning point in his fledgling political career that would lead to the Georgia Senate and eight years later to the governor's mansion.

After Carter completed his term as governor, politically savvy folks in the Lower Chattahoochee basin didn't think he could have been re-elected governor.

He shocked them—and much of the country, too—when he announced his candidacy for President in December 1974 and launched a campaign that was fired by his down-home Peanut Brigade that made the news when his supporters made forays into the East. At the Democratic Convention, he was nominated on the first ballot.

He campaigned hard and defeated President Gerald Ford by 297 electoral votes to 241 for Ford. Without this surprising victory and without his tenure as the thirty-ninth president (1977–1981), he would never have earned the Nobel Peace Prize. It all began across the river in little Georgetown after the political bug bit the West Point graduate.

An idealist, he announced his candidacy for the Senate after Georgia laws changed, mandating a special election to implement the U.S. Supreme Court's "one man, one vote" ruling.

"The 1962 campaign marked a turning point—the first real defeat for the old system on its own turf—that helped to end the legalized system of white supremacy, rural domination of government and deprivation of civil rights among our neighbors," Carter writes in *Turning Point* in 1992.

"A central political boss is a shrewd and incredibly powerful political boss, often benevolent, who considered the community his own and could not accept my encroachment on his domain," Carter continues in his fascinating book.

Confronting four square the rampant election corruption across the river from Eufaula—the reservoir dam at Ft. Gaines was 93 percent complete—Carter appealed on Oct. 30, 1962, to the Georgia State Democratic Executive Committee to hear his recount demand evidence—and there was plenty. He took this action after the Quitman Committee chairman, Hurst, refused to review alleged irregularities during the Oct. 16, 1962, election at the Georgetown box.

The turning point happened because, as the Nobel Peace Prize winner adds in his book, " . . . people in one small county in southwest Georgia who never became famous but who had an impact on history because of their courage and fears, their conflicting values and ambitions. Their actions were part of the great upheaval in American life that was the 1960s, and we are still struggling with the issues they confronted."

REAGAN IMPRESSED SCRIBES WITH WIT, WARM PERSONALITY

June 13, 2004

My most dynamic personal memory of President Ronald Reagan takes me back to the White House in March 1982.

Ann and I and our three young sons were attending the National Newspaper Association's Governmental Affairs Conference and sightseeing in Washington.

The highlight of that NNA conference was attending a gala reception hosted by the President. I'll never forget the imperial president, as some liked to call him then, regally descending that majestic stairway as the Marine Band played "Hail to the Chief."

Community newspaper editors and publishers danced lively around the mosaic presidential seal emblazed in the rotunda floor. Since I am an inveterate wallflower, I escorted the B. W. into the Gold Room, where

President Reagan was standing alone in the middle of the beautiful reception room. We shook his hands and were talking when the crowd of grassroots newspaper people enveloped the three of us.

There I stood in the face of one of America's greatest presidents, a little embarrassed because we were locked in by the press, right in the President's face.

"For the record," I wrote in "Candid Comments," March 25, 1982, "Mr. Reagan is vibrant, handsome and most personable, and he could get an aluminum siding salesman's attention when he talked about his economic policies."

After hearing Mr. Reagan plug his New Federalism, we visited in the Gold Room, the Red Room and several other beautifully appointed reception areas. We also enjoyed hearing the Marine Band play superb dance music. I even danced.

It was a heady experience for a small-town editor and publisher.

To jog my memories of President Ronald Reagan, I searched the March 1981 to 1989 bound volumes of the *Tribune* because the NNA's conference, which I once chaired, is held in March. I missed the '81 conference, but I editorialized that Barbour countians identify with the assassination attempt on the seventieth day of his administration: "Ronald Reagan's political antagonists, who seem to delight in pointing out he is seventy-years-old, must be astounded at the physical stamina and 'excellent spirits' he has shown after the assassin's bullet was removed from his chest. It is evident we Americans, who are appalled at the assassination attempt, have indeed a superior man in the Oval Office."

Barbour countians, perhaps, the editorial continued, are even more disgusted than the typical American because we could identify with that fateful day when Barbour native George C. Wallace was paralyzed by a would-be assassin's bullet while campaigning for the presidential nomination in Maryland.

The next year, the B. W. and I stayed at the Washington Hilton Hotel, near the White House. Mr. Reagan was shot outside this hotel, and I marveled again at his quick recovery and his return to duties of office.

During the twenty-fifth annual NNA Governmental Affairs Conference in March 1986, "I got the message from fiddle-playing Sen. Robert C. Byrd (D-West Virginia), with a new hair style, that he didn't believe President Reagan when he said our defenses are repaired during his re-election campaign. He said the President needed better advice than he was getting."

Another great memory I have of President Reagan is his July 10, 1986, visit to Dothan to come down-home and meet with some regular folks.

My son, Joel, home from Washington and Lee and working at the *Tribune* for the summer, and I secured press credentials to cover his speech on tax reform. I well remember the fervor, as the Dothan Dixieland Band and Troy's Sound of the South Band played patriotic music. The President brought tax reform down-home, and he was cheered mightily because Alabamians loved President Reagan.

Of the NNA March 1987 conference, I wrote it was an exciting time to be in Washington. I heard a "newsworthy briefing by President Reagan the day after he made his important address to the nation from the Oval Office, and I heard key senators and House members speak their piece." I also had a front seat to hear Chief Justice Warren E. Burger resign from the court to devote himself to leading America's commemoration of the Bicentennial of the signing of the Constitution.

These are memories I'll hold for a lifetime.

Chapter 9

The Chattahoochee: A River's Story

EUFAULA AND CHATTAHOOCHEE INSEPARABLE

This was written as a history of the Chattahoochee River and Lake Eufaula during the town's sesquicentennial celebration.
September 25, 1973

Eufaula and the Chattahoochee River are inseparable. There has been a Eufaula settlement along the banks of this "river of the painted rock" long before the first white settlers paddled down the river and set up camp here in 1823.

When the Lower Creek Confederacy was spread like a network along the rich, verdant banks of the Chattahoochee and its beautiful river like tributaries, the Indian village of Eufaula was a rather small settlement, an offshoot of a lower Creek Town, known as Eufallah, one of the main sites on the east bank of the river. Actually, Eufaula designated a number of Indian settlements; one was situated near the site of the present city.

Eufaula took its name from the largest of the aboriginal places that was located in the vicinity of the present Georgetown, Ga., across the river, with an Alabama site just above present day Eufaula. This last site must undoubtedly have been at St. Francis Bend, where evidence of an old Indian town remains, archaeologists and historians believe. Old Creek Town Park is located in this historic area where members of the Eufaula clan must have lived peacefully in their pleasant, temporary village.

It was across Chewalla Creek in that Indian settlement often called "Eufala" the first white man, Carson Winslett, is reputed to have settled. Legend has it Eufaula's first settlers, five white men, were floating down the river bound for Marianna in February 1823, when they discovered that picturesque Indian village of Yufala and its lush environs. The Eufaulees were our earliest farmers, cultivating the rich river-bottom lands on each side of the Chattahoochee.

Those first white men must have been enchanted with the beauty of the place, because they set up camp and decided to settle amid the virgin forests, the rushing creeks and the swift Chattahoochee. A Methodist missionary, Jesse Burch, had been here by 1816, and George Byrd, a Revolutionary soldier from Tidewater, Va., died here in 1817, early records show.

Soon other white settlers followed. The friendly Eufaula clan welcomed the first white families into their village. No attempt was made at first toward building a permanent white settlement, but gradually more white men moved into the Creeks' territory, and as their number grew, they began setting up trading posts and built crude homes from timber cut from the nearby forest. Inevitably, some settlers infringed on the Eufaulees lands. This ultimately led to a bloody conflict, the Creek Indian War. The treaty of evacuation was signed in 1832 with the Indians, and in that same year Irwinton was chartered. However, it was not until 1837—the year the Sheppard Cottage was built—that the last of the hostile Indians were moved to their new home, far away in Oklahoma, which they promptly named Eufaula.

With peace restored, Eufaula began to prosper and grow. The quaint village was officially named Irwinton on March 1, 1833, in honor of Gen. William Irwin of Shorterville, in nearby Henry County. He had been successful in securing a landing for riverboats in the frontier town as well as a post office. The spirit of Gen. Irwin was contagious, and the early citizens soon built the town into a center of commerce and agriculture.

The strategic location on the river, coupled with the post roads and stagecoach lines connecting Eufaula with Ft. Mitchell and Fort Gaines, proved to be exceedingly well situated. The changing riverfront town became even more accessible with the construction of the first covered bridge spanning the swift Chattahoochee in 1837. This marvel of engineering, built by John Goodwin for E. B. Young's Irwinton Bridge Co., made it easier for more pioneers from Georgia, the Carolinas, Virginia and the coastal lands to migrate to the frontier town.

Summerville Land Co. was soon formed with the idea of selling building lots to the influx of settlers. Eufaula was indeed fortunate these first land developers and leading citizens were men and women of vision, strong will, good judgment and much ability. Streets were laid out, beginning with old Front Street along the magnificent bluff overlooking the scenic river below. Other streets were planned, with wide parkways in the middle and the first letter of the four most important thoroughfares, Livingston, Orange, Randolph and Eufaula, spelled L-O-R-E, honoring Seth Lore.

Arriving in increasing numbers, the newcomers who came in covered wagons or flat bottom boats purchased lots and soon began to build substantial homes. The Tavern had been built earlier, around 1836, to accommodate the river traffic, and soon a wharf erected along the riverfront below to accommodate the riverboats which served the towns along the Chattahoochee.

Soon the frontier village of the Indians "river of the painted rock" was prospering. The economy of the town was based on land, cotton and slaves. Cotton was grown on the large plantations surrounding Eufaula.

Front Street, overlooking the river below, became a bustling little place. Taverns and other businesses were located along the street, and during these early days homes were built in the bluff area. Irwinton was renamed Eufaula in 1843.

In the 1850s, the prosperous Eufaulians began expanding, building on the hill west of the bluff in an attempt to avoid the "miasma" or fever, which they associated with the riverfront. The houses they built during this period were larger, with more detail. Greek Revival style was popular. Then during the opulent cotton-rich years which followed, planters shipped thousands of bales of cotton from the wharf. Steamboats carried cotton and passengers downstream to Apalachicola, where the cotton was transferred to larger vessels, bound for Mobile and eventually Liverpool.

Back then, as is true today, Eufaula and the Chattahoochee were indeed inseparable. River transportation contributed heavily to the prosperity. While the riverboats transported cotton downstream, on the runs upstream, they carried Italian marble, used in building some of the fine antebellum mansions, and furniture from Europe for the fashionable homes. The prosperous planters traveled and spent some of their wealth for education. This was the era of Chesterfield manners, great plantation days and luxury for the planters and merchants who prospered.

The two decades from 1830 to 1850 were exceptionally prosperous for Eufaula. The Greek Revival and Italianate-style mansions were built along the broad streets of town. This was rather unique, because most Southern planters were building their impressive mansions on their plantations. While the steamboats plied the Chattahoochee, they were soon challenged by the coming of the railroad in the late '50s, and this led to the development of industries. Those early industries included grist mills, brickyards, logging mills, cotton gins, planing mills and variety works, carriage factories and furniture making. Cotton was still king, but the industries continued to grow in importance to the local economy.

With slavery the burning issue of the times, Eufaula soon became a hotbed for secession. The Eufaula Regency, made up primarily of a number of prominent lawyers, was Alabama's second most powerful group of secessionists. They refused to make any concessions to the Union, and since they were such a powerful political oligarchy, they had great influence in Alabama politics.

When war came, Eufaula families contributed more than their shares to the Confederacy. Fortunately, the war ended when General Grierson's Cavalry was on its way to Eufaula. Youthful couriers were flying along the road from Eufaula to Clayton, bearing the flag of truce. At dawn the advance guard of the cavalry saw them. The Blue Coats marched into town April 29, 1865, and The Tavern and upper floors of the stores were overrun with sick and wounded Rebel soldiers. Dr. Hamilton M. Weedon, Mrs. Ross Foy's grandfather, was in charge of the hospital on the bluff.

Historian Anne Kendrick Walker's research reveals Gen. Grierson and his staff were entertained at dinner by Dr. and Mrs. J. C. Pope. Dr. Pope was the intendent, or mayor, and he and the General made arrangements soon after the armistice. Eufaula's public buildings and homes were spared; so was the cotton stored in the great warehouses. Financial stability was slowly reestablished in the post-war era, and surprisingly, Kendall Manor and other mansions started before the war were completed.

Reconstruction was a difficult era for Eufaula, but by the 1880s, trade was booming again, and the beautiful little river town soon became the trade center for Southeast Alabama and part of Southwest Georgia across the river. Eufaula Cotton Mill, the first cotton mill, was established in 1888. In 1895, Chewalla Mill was started and the growing operation was bought by members of the Comer family and renamed Cowikee Mills. This was Eufaula's largest employer until a year or so ago when American Buildings expanded its modern steel buildings manufacturing plant.

Actually, Eufaula changed little during the next three wars and the Great Depression of the 1930s.

The development of a navigable waterway on the Chattahoochee in the 1960s signaled a new era for Eufaula, when the aristocratic old town became an inland port. The river was impounded behind the dam at Fort Gaines downstream, creating magnificent Lake Eufaula, which transformed Eufaula into a virtual peninsula, jutting out into the 45,000-acre lake.

Eufaulians became excited about the town's future. The Chamber of Commerce was reactivated, and the town took on a more progressive attitude. At least six new industries, employing more than 1,500 workers, had been attracted to the Bluff City on the Chattahoochee by 1971.

Today, Eufaula is still progressive, yet Eufaulians are concerned with preserving the best of their goodly heritage, placing an accent on quality. They want to grow, but not just to become bigger—they want to build an even better town because they appreciate Eufaulians' enviable lifestyle of the 1970s.

And today, Eufaula and the Chattahoochee are still inseparable. Eufaulians call their giant, sprawling reservoir on the river "Lake Eufaula" but today the growing little city is a port-of-call for yachts and pleasure craft, not steamboats. Those sternwheelers are now legend, but recreation/tourist oriented Eufaulians are talking about bringing back those colorful days. There's much talk about forming a Lower Chattahoochee Valley corporation which would operate an old fashioned riverboat to make excursions along the modern waterway. And that would begin another golden era in our historic Bluff City on the Chattahoochee.

Chattahoochee should be named a Heritage River

November 23, 1997

With a sense of anticipation and enthusiasm, I second the nomination of the Chattahoochee as one of the ten American Heritage Rivers. The Chattahoochee: River of History has attracted people since prehistoric times. This has been well documented by archaeologists.

My research for the chapter on the Chattahoochee River in *Rivers of Alabama*, which was published in 1968 by The Strode Publishers, greatly stimulated my interest in this scenic river immortalized by Sidney Lanier's poem, "The Song of the Chattahoochee."

Actually, it was the impoundment of the Chattahoochee that attracted me like a magnet to the "Bluff City of the Chattahoochee." I frequently visited relatives in Eufaula during the days of my youth, and I was fascinated both with the Chattahoochee—reputed then to be the third swiftest river in America—and with the antebellum town's historic buildings.

Since becoming the editor of the *Tribune* in 1958, I've looked to the river and to Eufaula's rich past to find a way to ensure our town's future and the newspaper's financial security. What's developed through the years is a love affair. I find the history of the Chattahoochee a romantic story that is a continuing saga.

I have written, edited and published enough copy about our river to publish at least a trilogy, maybe more. I feel as if I've been called to inform and to interest citizens in the lower Chattahoochee Basin about the river—its past, its present status and its future.

Sometimes, I have felt that we take the Chattahoochee for granted and aren't aware of the dangers of pollution and the need to develop a formula to allocate the surface water resources. There is a great need to manage this God-given water resource that is Eufaula's lifeline.

The Chattahoochee has a goodly heritage that must be respected. It is important that we preserve a national treasure. The nomination of the Chattahoochee as an American Heritage River is a wonderful opportunity to preserve and protect this great river that has brought prosperity to the cities and towns along its fabled banks and historic basin.

It is important residents along the river's banks remember the history of the Chattahoochee, as well as its romance and its impact on the people living along the scenic waterway. The Indians, of course, were the first to put the river to work for man. From the days of the Mound Builders to the latter-day Cherokees in the north and the Creeks—including their Eufallah clan—in the south, the Indians used the river as a source of food and a means of transportation.

The first white men to camp on the banks of the Chattahoochee River were the Spaniards. They found the river four centuries ago and called it the River of Palms. DeSoto crossed the river's headwaters in 1540.

Early French explorers and fur traders paddled their canoes up to the Indian towns of Coweta and Cusseta. The territory remained under Spanish domination until the English established Georgia as a colony in the 1730s.

The Spanish established a fort at nearby Holy Trinity, and I recall the excitement in Eufaula and Columbus when some of the ruins from the old fort were discovered some years back when the archaeologists and the Corps of Engineers were making preparations to impound the Chattahoochee.

There's much history along the banks of the Chattahoochee that is constantly being interpreted through the efforts of the Eufaula-based Historic Chattahoochee Commission. Studies are being made that include an inventory of historical, cultural, archaeological and natural resources along the meandering Chattahoochee, which begins at Chattahoochee Gap, two hundred feet south of the Appalachian Trail, and flows past thirsty Atlanta to Columbus, the fall line, and to Eufaula and eventually joins the Flint River to form the Apalachicola River flowing into the bay at Apalachicola.

The Chattahoochee is indeed an American treasure that should be named one of ten American Heritage Rivers.

LAKE EUFAULA NATIONAL GEM THAT SHOULDN'T BE NEGLECTED

October 30, 2005

We should never forget Eufaula's fortune has always been dependent on the mighty Chattahoochee River.

From the steamboat days in 1846, when the Steamer *Eufaula* arrived at the city wharf with 405 barrels of merchandise and cleared the port of Eufaula with seventy-seven bales of cotton and passengers, to today when bass fishing boats, yachts and barges ply impounded Lake Eufaula, our economy has been enriched by the river.

This year, 2005, marks the fiftieth anniversary of the beginning of work on the Walter F. George Lock and Dam that created beautiful 45,200-acre Lake Eufaula and the navigable Apalachicola, Chattahoochee and Flint Waterway. Before the end of 1963, the huge project was completed at a total cost of eighty million dollars. Eufaula and environs experienced a renaissance.

This old river town with its historic homes, antebellum store buildings and aristocratic bearing was wide-awake and once again looked to the Chattahoochee River for an enhanced quality of life.

In 1963, a state inland dock facility was built at Eufaula at a cost of $196,500. State Docks Road was cut to the waterfront side. In the long run, the small tonnage of barge traffic made the continued operation of the Eufaula dock unfeasible. But an industrial park rapidly developed along the road, with an impressive number of diversified industries that are today

Tom Mann shows off an impressive string of the huge bass that quickly put Lake Eufaula on the map and lead the Tribune *to proclaim Eufaula "Bass Capitol of the World."*

the backbone of the area's economy.

That same year, the Eufaula City Council awarded a $346,869 contract financed under the Wallace Act for construction of a Holiday Inn at the corner of East Barbour Street and Riverside Drive. The sixty-unit motel with its excellent restaurant, banquet room and swimming pool accelerated our fledgling tourism business and put Eufaula on the travelers' and fisherman's map.

Sen. Jimmy Clark spearheaded a successful campaign to have the reservoir named "Lake Eufaula" by the Alabama Legislature and on June 14, 1963, the lock and dam was officially dedicated with much fanfare and dignitaries aplenty on the speakers' stand. A fight with Georgians ensued over the lake name. That's a topic for another column in itself.

Clark was also successful in convincing the powers that be to build Lakepoint Resort State Park, complete with a 101-room resort hotel and marina on Lake Eufaula. The once popular convention center is presently included on the timetable for enlarging and refurbishing the resort facilities that include a golf course.

When U.S. Fish and Wildlife officials were scouting for a possible refuge in 1960, a local refuge association led by attorney Sam LeMaistre was organized, and officials finally approved a tract of land on the west bank of the lake. In 1964, the Eufaula National Wildlife Refuge was completed, encompassing 11,600 acres of land and water north of Eufaula and Georgetown.

The swift Chattahoochee's muddy waters backed up into the deep creeks when the lock and dam became operational, creating an impoundment with an abundance of food to feed the fish. Fishing was so good, local people who never fished the river discovered the pleasure of pulling big bream and bass from Lake Eufaula and its tributaries.

The *Tribune* dubbed Lake Eufaula the "Bass Capital of the World." Tom Mann had the foresight to move the fishing lure operation he and his wife, Ann, started in 1960 on their kitchen table in Enterprise to Eufaula. Mann's Bait Company thrived as Tom Mann promoted his Little George and Wooly Bully lures at fishing tournaments on the lake and around the nation.

"My first bait company birthed many others that . . . collectively grossed hundreds of millions of dollars," Mann shared in his book, *Think Like A Fish*.

Allied Sports Distributors, the forerunner of Techsonic Industries, was Eufaula's newest industry, manufacturing depth finders and fish locators for the sports fishing industry. Last year, Johnson Outdoors, known for Minn Kota and other highly successful outdoors products, acquired Techsonic, manufacturer of the Humminbird depth sounder.

Numerous other successful industries are here today because the third highest lock and dam east of the Mississippi created Lake Eufaula and the navigable waterway.

Lake Eufaula, with all its enhancements—and several gated resort neighborhoods in the works or on the planning table—is the Lower Chattahoochee Basin's gem. We must continue to polish our prize and to protect its water resources because it is also a national treasure.

This fiftieth anniversary of the beginning of the all-encompassing Corps of Engineers project is worthy of celebration.

Chattahoochee River lifeline of Eufaula

October 1, 2000

The Chattahoochee River is Eufaula's lifeline. The river made famous by Sidney Lanier in his poem, "The Song of the Chattahoochee," was the reason for the settlement's being in the first place. The Lower Creek village of the Eufaula clan antedated 1733.

In 1823, five white settlers traveling down the river enroute to Marianna, Fla., discovered the Indian village called Yufala. The Creeks were friendly, and they returned and settled in the area.

This soon became the hub of a prosperous plantation region with a thriving river trade. As the planters prospered, they built imposing homes, and Eufaula became a distribution center for a wide tri-state area. The

Chattahoochee became an important artery of transportation.

In 1828, *The Fannie* became the first steamboat to travel up the river to Eufaula and Columbus, the head of navigation. This opened a prosperous era for Eufaula.

The City of Eufaula, built in Eufaula in 1845, was one of many paddle wheelers docking at the Eufaula Wharf. The steamboats on the Chattahoochee were fascinating and contributed to the planters' and the merchants' prosperity in Eufaula. The wharf, just below the River Tavern, was owned by the Eufaula Wharf Company. It had pine piling, a cap and deck and a warehouse.

The traffic and demand for steamboats could be measured by the cotton crop—and so could Eufaula's prosperity. In good crop years, cotton bales were stored along Randolph and East Broad until they could be transported down river to Apalachicola and then to New Orleans, New York or Liverpool, England.

After the war, in 1947, the *George W. Miller*, with its steam steering gear and accommodations for 736 passengers on her decks, was sold for debt to the Columbus Bank and Trust Company, then resold in 1950 and again in 1952 to Thurston Crawford and then dismantled. This closed the colorful, once prosperous era of steam boating on the Chattahoochee.

Eufaula's wholesale houses thrived, thanks to the river. A salesman would board a riverboat at the Eufaula Wharf and stop at Ft. Gaines and other landings downstream, taking orders from local storeowners. His orders would be filled at the Eufaula warehouses when he returned, and goods were dispatched downstream on the next riverboat.

During the 101 years between 1828 and 1929, more than two hundred stern and side-wheel riverboats plied the Chattahoochee between Apalachicola and Eufaula. Two hundred and forty landings were located along the 262 miles of river between Columbus and Apalachicola.

The railroads came to Eufaula, and the slower steamboats had competition.

The Chattahoochee, Flint and Apalachicola have been used as a means of transportation since the Indians populated the river system. This important waterway is still used today for commerce and transportation. Eufaula became an inland port again in 1963 when the state docks were built and industries began locating along State Docks Road. This was the harbinger of another prosperous era for the Bluff City of the Chattahoochee.

Passage of the 1945 River and Harbors Act authorized a nine by one hundred foot channel that was constructed on the Chattahoochee and Apalachicola.

The impoundment of the rivers behind three great dams proved a tremendous complement to the verdant basin's natural beauty. Eufaula is now recognized as Alabama's best outdoor town when it comes to hunting and fishing and enjoying the outdoors.

Limited flow of water during extreme droughts meant problems for the barges transporting agricultural and timber products and fertilizer and

Smith, right , a fervent booster of Lake Eufaula, and City Councilman Eugene C. Parker, Historic Chattahoochee Commission Director Doug Purcell, and Chamber Executive Director Jim Bradley discussing promotion of the speed boat races during the Summer Spectacular.

gasoline. In 1991, navigation windows were developed in cooperation with channel users to provide a deep channel when there was limited water.

However, this created a very low water level at West Point Lake, as well as Lake Eufaula. Apalachicola Bay on the other end of the waterway also has an environmental problem created by the dredging to maintain the channel. Consequently, Georgia U.S. Rep. Bob Barr proposed to de-authorize barge navigation on the Tri-Rivers. This action, ironically favored by some high U.S. Corps of Engineers officials, has been stopped at least for this year.

But the Chattahoochee's future as an artery of transportation and a rec-reating paradise in its magnificent reservoirs is threatened. It is endangered when there is prolonged drought.

These navigation windows this summer, coupled with the relentless drought, have endangered Lake Eufaula and the waterway.

Thanks to Congressman Terry Everett and Sanford Bishop of Georgia and Senators Richard Shelby and Jeff Sessions, the proposal to de-authorize barge navigation has been derailed—at least for now.

River that once divided now connects basin

May 17, 1998

The seven-boat "Chattahoochee to the Sea" flotilla and entourage with its accompanying floatplane overhead, four motor coaches on land, canoes and sea kayaks trailing probably didn't create as much excitement as in the days when a steamboat docked below The Tavern or at the Ft. Gaines wharf. However, as O. B. (Buck) Earnest, Apalachicola, Chattahoochee and Flint project manager, says, "there has developed a new spirit of cooperation today that binds together each side of the river."

Becky Champion, director of Oxbow Meadows Environmental Learn-ing Center in Columbus, says the three-day voyage down the waterway has been "spectacular. It was a river that divided us, but now it's a river that connects."

After enjoying old-fashioned hospitality at Kendall Manor and touring the Seth Lore and Irwinton Historic District, the fifty-seven passengers floated downstream to tranquil, secluded Bagby State Park and Ft. Gaines, Georgia's third oldest town.

It was at the park, near the Queen of the City of the Chattahoochee, that Corps of Engineers project manager Earnest told the journalists and TV camera men, political and civic leaders and resource support and personnel candidly: "It is gratifying to see this group has folks from both sides of the river. It was not always so. When this lake was first impounded in 1963, people from Georgia and Alabama had some disagreement over the name of the lake and maybe a few other things.

"That is all in the past. In recent years, there has developed a new spirit of cooperation that binds each side of the river. There is no doubt this river links us together and establishes us as a community. Not only a community in a geographic sense, but also a community in an organizational sense. No one group of us can do anything with the river system without impacting the interests of others. We need to remember that."

Even so, I didn't feel that comfortable: I'm glad nobody introduced me as one of the "colorful characters" along the river that Joe and Monica Cook captured on film during their one-hundred-day canoe expedition down the river system that began in the mountains of North Georgia, ending at St. George Island near Apalachicola. None of the Chattahoochee River experts present were aware that I wrote the chapter on the Chattahoochee for *Rivers of Alabama*, published in 1968. It's just as well I was the working press, covering the voyage of discovery for the *Trib* and its sister publication, the *Cuthbert Times and (Ft. Gaines) News Record.*

Fred Brown, co-author of *The Riverkeeper's Guide to the Chattahoochee*, was among the elite. It's a book any river buff will treasure. The section on "Walter F. George to Seminole" is rather accurate and candid. It includes a sidebar about "A Lake With Three Names," detailing the awful squabble between Georgia and Alabama river proponents who fussed over the name for the magnificent new reservoir. However, the authors didn't say that Eufaulians finally got fed up with our Georgia neighbors claiming every darned new lake, barreling full throttle ahead naming every lock, dam, bridge and impoundment on the river system.

We took our stand and insisted on the name "Lake Eufaula," not just for our beautiful, historic hometown but for the Creek Indian clan that settled both sides of the Lower Chattahoochee.

"For over thirty years, the reservoir impounded by Walter F. George Lock and Dam has not had one common name with which people on both sides of the lake could be happy," writes Brown and Sherri M. L. Smith. "Signs welcoming visitors to Eufaula, read 'Welcome to Historic Eufaula, AL: Home of Lake Eufaula' while similar signs in Ft. Gaines, Ga., read 'Welcome to Historic Ft. Gaines: Home of Lake Walter F. George.' A lone Lake Chattahoochee sign further complicates the issue."

The guide notes the U.S. Supreme Court in 1859 established a boundary with Georgia owning not the lake but the river up to the western boundary. (There was no lake in 1859, but a high river bluff on which the Indians and white settlers built Eufaula.) When the river waters were impounded, spreading out into the Alabama flatlands, our area of the lake rapidly grew in size. The fuss died down, and today there is a new spirit of cooperation between neighbors along the river. But for the record, the Alabama Legislature on June 25, 1963, named the reservoir Lake Eufaula and the entire Alabama Congressional delegation endorsed the name Lake Eufaula.

Alabamians revered Georgia's U.S. Sen. Walter F. George and Sen. Richard Russell for whom the Alabama-built Eufaula-Georgetown bridge was named, but it was the last straw when Georgians insisted on naming the next to the last reservoir in the system. The Eufaula clan put on their war paint and hung tough while working overtime to capitalize on the new navigable channel and beautiful new lake.

As the *Atlanta Journal* editorialized some years later, Ft. Gaines kept waiting for the boat called "prosperity" to dock while Eufaulians upstream rolled up their sleeves and revitalized their old river town.

We're all "Chattarats," as the voyagers' caps proclaim, and the river does connect and bind us together. There is a new spirit, and it is high time we build more invisible bridges of friendship between Alabama and Georgia. We're all in this beautiful basin together. Let's make the most of it.

Steamboat perilous but grand way to go

October 14, 1990

Water wars aren't anything new along the Chattahoochee River, says Edward A. Mueller. The author of a new Tri-Rivers steamboating book says low water in the fall of 1887 seriously disrupted steamboat travel between Eufaula and Columbus. Folks down stream, not unlike today, were pointing fingers at thirsty, bustling Atlanta.

"Columbus citizens believed the low water was caused by the fact that upstream Atlanta had constructed a water system that diverted seven million gallons a day from the Chattahoochee," Mueller writes in *Perilous Journeys: A History of Steamboating on the Chattahoochee, Apalachicola, and Flint Rivers, 1828–1928.*

Some four million gallons was used for domestic purposes and three million for flushing her sewers. The *Enquirer Sun* argues, 'This thing is already becoming quite a serious matter with us and it is high time some steps were being taken to see what can be done about it.'"

Now, ninety-three years later, that's hardly a drop in the bucket compared to the 529 million gallons a day—increasing the diversion by fifty percent—advocated by the Corps of Engineers's controversial plan.

The Corps's involvement in water wars and navigation controversies isn't anything new, either. Mueller said during a lecture at Lakepoint Convention Center Tuesday that the Corps of Engineers took an interest in the river in 1873 and tried to regulate the stream.

The author's slide presentation and lecture on one hundred years of steamboating on the Tri-Rivers provides historical perspective on the proposed reallocation of Lake Lanier, one of the waterway's sparkling reservoirs connected like a mammoth string of pearls along the Alabama-Georgia border.

That year in history, 1897, saw the demise of two Chattahoochee River steamboats within two days, the *City of Columbus* and the *J. F. C. Griggs*. "The condition of the river forced the 'pool' to adopt the strategy of abandoning travel on the upper river for a spell. They were ruining the vessels and working their crews to death. The steamboats would only come as far north as Eufaula. The Central of Georgia would convey river freight by rail to Eufaula, and the boats would take it from there."

Those were perilous journeys: Steamboating on the Chattahoochee did have its romantic appeal, but "in those days people were interested in things other than nostalgia," Mueller says. Riverboat owners like John W. Callahan of Bainbridge, who named one of his steamboats for himself, "was the richest man in Georgia at the time," and W. C. Bradley, who was "a steamboat man," also "became wealthy and endowed lots of things in Columbus."

The average life of a riverboat was seven years. "The water was swift and there were lots of snags in the river." When a boat sank, often its cabin was moved to other hulls.

As perilous as it was, it was "a grand way to travel for the times." Ladies and gentlemen would make excursions downstream to Apalachicola where the cotton was transferred to seafaring ships that carried the cargo to Eastern Seaboard and European markets. At the time, Apalachicola was the third largest market in America, and sometimes when a Chattahoochee steamboat's passengers arrived at the port "fifteen or twenty sailing ships would be in the bay."

Between 1900 and 1910 and the early '20s, hunting and fishing parties would board steamboats at the Eufaula City Wharf, one of the more advanced landings, and cruise to the Dead Lake area on Owl Creek, "frankly to drink."

Staterooms, seven feet square, had "a slop jar, no bath," and opened on the outside and the inside where sumptuous meals were served on tables covered with white linen.

From 1828, when the *Fannie* made the first trip to Eufaula and up to Columbus, until 1939, when the *George W. Miller* was the last boat on the river at Columbus, a total of 200 steamboats plied the treacherous, swift waterway.

Chapter 10

Hot Type, Heartache & Happiness

WHAT DOES NEW COLUMNIST WRITE ABOUT?

December 11, 1958

This business of column writing has its occupational hazards. For this reason, I've been a little hesitant about beginning ye ole column.

What does a new columnist in town write about? Should he take out after the mayor and city council, launch a crusade to move the county courthouse into town, or advocate pullin' down a Confederate monument in an effort to alleviate traffic congestion? He does if he's a traveling man or if he likes the smell of tar and feathers. But since I'm here to stay—and anxious to become part of the town—none of the before-mentioned crusades appeal to me at this time.

Our friend Jim Waldron, a newspaper promoter with a great deal of experience who has fairly recently settled in town, tells me to write about my impressions of the town and its people. A good idea . . . but since I've been visiting Eufaula for years, they would hardly be first impressions.

What to call the column? Should I steal Walter Croker's "From the Bluff" title or how 'bout "Our Town"? Giving a thought to the river development and the way the area will be covered with water, I've kinda wondered if we'll be the Bluff City. "Our Town" sounds pretty good to me . . . lots of folks around town certainly remind me of the characters in that famous play. But then "Our Town" sounds a little small townish and Eufaula's liable to outgrow the title.

So you see, it looks like I'm stuck with that old heading, "Candid Comments." For over three years, I've batted out a weekly article under that title. At first I intended to have a rather objective approach, to perhaps do a little crusading.

But looking back over some of our past efforts in the *Geneva County Reaper*, I noticed little effort made urging reform. Reminded of the words of Edgar H. De Lesseps, managing editor of the *Daily World* in Opelousas, La., and somewhat an authority on column writing, I've decided that crusading should be done through the editorial columns.

Says De Lesseps, "We feel that above anything else a column should entertain. Weighty editorial comment should rest in the columns of the editorial page, leaving the 'original column' free." Bearing this in mind, I'll strive to write lightly—and be just a little entertaining. I'm the first to admit, I'm no Earl Tucker. But at least I'll try to leave "weighty editorial comment" in the editorial columns.

Editing small-town weekly no bed of roses

August 3, 1980

Editing a small-town newspaper isn't exactly a bed of roses. The editor's life is full of ups and downs, and some weeks there are more downs than ups. Everything is so personal in a small town—including the local newspaper.

During the quarter of a century I've edited and published community newspapers, I continue to be fascinated with people and how they react to all sorts of situations. Small towns are filled with some of the finest people anywhere, but they're also the homes of little people who vastly overestimate their importance. It's these little people who can give a newspaper editor fits.

There's the garden clubber who has an exalted opinion of herself who delights in not only trying to run the good ladies in her club but the editor of the local newspaper as well. Her beef is the newspaper doesn't give enough space to her garden club's meetings or the club's projects.

Like most "federated" ladies' clubs, her garden club keeps a scrapbook, which is entered into competition with other clubs in the district. If the president is a real go-getter, woe be unto the newspaper staff if they don't print every word the secretary writes in her detailed account of the last meeting.

This might include how the members answered to roll call with their favorite flower or a line from a favorite poem, who won the attendance prize, the visitors, the refreshments served and how the house was decorated with Crowned Imperial lilies or some other seasonal flower. The week before the club meeting, the Bookmobile does a booming business checking out books to club members so they can come up with something appropriate to answer when their names are called at the next meeting. In fact, the write up contains everything but what the speaker had to say, and usually that's the only real news involved in the meeting.

Then let the club sponsor an event and the editor gets chewed out by the would-be gracious lady who is mad as hops because the newspaper won't print the same story promoting the event three weeks running. But the best part is the good sister doesn't stay mad. The next time she wants some publicity she doesn't hesitate to demand space. And seldom ever does the newspaper please her or live up to her expectations—even after the newspaper's photographer takes up half a morning making her picture to publish along with another story in the series about her club's big news event.

Thank heavens all the clubwomen aren't so pompous. Most are truly delightful ladies, the backbone of the community. They pay their civic rent, as well as their husbands' year after year after year. In fact, small towns wouldn't be much without the civic-minded ladies or the Jaycees or the Lions.

But for every ungrateful greenthumber, there is a public-spirited individual who works overtime for the town. He is a member of the city council and attends out of town meetings of the economic development district, working to improve the quality of life in his town. His actions are the subject of much conversation at the barbershop or wherever two or more congregate around the square or at the courthouse. Newspaper editors couldn't survive without the moral support this fellow gives.

There is the merchant or the banker who ought to be the hometown newspaper's regular advertiser and big booster who has taken exception to something the editor wrote or didn't write years ago and he hasn't advertised since. Of course, his business continues to lose ground, but it hasn't dawned on him this is the age of advertising and that a weekly ad in the local newspaper is what he needs to increase his volume or his deposits.

There's also the grocer or the local official who has his neck out of joint because the production manager in the make-up room cut the nine-and-a-half foot long article about his daughter's three-week old wedding.

Then there are the former residents who still subscribe to the hometown newspaper even after an absence of many years who are the first to renew their subscriptions and include a pleasant note, along with their checks, saying how much they enjoy reading the paper. Of course, there are those delightful folks in the town who are cordial and take the time to thank the editor when he writes an editorial which happens to coincide with his philosophy or political leaning.

Editing a small town newspaper will try a man's patience, but after writing for a weekly or semi-weekly newspaper the last twenty-five years, I wouldn't even think about going back to the city to work for a daily newspaper. That would be too boring, because I'd never get to know the green thumb set, the banker or the grocery store owner.

WE'RE FRESH OUT OF GIDDLE-DOOPER

February 28, 1963

Mac Dixon wants to swap a used doginpin, which is in good condition and has just been overhauled, for a used giddle-dooper. And Sig Bloom is in the market for a second-hand giddle-dooper to match up with one he already has.

If you, dear reader, have a used giddle-dooper—even one that's not in good condition—the *Tribune's* classified department can sell it for you, and at a premium. There must be fifty folks around these parts who are splittin' their pants for a giddle-dooper.

Why all this sudden interest in giddle-doopers? It all began as a small-scale promotion gimmick for the "Fishwrapper's" classified section. At my instruction, our classified ad manager, Betty Peterson, ran the following little classified under the "Wanted" category: "Used giddle-dooper. In good condition and priced to move at once. Must be seen to be appreciated. Opportunity to re-sell at a good profit if slightly modified. For full details, write Box 420, Eufaula Tribune."

Before the last run of the paper was off the press, Martha Jefferies was on the telephone wanting details on the used giddle-dooper. This little $1.40 ad created a mild sensation. Readers rushed to dictionaries, encyclopedias and to the library to find out just what this white elephant item really is. Giddle-doopers were the topic of conversation at parties, the local doctors' waiting rooms and at the coffee clubs.

The second time the classified ad appeared, the *Tribune's* telephones—all five of them—nearly rang off their hooks. Folks were curious. Surely they must need a giddle-dooper, and they were anxious for full details.

Principal Albert Killian, just back from a flying trip to Pittsburgh, called after hours to find out "just what is this giddle-dooper?" One man called our advertising manager three times—at home—after office hours. Another lady wanted to come down to see the giddle-dooper.

Gorman Houston thought it was that antique organ that stood in the editor's yard for months. One caller, who didn't identify himself, said that advertisement sounds like "something one of those Damn Yankees might place." Still another caller thought that "one of those German scientists at the radar base" might have put the gizmo up for sale.

The little ad even aroused the curiosity of a *Birmingham News* reporter who called long distance to find out about the giddle-dooper.

Sig Bloom Jr., in his letter, wanted to "no yore lowest price, please."

So, if you have used a giddle dooper, fizgig, or a used doginpin—in good condition—call us, please. We've found you a market!

It was 'one of those days'

Circa 1968

I had the feeling it would be "one of those days." Oh, the joys of editing a small town newspaper!

I've been as proud as a speckled pup with the full editorial page we've been publishing for the last couple of months. Of course, we've always had an editorial page, but limited advertising revenue dictated some ads appear on the page. However, thanks to a healthy increase in advertising linage, it is now feasible to publish a "big city" style editorial page. The staff has agreed to make an all-out-effort to fill one whole page with editorials, columns, editorial cartoons and letters to the editor every issue if possible.

Things were going too well. We were putting out a twelve-page edition on Tuesday. A new column had been added to the editorial page line-up giving voice to still another columnist's opinion. The regular columns were timely, offering the writers' opinions and advice on the opening of the public schools.

For a Tuesday, it had been rather hectic around the *Tribune* offices. Then that afternoon the newspaper boys began delivering the day's edition. The telephone started ringing. One irate caller disagreed with my new columnist's observations on the hospital situation. A chamber of commerce committee meeting, thank goodness, took me away from the office for the rest of the afternoon.

Then after a hectic day, I dragged home and hadn't settled down before another irate caller registered his complaint about one of the columns devoted to the opening of the school. My explanation of how I like to think of the editorial page as a forum for exchange of ideas and opinions went over like a lead balloon. He thought the editor should have "banned" the writer's column.

The next caller commended the *Tribune* highly and praised that same columnist. Wednesday morning my faith in the *Tribune's* subscribers was restored. Seven or eight readers called to commend the controversial new columnist, and one letter arrived opposing the writer's stand.

On days like those, it isn't much fun to be the editor—not if you're the kind of person who really doesn't enjoy controversy.

Yep, a couple of calls from indignant readers, who happen not to agree with your editorial or the columnist's opinions, can ruin an otherwise pleasant day. But then that one letter in the mail or a series of several favorable calls can be rewarding.

That's small-town newspapering.

Small-town newspaper editors who print the news and write hard-hitting editorials don't win popularity contests. Of course, some joker is apt to ruin the editor's coffee break on any given morning. And seldom do communities hand over their coveted "Citizen of the Year" trophies to a newspaperman.

That's one facet of the life of a small-town newspaper editor. The job has its rewards, too, because everything is on a personal basis. That's why I wouldn't swap places with any big city editor even if he can climb into his ivory tower and tell his receptionist "he's in conference" the morning after he prints a stinging, toe-stepping editorial.

I like to think of small-town newspaper editing as character building, but then some days it's enough to make you lose ALL your religion. Tuesday was one of those days.

Old files tell story of Tribune's progress

June 13, 1972

The clean-up job after moving the *Trib* continues. Actually, everybody seems to be fairly well organized but me. After going through six orange crates of papers, my office still looks like a whirlwind has just passed through. While my desk is usually cluttered with papers, clippings, correspondence and things people bring for me to see, now it is brimming over with clutter I've salvaged and hope to file.

My excuse for not filing the miscellany is there's no room in the filing cabinets. So, now I'm plowing through the file folders and dumping things that aren't needed anymore. I run across so many interesting things it is hard to make much progress. Right now I am stuck in the E section.

Looking through the "equipment" files is almost like reviewing the progress of the *Trib*. And it brought back so many memories. I pulled out all sorts of literature on equipment that has long since been outmoded—like the Photo-Lathe and the Ludlow. When we added these pieces of equipment a number of years ago—back when we were printing the paper on the old Babcock press—we thought we had really gone modern.

The staff thought we had arrived when we could make our own engravings from pictures on the Photo-Lathe. No longer did we have to send our pictures to the *Columbus Ledger* via the bus and hope the expensive engravings would arrive in time to meet our deadline. And the Ludlow was a marvel, because we could cast new type each time we set a headline and simply dump the type into a casting box after it was used. This made the old beat-up wooden type obsolete.

And there was the information on the Babcock Optimus, a monstrous second-hand sheet-fed newspaper press, which we purchased after a similar but older model press bit the dust. We really thought it was a speed demon and proudly announced the good news to our readers after it was reassembled in the pressroom. Now, this relic of those "hot type" days is something of a white elephant, the victim of automation. It still stands in the former *Tribune* building. While it is still in perfect working order, there's not much demand for such a cumbersome piece of old printing equipment.

Someone has suggested the old press and one of the Linotype machines be given to the Eufaula Historical Museum, but we haven't heard a word from Mary Wallace Martin, museum curator. The files are also filled with literature on all the many, many new pieces of equipment that were put on the market after offset printing became practical for small newspapers.

For years, few mechanical improvements were made for newspapers, and the few new pieces of equipment made were so expensive not many hometown newspapers could afford them. However, the "offset" revolution changed all this. True, the sophisticated equipment was expensive, but it became vital for small newspapers if they were to survive or make a decent profit.

I smiled "like unto a possum," as Tom Culpepper would say, when I came across all the promotion pieces on the Justowriters, the electric waxers and Headliners, all new equipment we eventually purchased. The computerized typesetting machines, which punch tape that is automatically run through a companion machine and justifies the lines of type, and the machine for setting headlines, were really something. They still are.

Tomorrow I'll try to finish on the E's in the file. Maybe before the summer is over I'll get through the alphabet and file all that important material that's covering my desk. The *Trib's* faithful maid, Mittie, hopes so.

COMPUTERS LACK EXCITEMENT OF HOT METAL

December 9, 1990

Sooner or later, it looks like I'm going to have to abandon my trusty typewriter and switch to a computer. I've put this off for years, making the excuse that computers are so expensive I shouldn't monopolize one just to write editorials and columns.

The latest threat came recently when we bought a fancy Apple Macintosh with a scanner. Some progressive newspapers are using the scanner to put typed news releases and legal notices into newspaper form without having to retype them. Since I'm the one who edits most of those news releases, somebody on the news staff suggested that maybe I should learn how to set type on a computer so that I could then learn how to use the scanner.

I don't like the idea.

I'm a hopeless stick-in-the-mud. That's why we moved into our pioneer cottage from the building that now houses Dale's Lounge. If we could have bought the old place at the time, I'd have been content to restore the vintage red brick building.

For all its inadequacies, I loved hot type and the sound and the smell of publishing a newspaper on a flatbed press. The cantankerous Linotype machine, I guess, was the main reason I embraced offset printing. For years, I depended on hot metal type and that old flatbed Miehle press to print the *Tribune*.

It was a struggle, but it was also exciting. After pounding out copy on an old Royal manual, I finally advanced to an electric typewriter. But it nearly drove me bananas. I had, and still have, a touch like an elephant. If I knew music like I know the touch system, I could play a piano as loud as a revival musician and sound about as melodious, too.

Yes, I was perfectly content sitting in my little office, with a big window facing Broad Street, watching the comings and goings at the chamber of commerce office next door. I usually got one of the first peeks at a newcomer in town because he would buy the *Tribune* from the only hometown news rack in town, just outside my window.

I'm half deaf and a little daffy too because of years of listening to that old press slide back and forth, back and forth, cranking out *Tribunes* on huge sheets of newsprint. And after the printing was finished, the tricky part came in running the printed sheets, four pages wide, through that temperamental folder. It always broke down.

Backing up a bit, the Linotype was also enough to drive a young editor crazy. In fact, Mergenthaler, the German who invented it, did go stark, raving mad. It was a remarkable typesetting machine in that it justified the type into neat column-width lines that were cast in lead from tiny molds.

After the type was run through the press, it was tossed into the devil's box and recast into large metal pigs. The pigs were hung on a chain by the Linotype operator, usually a prima donna, on the side of his marvelous machine and were melted by an electric pot. The molten lead was squirted into the molds and provided a fresh typeface every time.

The melting lead was pungent, and the casting room was like a fiery furnace.

What an accomplishment it was to publish an edition of the *Trib* using that antiquated equipment. Even with computers and scanners, printing a newspaper twice a week is still a miracle. It takes a publishing house a year to publish a book, so don't expect your semi-weekly newspaper to be letter perfect.

Learning to use a computer and scanner would be enough to drive me to drink. The cycle would be completed and I'd wind up back at Dale's Lounge.

EDITOR'S JOB GREAT—95 PERCENT OF THE TIME

November 13, 1994

Ninety-five percent of the time, I love my newspaper job. It's more interesting than selling insurance.

I don't know what personality type I am, but I'm different from my late friend, Sig, who loved talking to his clients so much that he should have paid Liberty National for the privilege of working his debit.

I say I'm different. I gave up a comparatively good job with the *Birmingham News* to be my own boss as editor and general manager of the weekly *Geneva County Reaper*. It has been an adventure ever since.

I can identify with the staff that published *The Paper*, but we normally don't work under quite as much pressure as the interesting characters in that movie. Publishing in a non-conventional town like Eufaula, where the men are candid and most of the women are gracious, I get my comeuppance at least a couple of times a week.

That's fair, I guess. I believe so strongly in our First Amendment rights I'm continually asking for trouble. One friend confided that I make a better S _ _ than he does, and another observed early in my small-town newspaper career it was apparent I'm a J-School grad because I document my gossip.

I've also learned that the coffee club is a good place to pick up leads for stories and that the "news" is usually pretty factual. Even so, the coffee crowd I hang out with has an unusual motto: "If you can't say something bad about somebody, don't say it." They are irreverent and never pass out compliments.

There's also nothing dull about newspapering: From covering politics to publishing a daily ballpark edition during the Dixie Boys World Series, there are plenty of interesting things to do. It's hard to tell where my job ends and my private life begins, but then I get paid for doing work that I thoroughly enjoy. Most of the time, that is.

This week, for instance, was frustrating but exciting. The staff and I were almost consumed by politics. Reading the mail about the candidates and the latest fax about the political polls was addictive.

Returning from my early morning walk, I was surprised—but I shouldn't have been—to notice some joker had neatly printed in freshly poured concrete on the sidewalk: "Home of King Smith."

That wasn't the most pleasant way for an editor to start a busy week.

The next day, I got cut down again by a bold woman who wrote in a letter to the editor that she is bored with my articles on Egypt and the Middle East peace efforts. "Of course, when the editor has a fleeting, long distance glance at a national leader or representative it is strictly an ego builder . . . We oldsters hate to use our fading eyesight on unimportant things. Many people have big egos, but please improve the paper."

That woman in Winding Way estates knows how to hurt a hard-working, small-town editor, but the good news is she adds, "we read the paper every issue always hoping to find some worthy news or society item."

Sometimes, when reading the mail is burdensome and dull, a regular, anonymous letter writer gets my attention when he cuts me down to size with his acid commentary on our editorial stance. Too bad the coward doesn't have the guts enough to sign his letters like the woman from Winding Way. Readers would find his comments interesting, and in a vitriolic sort of way, he would contribute to the editorial page dialogue.

However, those confidential, not anonymous letters—and telephone calls—that fill me in on local issues sometimes give me insight, if not answers. I've kept some of the best ones. They're chocked full of juicy stuff that will help make me rich and famous when I publish my novel.

TRIBUNE SOON TO SPAN FROM TYPEWRITER TO CYBERSPACE

January 11, 1998

It's deadline time, and I'm staring at a blank sheet of paper in my lonely, decrepit typewriter. I say "lonely" because it's the only functioning typewriter at the *Trib*.

I feel pressured to get this "copy" back to the sole typesetter, Debbie Kite, who sets the well written, edited news releases and my copy. All the other staff writers and editors key in their articles on the newest computers.

I feel like a lively but living relic pecking out columns, editorials and an occasional news story. Our youthful general manager-associate editor has already taken us to the next level in newspaper publishing; soon we'll be spanning from typewriter to Cyberspace.

The *Tribune* has pioneered Alabama's grassroots newspapers with Audiotext. Just this week the update on the South Eufaula Avenue tragedy, when two young Eufaula men were killed in an accident, 1,131 anxious readers responded to a page-one story's postscript to call Trib Talk 24, our round-the-clock Audiotext service, for an update.

The midweek edition, dated Jan. 7, had been "put to bed" when the telephone rang a little after nine PM bearing the bad news. The managing editor and sports editor-staff writer rushed to the scene of the fiery fatalities. With notes and film in hand, they rushed back to their computers and wrote how "the small pick-up truck erupted into flames after a violent collision with a tractor trailer on Highway 431 South Monday night, killing the truck's two passengers."

Computer-paginated page one was revamped, deleting a less important story—replaced by the lead story headlined: "Trucks collide; two dead."

That kind of update would be credible newspaper reporting for a lively daily: It's plenty remarkable for a twice weekly serving a community of 13,400. Throw in discreet, full color accident photos in the next edition, and that's real high-tech newspapering.

Although Ye Olde Editor continues to cut and paste up the editorial page Mondays and Thursdays, week after week, I feel threatened by automation. (However, for the record, this page did win first place in the last Alabama Press Association Better Newspaper Contest.) I'm darned lucky to be the publisher, though. I'd hate to start looking for another job at my age.

Earlier this week, the production manager made up the *Cuthbert Times and (Ft. Gaines) News Record's* editorial page, the *Trib's* sister publication, on the screen of his intrepid computer while this low-tech redneck watched. He's not an experienced headline writer, though, and I stood by and scribbled heads to complete his dummy.

But I'm getting with the program: I now receive E-mail letters to the editor, and for a couple of years I've edited letters received via Fax.

Among the *Tribune* staff's New Year's resolutions is one to launch a Web page sending out local news and features over the Internet to thousands outside our geographic coverage area. I haven't personally resolved to junk this typewriter and its worn ribbon, but I'm for crawling on the Cyberspace bandwagon and encouraging our bright, computer-literate staffers.

They make an old codger like me look fairly presentable, to the disdain of my long-time critic—ATTE, Eufaula, AL 36027—and insensitive readers like the gentleman who recently buttonholed me at a reception and grabbed me by the arm and told me to leave him out of my book and keep on writing about myself. He once told me, folks read the *Tribune* "like a letter from home," but he's changed his tune when he disagreed with our editorials supporting a western alternate route for U.S. 431.

The continual, phenomenal success of John Berendt's book about Savannah, *Midnight in the Garden of Good and Evil,* tempts me to write a book about our old town and its delightful characters, past and present.

I could sock it to 'em and buy a cottage in Maine or a condo in Florida with the royalties. That would beat facing relentless deadlines, twice a week, every week for forty years.

Typewriter-less, he'll muddle through Renaissance

July 29, 2001

For the first time since as a boy I typed articles hunt-and-peck style for my neighborhood newspaper, I am without a functional type-writer.

Now that's a frustration for a life-long newspaperman who began his journalism career as a copy boy, taking his mother's articles to the weekly *Samson Ledger.*

It's ironic. My heretofore-faithful typewriter gave up the ghost near my forty-third anniversary with the *Eufaula Tribune.* While I pulled down several discarded typewriters from the storage room, none would work. Jack, the editor and general manager, and Ann, the associate editor and associate publisher, took my typewriter away and quickly plugged in this obnoxious one-eyed monster that stares at me from behind my desk.

That's the downside of working for a family-owned newspaper.

When I came to the *Tribune* in July 1958, we used manual typewriters— that is, "Miss" Willie Couric, the society editor-reporter, and I did. Even so, we turned out more copy than Gene Smith, the Linotype operator, could handle on his antiquated Linotype.

Publisher H. L. Upshaw, the Southern gentleman who lived in the Shorter-Upshaw mansion, gave me the go-ahead to buy a second used Linotype machine. The cantankerous typesetting monster invented by Mergenthaler used hot metal to set type. The technology hadn't changed since I was a boy in Samson pecking out my stories for my newspaper on an upright L. C. Smith typewriter my grandfather, Dr. Joel Carter Sellers, used in his medical practice at Enterprise. (My brothers and I also used his instruments stored in the bottom drawers of a large cabinet with glass doors. His small stainless steel saw—used for amputations—was great for cutting out wooden slingshot stocks.)

The Linotype machine was a marvel, because it used molten metal to cast lines of justified type. My late father-in-law, W. E. G. Sutton, as a young man worked in the Jackson newspaper's back shop where he set body type for stories by hand—a slow, tedious process. The newspaper was printed on an old Washington hand press.

The *Trib's* flatbed press closely resembled Guttenberg's printing press. Well, I'm out-dated, along with the Washington hand press and the typewriter. I'm making a feeble effort to survive in this digital universe. Why, I can remember when our editor, Jack, stuttered when he tried to say digital. Now, I'm the one stuttering in this new age of Renaissance journalism.

I thought our young general manager was truly progressive when he contracted for Trib Talk 24, the free Voice Information Service, available to you gentle readers twenty-four hours a day, seven days a week. Simply by dialing the telephone our readers can get all sorts of information: weather, time, news, sports, church information and devotionals, obituaries and chamber of commerce events. We also made schoolteachers available after school to confirm homework assignments. I guess that didn't go over so hot with the students.

Now, just as my typewriter conked out, they've run in something else new. The *Eufaula Tribune* is now online with local news, weather, classifieds, sports and who knows what else on our new website, eufaulatribune.com. That website name looks like some of my typesetting on my new (old) Macintosh.

This enables the *Tribune* to provide local news twenty-four hours a day, worldwide. I wasn't so sure about this expensive innovation until the B. W. and I cruised the Mediterranean. Somewhere in the Adriatic Sea, she suggested we go to the Splendour of the Sea's Internet lounge and dot.com the *Tribune* back home to read the latest news—or to learn if they were still publishing in our absence. Darned if Ann didn't conjure up our new website, and she printed out four pages of Bluff City news I could hold in my hands and read as we cruised thousands of miles from home.

I still find it hard to comprehend that our twice-weekly newspaper is now hourly. Truly, the Eufaula area's source of local news and information has gone digital—and it doesn't cost subscribers a dime more. For a buck more, those placing classifieds can connect to the world.

Small wonder the *Tribune* won second place for general excellence and a beaucoup of other awards in the Alabama Press Association's Better Newspaper Contest last weekend. Here's to our intrepid leader, Jack, and our savvy staff who are all caught up in this age of Renaissance journalism.

Somehow, without my faithful typewriter—the modern one that operated with electricity—I hope to muddle through, to hang in there and continue this string of over 2,350 "Candid Comments." Cheers, gentle readers.

Rich memories abound after 45 years in Eufaula

July 13, 2003

Forty-five years ago, I edited my first edition of the *Eufaula Tribune*. The week will also mark my fiftieth year as a newspaperman. I never won a Pulitzer Prize, but I could claim a prize for persevering.

I've written more than 4,680 editorials for the *Tribune* alone—and that's a conservative count of one editorial per edition. I've written half that many columns, never missing a week after beginning to write "Candid Comments" for the *Tribune*, open heart surgery notwithstanding. Being a local history buff, I can't pass up the opportunity to share with you faithful Gentle Readers some of my observations during the last four and one-half decades in our beloved Bluff City.

The Chattahoochee's impoundment lured me to town, a place where I had visited family through the years.

As a schoolboy, I would take a short cut behind the Shorter-Upshaw House to reach my Aunt Sally's apartment on Colby Street. Little did I dream the mansion's occupant, courtly Col. H. L. Upshaw, would cut a deal some day and name me editor and G. M. with an opportunity to acquire ownership of the *Tribune*.

Construction of the dam began in 1958, the summer I took the reins as editor and general manager. The public schools were segregated, and the town, the *Tribune* and I weathered integration, me as a member of the city board of education.

Had I read then Auburn journalism student Marcus V. Mulkey Jr.'s survey of the *Tribune* made a year before, I may have thought twice whether I should cast my lot with the *Tribune*. But as my departed aunt said, "Everybody reads it." It had also seen many good times with Upshaw in charge. In Mulkey's documented evaluation he concluded: "The *Tribune* is not a good weekly newspaper" but he felt it had "great possibilities if it were run correctly."

This is not to say I ran the *Trib* correctly, but I can assure you the best thing I ever did for our local newspaper or our town was to marry my B. W. in 1966 and offer my son the editor-general manager position in 1999, along with a chance to acquire part ownership.

Wooden storefront sheds in need of paint and parkways lush with sandspurs impressed me in 1958, but so did the excitement created when construction began on the lock and dam downstream at Ft. Gaines.

Eufaula's hallmark, then and now, was its beautiful homes and gracious people. The Monarch oaks and graceful elms formed a canopy on North Eufaula and North Randolph, and ten or eleven houses were for sale on those pretty old streets when I came here.

Those were the Camelot Days when spirits were high and Eufaula was awakening from a twenty-five-year hiatus. Those were the days when downtown stores and offices closed at noon on Wednesdays. Downtown shut down for the day, and the business and professional people played golf or went fishing or boating on the muddy river underneath the cantilever McDowell Bridge.

Wednesday's closing was a longstanding tradition when many gentlemen maintained second story offices downtown. They probably played more cards and socialized with close friends than they conducted business or practiced their profession. I remember one dapper middle-aged lawyer who wore a camellia or rose in his lapel. I found it challenging to make the Bluff City Inn or Buck Abbot's Café coffee clubs—the oldest club in town moved to the swanky new Holiday Inn when it opened on the Bluff overlooking magnificent Lake Eufaula.

I also recall the years of squabbling with southwest Georgians about the name of the new impoundment. Eufaulians who had never fished in the Chattahoochee grabbed a line and a pole and caught long stringers of bream in the lake or its flooded tributaries. I also remember water moccasins washed from their murky habitat that tried to crawl into fishing boats. Lake Eufaula produced so many trophy bass the *Tribune* dubbed it the Bass Capital of the World.

How excited the young editor was in 1963 when Dixie Shoe and American Buildings built new plants. It was the opportunity of a lifetime for many of us. Eufaula blossomed and happy days were here again in this old aristocratic river town. Progress was rampant with the revitalized chamber of commerce, Clio native George Wallace in the governor's chair and youthful Senator Jimmy Clark in the Legislature. Clark took office the same year I came to town, and what a difference he made. Wallace also worked with us to land the Chauncey Sparks State Technical College, and Gov. Lurleen Wallace and Senator Clark made Lakepoint State Park and Convention Center a reality.

Growth happened so fast Gov. Jelks's mansion was demolished, along with several other antebellum buildings. In 1965, good citizens rebelled and bought the Upshaw-Shorter House at auction for $33,000. The next year, the Eufaula Pilgrimage attracted thousands of visitors to its tour of historic homes and buildings. The tradition continues thirty-eight years later.

This aging newspaperman and this newspaper have survived forty-five years together through good times and not so good times. I couldn't have made it without my wife, the associate editor and publisher, and my sons, especially my partner, the editor. I look forward in April to celebrating my seventy-fifth birthday and the *Tribune's* seventy-fifth anniversary.

I have been challenged during my forty-five years in Eufaula. I have been rewarded and supported beyond measure by our classy community. It's been a wonderful life and I enjoy my family, especially my five beautiful grandchildren, who are fourth generation Eufaulians. I thank God for each new day.

Editor understands family's heartbreak

December 6, 1991

A few weeks ago, as a board member of the Alabama Press Association Journalism Foundation, I participated in a panel discussion with Auburn's community journalism class. The students asked sensible, intelligent questions. Like the other three editors and publishers on the panel, I tried to give sage advice.

I confided that, yes, it's sometimes tough editing a small-town newspaper but threw in the disclaimer that if you are fair when publishing controversial issues, I've usually found readers who take exception usually come around.

John Cameron, *Selma Times-Journal* editor and publisher, laid it on the line for the budding community journalists. He minced no words. The former weekly editor explained how difficult it can be for the small-town editor to publish some local news. It's not like writing for a big city daily where the writer probably doesn't personally know the principals in a news story. In a small town, the editor or reporter runs into the newsmakers in the grocery or sits by him at a civic club the next day.

Mr. Cameron makes a good point. Even after editing the *Tribune* for thirty-three years, I sometimes find it difficult to take the editorial stands we do. I've become accustomed to reporting the news factually and impartially, but here of late this has been a downer, too.

How do you publish bad things about your good friends?

There was no joy in Eufaula last Monday as our former district attorney and two former police officers appeared for sentencing at the federal courthouse in Montgomery.

The courtroom was filled with the former DA's, and his family's friends. There were lawyers and judges and law enforcement people with whom he had been associated professionally, and there were many solid family friends.

I wimped out. I wasn't in the courtroom to hear Judge Truman Hobbs sentence my good and loyal friend's son to twenty-four months in prison. Which hat would I have worn if I'd been in Montgomery? Would I have sat on the benches with the defendant's family? Or would I have bunched up with the news media and covered the sentencing like any other big news story?

I'm a father, too. I know first-hand about that bond between father and son. I have nothing but admiration for the father, who is also an attorney. Surely this fine, decent man, my lawyer and one of the most ethical attorneys I've ever known, was the perfect role model for his bright son. Certainly, this father has handled the terrible charges against his son very well. He has been an inspiration to this father.

The only logical explanation that makes sense is the former prosecutor's confession before the packed courtroom: Expressing sorrow for what he has done, he told the judge, "I've lost a great opportunity given to me in life because I couldn't control my gambling.

"I have been diagnosed as having mental illness, compulsive gambling." He added that he sought treatment at a Maryland hospital this summer and he attends Gamblers Anonymous meetings regularly.

Personally, I think my friend's son is on the road to recovery. He has acknowledged he has a psychological problem, and he has sought treatment. He also had the decency to apologize publicly to his ex-wife, his children and his wonderful parents.

Earlier, he was big enough to thank me, the town's editor, for the *Tribune's* fair coverage of the story, which included the U.S. attorney's office dropping fourteen counts of extortion against him and accusations he solicited money from defendants in drug cases in return for his recommendation defendants be given lenient sentences.

I would have understood if he had spit at me. And I wouldn't blame his supportive parents if they didn't speak to me. I'm also a loving father. I would have understood.

Publisher finds happiness through family, newspaper

"The Constitution only gives people the right to pursue happiness. You have to catch it yourself." — Ben Franklin
July 17, 2005

I'm with you, Benjamin, founding father and writer. On July 16, 1958, I took one giant step to pursue happiness and a lifetime livelihood when I came to work as the editor and general manager of the *Eufaula Tribune*.

As I look back over my life's story, forty-seven years later, I've caught happiness right here in the Bluff City. Bear with me again, gentle reader, as I look back over the years.

There have been plenty of good times—and some not so good times. I love my adopted hometown, though. It's one of those places of the heart: Samson, my birthplace; Panama City, my growing up place; and Tallahassee, home of my alma mater and Eufaula, my wonderful hometown.

Life's a bowl of blueberries these days. I say blueberries, not cherries, because I'm enjoying harvesting a bumper crop of blueberries out at the Fourth Estate. Son has taken the *Tribune* to new heights. Later this month, the editor will accept the Alabama Press Association's General Excellence First Place award while the staff and I cheer. Now, that brings much happiness for me, because I've dedicated the best years of my life to publishing the *Tribune* and rearing my family.

Years ago, I would muse how great it would be to wear just one hat: Either the editor's or the publisher's. What a happy celebration it was in 1999 when we observed the paper's seventieth anniversary. How satisfying it was to promote my second son, Jack, to editor. Happiness was keeping the *Tribune*, my pride and joy, in the family as an independent family-owned newspaper.

On my forty-seventh anniversary with the *Tribune*, the challenge I face is editing a collection of columns, "Candid Comments," for a forthcoming book. I opt to do this rather than write a novel or a "tell all" book about

Smith frequently attended the National Newspaper Association's annual Governmental Affairs Conference in Washington, meeting speakers prominent on the national scene. One of his favorites was Senator Bob Dole.

life in Eufaula. (Bobby Jennings attempted this in a *Playboy* magazine article years ago.)

This week, I settled down in my spacious new office and studio upstairs at home, in my first son's former room. We finally moved his trophies out. I'm overwhelmed with making selections from more than 2,444 columns we've published in the *Tribune* on a weekly—sometimes twice-weekly basis. And three years before that, I wrote "Candid Comments" for the weekly *Geneva Reaper*. Granted, many of those columns—all written under pressure of a deadline—aren't so hot, but they often captured, somewhat, what I had on my overworked mind. Like a journal or a chronicle, they record one small town editor's observations. Together, they give a social history or a historical record of events in Eufaula and Alabama. Often the columns take a broader view of our country and countries around the world.

While editing and publishing a small town newspaper is plain hard work, it also opens doors to adventure and travel—if the independent newspaperman is so inclined and the receipts hold steady.

As a young boy growing up in Samson during the Great Depression, I yearned to travel. I loved taking the train to Montgomery to visit my grandmother and four young, adoring aunts. I so envied my friend who visited the World's Fair in New York City.

One day I would attend the World's Fair in the Dominican Republic when Trujillo was the not-so-benevolent dictator. His party was a lot like "Smarty Arty who gave a party but nobody came but Smarty Arty."

I was among the few who checked into the five star, state-owned hotel in Cuidad Trujillo. Jamaica was next, and those adventures happened before I came to Eufaula. I've been with the Alabama press in Cuba, in the presence of Fidel Castro. Meeting with the Communist dictator's press corps was exciting—and a little frightening.

Congressman Terry Everett, before he ran for Congress, was in our tour group. He would pull out his portable computer—the first I'd ever seen—and pull up information on Cuba and question Castro's cabinet members. He was so straightforward with his controversial questions, I was uncomfortable.

Then the day he got fed up with the Cuban press, walked out of the room and slammed the door, I thought I might never return home to my wife and three sons.

My trip to Cairo, Egypt, with several National Newspaper Association journalists was also insightful. There I also met with several cabinet members and attended a press conference with President Bill Clinton and Egyptian President Hosni Mubarak during Clinton's first official visit to the Middle East.

With an NNA delegation, the B. W., young son Bill and I were entertained in Ireland by the American ambassador in his spacious residence in an impressive park-like setting. The wife and I enjoyed similar hospitality in Madrid and the World's Fair in Seville. Chairing the NNA Governmental Affairs Conference in Washington gave me the opportunity to introduce Sen. Howell Heflin, and the B. W., the honor to introduce Admiral Thomas H. Moorer (former Chairman of the Joint Chiefs of Staff), to our newspaper friends from around the country.

It was a privilege also to serve on President Nixon's Alabama Committee on Education at the height of integration, to meet him in the Oval Office and to confer with members of his cabinet.

All this is chronicled in my columns, along with meeting Presidents Ronald Reagan, George H. W. Bush and Bill Clinton at receptions in the White House. Covering George W. Bush's recent visit to AUM in Montgomery was also exciting. I reveled in his referring to my remarks from "Candid Comments" to an NNA audience about eliminating death taxes.

Personally meeting Arkansas Gov. Bill Clinton in Little Rock and coming home with the scoop that he would run for president was a coup. Later following him and Al Gore on their eleven-bus campaign motorcade from Columbus and through southwest Georgia was also challenging.

Karl Rove, senior advisor to the President, is my contact in the White House. He thoughtfully gave Bush one of my columns about his re-election, and the President wrote me a personal note that I promptly framed for my office.

Yes, Ben Franklin, I've managed to catch my own happiness thanks to my beautiful wife and our close-knit family, all wrapped up together in this family owned and run newspaper.

Chapter 11

Buck Dancing & Sunsets

HE'S GRATEFUL FOR ANOTHER RING ON TREE OF LIFE

February 16, 2003

H ere I sit at my iMac on the eve of a milestone birthday. I say milestone because at this stage in my life every birthday is a milestone. Perhaps I should reminisce a bit and recall some of the wonderful people and past events that have impacted my life.

I'm grateful my seven-year-old pig's valve keeps my irregular heartbeat going strong and upbeat. Some gentle readers probably surmised years ago that I walk to a different heartbeat—and I do. Yesterday my cardiologist, during my annual checkup, found me fit as a fiddle, but since my porcine valve's life expectancy is twelve years, more or less, the good doctor has scheduled an outpatient cardiac testing for me in the hospital's Heart Institute as a precautionary measure.

Even so, I'm enjoying a wonderful life in a troubled world. I am grateful to be alive and in relatively good health. My ever faithful B. W. and five beautiful grandchildren, each four or under, living in close proximity, are the joy of my life.

I've suggested a banana pudding, sans candles, in lieu of a birthday cake, but this morning I noticed five eggs and a stick of butter on top of the counter by the stove. As I say, it's a wonderful life and I look to the future, even as I resume work to publish a book of selected columns from forty-five years of writing "Candid Comments." I'm among the eighty-one percent of Americans who feel they should write a book: I hope I'm also among the two percent who do.

I've been advised to include a memoir in one chapter. Building the other chapters will be challenging because there are hundreds of columns from which to choose. An advisor calculates reading the 2,340 columns I've written would be like reading three big novels. Maybe with careful selection and dutiful editing the book will be worth printing.

My life for almost half a century as a newspaperman has never been dull. It may sound preposterous but I can identify somewhat with the *New York Times*'s James Reston—the "Prince of Peace," *Time* magazine dubbed him on the publication of his biography, *Scotty: James B. Reston and the Rise and Fall of American Journalism.* The *Times*'s Jan. 13 book review is a little unkind, even to a tough journalist: "Because he stayed on the public stage long past his prime, and because journalists' work and reputations fade with amazing speed, Reston is undervalued now."

Maybe I can avoid a drastically scaled-down, similar situation here at the *Trib* if I listen to my editor, who works hard to keep us current and relevant. I'm on the lookout for new topics to write about and for new interests to broaden my narrow horizon. A cranky disk has nudged me to slow down with my gardening and the threat of terrorism and a war with Iraq have dashed cold water on my bent for foreign travel. That and to cope with stress, a newspaperman's nemesis, have moved me to take up painting. No, I don't mean painting my old house, but painting watercolor landscapes.

Believe it or not, I continue to live an interesting life because I'm still addicted to newspapers—this one you're holding in your hands in particular. Yes, I do still have the old house bug. My old house is still my beloved home and my hobby. And yes I still want to renovate or restore every great but neglected architectural treasure in town.

Can I help it if I'm hooked on historic preservation? The Home &

Garden TV channel keeps running the segment they filmed a couple of so years ago of my family and our old Eufaula homestead. We keep hearing from old friends who see it and are kind enough to call or email us about it. I also take pleasure in hearing from displaced Eufaulians who read selections from the *Tribune* on our web site. Jim Conner recently emailed me to say hello and to say he is enjoying the web site: "It brings back so many fond memories of home. Thanks for doing this."

Long time readers like Mrs. Willie T. Martin in Oakland, Cal., now in her nineties, keep in touch, too. Recently I mailed her a Eufaula "phone book" so she could "see if anyone I know is listed." As I complete another ring on the tree of life, I look forward to the future and I have faith in Eufaula and its people. They're kind, compassionate and confident. They may talk about you but they will pray for you if you're in need of prayer. I know because during my open-heart surgery, God heard them.

Can an old man learn
to buck dance gracefully?

January 6, 2002

The New Year, 2002, is looking up for me, and you gentle reader. I hope your New Year is off to a promising start, also.

On the occasion of Christmas 2000 my steadfast and scholarly Sunday school teacher, Barbara Smith, gave my classmates and me copies of Oswald Chambers's classic daily devotional book, *My Utmost for His Highest*. I have read through this book that has a 1935 copyright with daily readings selected chiefly from lectures given at the Bible Training College, Clapham, during the years 1911–1915. It is the most popular book of daily devotions ever published.

With the promising New Year, I'm starting over again. The author is British; the writing is sometimes difficult to comprehend, requiring careful re-reading. But I find comfort and inspiration in the daily devotionals.

The Dec. 31 devotional has wonderful food for thought: "Our yesterdays present irreparable things to us; it is true that we have lost opportunities which will never return, but God can transform this destructive anxiety into a constructive thoughtfulness for the future. Let the past sleep, but let it sleep on the bosom of Christ. Leave the irreparable past in His hands, and step out into the irresistible future with Him."

What marvelous words on which to close 2001, a year like no other. Flipping back to day one, Jan. 1, I reread what the Apostle Paul says: "My determination is to be my utmost for His Highest." During 2002, I hope I too, can be my utmost for His Highest. I do have new resolve, although I've given up writing resolutions and have come to rely on my weekly list of "Things to write and do." Sometimes I feel I'm spinning my wheels. I flip back through the stack of collected lists where I've checked off items.

Now on the lighter side—I don't intend for this to be a devotional, our guest ministers to do this quite well—I proclaim this the Year of the Seminole in Alabama before some Chinaman designates 2002 as the Year of the Rat or something. We can all take heart in the plight of the 'Noles (8-4). After a disappointing season, my alma mammy beat Virginia Tech in the Gator Bowl and Alabama native Bobby Bowden matched Bear Bryant's victory total of 323 wins, only four behind Penn State's Joe Paterno.

And what's more, my FSU class of '52 will celebrate its fiftieth anniversary in April. That's the second class to graduate after the college's name change to the Florida State University. So bear with me, gentle reader, we minorities can celebrate, too. More about this in a future column.

I say I'm off to a good year, but on the horizon charity commitments could be challenging. Somehow I got sucked into co-hosting a barbecue that was sold at the Rotary Club auction for nine couples out at the Fourth Estate. The successful bidders want to chow down Saturday night and it may be too cold or rainy to gather on the patio. But that's not the worst. The *Trib's* extroverted, enthusiastic, community-minded editor and advertising staff sold a barbecue at the Whitehead's ranch to help raise money for the Wallace College Sparks Campus Foundation.

In a bad miscalculation to encourage bidders to be higher, I told the wily auctioneer, Albert Adams, I'd buck dance for the entertainment. That did it: number-cruncher John DeLoach and jelly-worm maker Terry Spence topped the bidders.

Now I've got to learn how to buck dance, along with all the other challenges facing me in '02. I was rudely reminded of that commitment when I read about the tribute paid to Hank Williams in Montgomery the other day. A fellow, who looked about my age, wearing a cap and tight blue jeans, was pictured dancing solo to the music of a Hank Williams tribute band. What was I thinking, I was the biggest wallflower in my high school graduating class, and I have regressed with age.

Every time I see that successful number-cruncher DeLoach, he comments about my buck dancing performance. Then I think about what my mentor, the late *Tribune* publisher Col. H. L. Upshaw said: "Some folks grow old gracefully, and others learn to dance."

Thoughts of life and love shared during February

February 18, 1996

D eep in my damaged heart I have thoughts of life and love I must share this Valentine's Day, this February—my birth month and the American Heart Association's officially designated "Heart Month."

As I peck out this column—my fortieth year of writing "Candid Comments"—I realize I'm one year older. I was a valentine arriving a day early in the Rose Sellers and Abb Jackson Smith household on the eve of the Great Depression. I arrived with a defective aortic valve, but the doctor didn't know it and my mom would have loved me just the same. If my doting parents were disappointed that I was their third little boy and not that girl my mother must have dreamed about, they never hinted.

I came into this world loved: I can't understand why all babies aren't loved, but I know deep in my heart some aren't. Of course, I understand sibling rivalry since I was a middle child. I have two older brothers, two younger and a younger sister.

The Smith home was a happy lively place. My father was in the mercantile business in the small farm town of Samson and my bright, beautiful mother was a newspaperwoman. She didn't keep regular hours at the weekly—that's "weekly" not "weakly"—*Samson Ledger*. However, she did slip out of the house and type her copy down at City Hall or scribble her notes on of the tables in the Tip Top Café, a Smith family enterprise on Main Street downtown.

She didn't just write about "recent brides," although I well remember looking up from the *Ledger* and asking her what actually was a "RE-sent" bride? I also remember our rotund cook Mrs. Ryals sitting by the wood cook stove reading her favorite magazine, "MO-DERN Romance."

Being the younger brother, I had the job of dropping Mother's stories off at the newspaper office on the way to school. That old flatbed press and Linotype machine fascinated me. In between rounds of playing cowboys and Indians, I pecked out a neighborhood newspaper on my grandfather's, Dr. Joel Carter Sellers's, upright L. C. Smith. Other than aspiring to be a "popcorn popper" at Mr. Pate's Royal Theater, I never wanted to be anything but a newspaperman. I did daydream once about being an architect, but algebra and plane geometry convinced me I'd better stick with the printed word and leave the figures to brothers Jack, Maury and Bob.

My mother's death in 1940 and World War II interrupted my otherwise wonderful childhood. Ten years later, tragedy struck the family again when my father died during my summer break from Florida State, where I was majoring in journalism. Those were tough years: My heart must have been calcified then, else it could have surely broken.

Monumental years following included my ongoing love affair with newspapers that blossomed when I went to work for the *Birmingham News,* the *Geneva County Reaper* and the *Eufaula Tribune*, and my romance and three-year courtship with my B. W. My bachelor days ended in Eufaula with a six-month engagement, followed by a wedding in Springville with more groomsmen than bridesmaids because every brother and several friends were members of the jubilant wedding party.

There have been many special people and places in my heart. My Valentine turned my life around, and what could compare with fatherhood? The birth of three sons gave meaning to life and taught me about the depth of a father's love. Only days behind my middle son's marriage last summer, I suffered a heart attack downtown while taking my morning constitutional. To paraphrase the Heart Association's 1996 theme, "I could have died of embarrassment."

I had that "uncomfortable pressure, fullness, squeezing and pain in the center of my chest." I did have the presence of mind to sit on a bench. Another walker also didn't recognize the tell-tale symptoms. "It's that wedding that's got you down!" the walker mused as she scurried along.

I could have died of embarrassment if my wife Ann hadn't called Lakeview Community Hospital emergency room. If you ever experience similar chest discomfort—or lightheadedness, fainting, sweating, nausea or shortness of breath—get help fast.

PUBLISHER GRATEFUL HIS LIFE WAS IN GOOD HANDS

September 3, 1995

If you're over fifty-five, slow your lifestyle to a gentler pace: Don't pile one travail upon another. (This is your Dutch uncle speaking.) I've survived a heart attack induced last Thursday during my regular morning constitutional. That's the bad news.

The good news is our Lakeview Community Hospital emergency room staff recognized the seriousness of my chest pains. I took comfort when Dr. Ted Morgan appeared, followed soon by Dr. Danny King. I knew I was in good hands and tried to relax, but the pain didn't go away until Dr. King placed a nitroglycerin tablet under my tongue. Like a phantom, my longtime friend and retired doctor John Jackson appeared, along with hospital administrator Carl Brown.

"You may have had a heart attack," Dr. King advised, noting he detected a heart murmur. The correct decision was made to transfer me to Flowers Hospital under the care of cardiologist Dr. Roland Brooks. Paramedic Dave James and ambulance driver Donnie Ezzell quickly transported me to Dothan. Professional and courteous from the word go, Donnie navigated—maneuvering to the head of the line of traffic stopped by a train in Dothan and passing a huge house in the middle of the road.

I knew my life was in good hands as Dave monitored my heart rate and vital signs, using the city ambulance's special equipment. As we sped down U.S. 431 South, he alerted me that Donnie would turn on the siren, and I allowed, "I want the full treatment." That's what I got, too: The full treatment from Day One to the day of discharge from Flowers Hospital.

Just as my RN friend Janie King assured me before leaving the Eufaula emergency room, it was best that no time be lost and I undergo a heart catheterization. Walter Matthau, via video, assured me it wouldn't hurt and I would feel better than ever after the procedure.

However, my expert cardiologist had turned cinematographer, I feared, as he projected images of my poor heart on the screen monitor and maneuvered a tube through my groin into my fist-sized ticker. The process took much longer than usual: It was like watching a silent suspense movie. The blocked artery was easily detected. My thoughts were, "This will be a piece of cake. The doc is now working his balloon catheter, and this will be a one-stop operation."

Not so. Dr. Brooks, after another round of typecasting and filming, had me rolled out of ICU again for more cardiovascular film. The diagnosis followed, after his careful study of the results. My aortic valve had been damaged by rheumatic fever when I was a child, or I was born with only two of the three "leaflets" fluttering on top of the valve.

The valve must be replaced. Without open-heart surgery, my chances of surviving two more years would be less than fifty percent. The only debatable decision left was whether to implant a pig's valve or a metal one in my heart.

I chose the metal plumbing, remembering columnist Lewis Grizzard's pig-valve implant. The Atlanta humorist wrote that every time he drove past a barbecue stand he got tears in his eyes. And after the valve replacement he developed a fondness for mud wrestling.

Minutes after my telephone conversation with long-time doctor friend Melvin Oakley, who told me UAB was "the best place in the world" to have the operation, Dr. Brooks handled the details. My nurturing family was already researching heart surgeons and their hospitals, UAB won hands-down, even though in my heart I also know Dothan cardiovascular and thoracic surgeons could get the job done well.

When I gave Dr. Brooks my decision—enforced by Virginia native Dr. Oakley's recommendation—he delivered just as he said he would do. He made an appointment for me to meet Dr. Al Pacifico, a world-class heart surgeon, and to have my faulty valve replaced in Alabama's nationally ranked teaching hospital. My cardiologist is the greatest.

The wait has been cushioned by cards, letters, calls, food and flowers from well-wishers. I never cease to be amazed at the goodness of people—especially Eufaulians and Barbour countians.

I'm not so cavalier as was Lewis Grizzard: He was a humorist and I'm a hack columnist and editorialist. I have a sense of humor, but you can also read my plain face like a dull textbook. I sometimes wish I were more sophisticated, but like Popeye—well, a sixty-pound weakling version—"I yam what I yam."

A fellow columnist made a "telephone prayer" for my recovery. I covet the prayers and positive thoughts, no matter what the manner or delivery: God hears them all. I deeply appreciate the prayers and kindness to me, my devoted wife and nurse Ann and my three wonderful sons and new "daughter."

I am comforted. I have full confidence in God, Dr. Pacifico and the goodness of family and friends.

Pilgrimage home
will bring back memories

November 5, 1982

Thanksgiving in the Lower Chattahoochee Basin is a time for remembering as well as giving thanks and enjoying family reunions. For many, it's a time to make a pilgrimage home.

For those fortunate enough to make a visit to the old home place or to feast with family and old friends, Thanksgiving includes a bonus. For me, this Thanksgiving will be tinged with nostalgia as my four brothers, a sister and their families, three devoted aunts and I make a pilgrimage to Geneva County and our little hometown of Samson.

Mingled with the joy of a festive reunion and a convivial family feast will be a quick trip to my birthplace and the cemetery where our beloved parents, Rose and Abb Smith, are resting. A newer and more grand family marker made of beautiful Georgia marble has been erected only days ago. While I haven't seen the finished product of two older brothers' efforts, already I know no monument could be designed or sculptured that would adequately honor the memory of our dear, departed parents.

So, when I think about giving thanks on our national day of Thanksgiving, I'll have to remember those early years of my life when my parents and other close members of my large family did so many things to make my childhood happy, even during the depths of the Depression.

Back in those days, I don't recall too many Thanksgiving dinners when a turkey was carved, but the hen our cook roasted in the old wood stove— along with the rich oyster dressing, fresh cranberry sauce and pans full of homemade rolls made by our mother—was as good as any Butterball turkey.

Those surely were hard times for our father, a merchant, but he didn't let the state of the economy cast a spell of gloom over our happy home. And our lovely mother, whom folks said "looked like she stepped out of a band box" when she dressed up to host her bridge club, had to have been a super manager. Somebody in the family once quipped she could take a

For several decades, the six Smith siblings and their families gathered in Geneva at the home of Jack Smith, pictured with Joel, Doug, Sarah Margaret Smith Price, Maury Smith and Bob Smith.

five dollar bill on a shopping trip to Montgomery and buy all the children outfits—and even a small surprise or two.

When we pause at the big white house on Main Street, now a little shabby and treeless, a thousand thoughts will rush through my mind. A glance at the narrow, almost denuded parkway out front will recall those happy days when the rock-lined median was filled with hundreds of blooming rose bushes and Samson was indeed the City of a Million Roses.

There were those carefree, happy days of our youth when my brothers and I played in the cool, green woods nearby, swinging on vines like Tarzan and catching minnows and turtles in a stream. There was the time I wore my new shoes to the woods and almost lost them in a mud bog. I washed them off, sneaked in the backdoor, and put them in the oven to dry with disastrous results.

Then there was the time a playmate and I got our clothes wet in the creek and hung them up to dry. My older brother and a friend stole our duds, and we bunched dog fennels around our naked bodies. Just as we dashed across Main Street, in front of our house, a group of girls on roller skates approached. We dashed behind the thorny rose bushes in the parkway, with dog fennels flying, just in the nick of time.

Then I'll recall those sad days when as a young boy I would swipe beautiful rosebuds from the parkway to take to our sick mother. Rumor was it was a major fine to pick a rose from the parkway, but I gladly ran the risk.

Our mother died while we were all children, but our family survived. Our wonderful father and wise grandmother and two devoted aunts supervised our upbringing. Each of the five boys and the girl received college educations, and each has lived a productive life.

Yes, Thanksgiving is a time to reflect, as well as to give thanks to Almighty God. This Thanksgiving finds me truly blessed with my own three sons and devoted wife. My prayer is that I shall pass on to my children some of the principles and many of the lessons I learned from my parents and my aunts.

HIGH SCHOOL REUNIONS COULD TRIGGER NOSTALGIA ATTACK

October 29, 2000

At my age, attending two high school class reunions within a month's time is enough to bring a nostalgia attack. My wife had to bear the burden of mingling with strangers at two reunions because I became a displaced person during my high school years—thanks to Adolf Hitler, Tito and World War II.

I enjoyed seeing classmates Sept. 30 at my Samson High School reunion, actually part of the All Class Reunion 2000. We grew up during the Great Depression in the south Alabama town. The outbreak of war in

1940 dramatically impacted even the smallest of farm towns.

First, Daddy joined the war effort at Fort Rucker, then at Biloxi where he engaged in construction work, drawing on skills learned from his father. This was a particularly trying time because my lovely mother also died that year. Well I do remember as an eleven-year-old visiting my father and older brother in Biloxi and riding the Greyhound bus alone through the tunnel under Mobile Bay.

Soon we moved to Panama City, where my father helped build Liberty Ships at Wainwright Shipyard. Christening a ship was memorable, and so was the death of President Franklin D. Roosevelt. Well do I remember that impromptu school holiday and joining classmates at the beach April 12, 1945, when our beloved wartime leader died.

Only weeks later the Germans surrendered unconditionally at Gen. Eisenhower's headquarters in Reims, May 7, 1945. This was followed by the Japanese surrender ceremonies Sept. 2 aboard the battleship *Missouri* in Tokyo Bay. My older brother, Jack, was with the navy in Japan at that momentous time. Those were challenging days for schoolboys and girls growing up as older siblings performed admirably as members of "The Greatest Generation."

Under the circumstances, there couldn't have been a better place to be than Bay County High School, unless it was Eufaula High. However, my brothers and I often rode the bus from Panama City to Eufaula to visit the other half of our displaced family, who lived with my indomitable maiden aunts. Daddy saved gas ration stamps and conserved his tires so we could drive here as often as possible.

When the war clouds settled, life became a joy as I enjoyed classes taught by remarkable teachers. There was the exception though, thanks to retired teachers pressed into service during the war. My algebra teacher was of that vintage, and the dear old lady was most tolerant of my inadequacies when it came to mathematics.

During the reunion last weekend, I remembered fondly my high school principal J. T. Kelley, who later became my boss on a part-time job during my FSU college days, and his wife Cornelia, who taught me high school English. Gladys Christo Pickett, the class beauty, and I recalled senior

English in Miss Marjorie Fay's class. Each Friday, sometimes when Gladys was class monitor, classmates recited lines of poetry until we fulfilled the requirement. I still remember, "My love is like a red, red rose," an easy poem, and verses from *The Lady of the Lake*. I remember reciting, "The stag at noon had drunk his fill" when I visited Loch Catherin in Scotland last July.

Favorite teachers were Alma Barkmeyer, who taught me speech, and Jane Bailey Clothier, who tried to teach me Spanish. Speech classes didn't take too well, either, but it wasn't Miss Barkmeyer's fault. She made me act in the Senior Class Play, *Brides to Burn*. In one scene, I was disguised as Princess Boogie Woogie and muttered indistinguishable lines.

Journalism was my favorite subject, and I thrived as business manager and later editor of the weekly *Tornado Whirl*. Rebecca George was the patient teacher.

It was interesting greeting classmates. Many did look old enough to have been my teachers—as my wife and another class member's spouse joked during our reunion days in 1988. Gladys still looked glamorous, but I couldn't quite picture the Stephens College graduate living in Stewartsville, Mo., as a retired farmer's wife. She grew up living in a mansion overlooking St. Andrew's Bay.

Visiting with Basil Drake, the former captain for the Bay High Tornadoes, brought back many memories. Though he was the big athlete and I was the skinny high school journalist, we were friends.

Travis Scott, whom I helped elect student body president, has aged the least of any of the men. I followed in my father's footsteps when it came to political news and interest in politics. Our homeroom elected Travis, who lived near Bear Creek out Fountain way, as our candidate and then chose me as his campaign manager. I took on the job with great enthusiasm. I painted huge signs on butcher paper and came up with the "clever" winning slogan: "Make Your Ballot Count a Lot: Cast Your Vote for Travis Scott."

I helped manage my younger brother Bobby's successful campaign the next year. No wonder I took an interest in politics at an early age. I have to fight the urge now to run around and put up Bush-Cheney signs.

Among my close chums at the reunion were twins Anne Godfrey Weeks and Jane Godfrey Becker. Anne was most entertaining and Jane was fun, too. Jane is the volunteer class executive secretary who called when I didn't show up for the fiftieth reunion. They were among the few who drove their own car—a sleek blue Chevrolet convertible. On a jaunt to Florida State, I decided I wanted to be a Seminole.

To refresh my memory, I pulled down the Pelican, my annual, and read inscriptions classmates penned inside the cover. As the "Boy Most Likely to Succeed," among Class Favorites, whom the class prophecy predicted would edit the *New York Times* one day, I must have been a disappointment.

However, I've enjoyed forty-two years with the *Tribune* just as I did those golden days at Bay High School with the Class of '48 after the memory of those WWII days faded.

Pangs of sadness creep into each class reunion, I suspect. The "In Memoriam" page printed in the reunion directory informed us forty-one out of a class of 204 died. I was shocked to learn Ton Sizoo, a Dutch immigrant who moved to Panama City during the war, had died in Boston. We were close friends and roomed together our freshman year at FSU. We pledged Sigma Nu.

"My name is Ton, like a 'ton of bricks,'" he would introduce himself. He carried messages in a capsule up his rectum for the allies in German-occupied The Hague. A war orphan, he survived by eating tulip bulbs. In an American government class in college we attended with a German girl, Ton's blood vessels in his head would almost burst when she spoke. Imagine my surprise when I called his home while visiting Boston and learned he had married Greta, a German.

During the fast-paced changing of the millennium year 2000 it is good to take time out for class reunions. Let's not forget from whence we came, nor those who helped us along.

Let's take time to cast our eyes to sunsets

January 5, 2003

The Year 2002 slipped quietly away the afternoon of Dec. 31, but not unnoticed: a magnificent double rainbow formed in the eastern sky above beautiful Lake Eufaula.

Only minutes earlier, rain fell and the wind blew falling leaves about the historic townscape. That dreary day—the last day of 2002—was perhaps an appropriate farewell to the old year. I took the magnificent display in the late afternoon skies as a good omen for the New Year, as I excitedly left the office to mail envelopes containing my property tax checks for '02.

I dropped the first envelope into the post office slot without a stamp but I realized my mistake as I searched for the right slot to mail my Henry County taxes. An affable postal employee heard my lament and rescued the stampless envelope that could have cost me a penalty. As I stepped back outside, the sun was setting over the Bluff City in the west. The western sky was aglow with the most magnificent coloration along the horizon: Vivid shades of light blue with unusual formations hugging the earth attracted attention to the west. The sky seemed to enclose the world as I saw it inside a spectacular dome, as if to capture and preserve Eufaula and its envious place as the center of the globe.

The next day a large picture of the sunset and the rainbow graced the front page of the *Columbus Ledger Enquirer*, and it jarred me to my senses: Eufaula isn't the center of the universe but it is beautifully situated on a high bluff overlooking the impounded Chattahoochee River. But how beautiful it was to close the day and the challenging year in such a spectacular way. Surely God is communicating to us. I take it as a good omen for the New Year.

It inspires me to continue my watercolor classes taught by Wayne Spradley. However, not a single horizon or cloud formation I've painted into my landscapes can hold a candle to the magnificent displays I saw at the close of Year 2002. I'm reminded that I have to be more creative, more aware of the real world around me when it comes to painting my next landscape on paper.

God's double rainbows created in such vivid color and the marvelous sunset inspired me. I'm reminded that we have many beautiful sunsets, if we but take the time to cast our eyes upon the horizon late in the afternoon.

I'm also inspired by Winston Churchill's great little book, *Painting as a Pastime*, I received as a Christmas gift from my son and lovely daughter-in-law. If that busy man found time to paint beautiful pictures, beginning in his forties, surely at my advanced age I can crowd lessons into my work schedule—I go to work at ten AM!

My hero gives good advice: "The first quality that is needed is Audacity. There really is no time for the deliberate approach. Two years of drawing lessons, three years of copying woodcuts, five years of plaster casts—these are for the young . . . We must not be too ambitious. We cannot aspire to masterpieces. We may content ourselves with a joy ride in a paint box. And for this Audacity is the only ticket."

I'm inspired to look upward and to paint beautiful pictures during the New Year. As I pull out the hand-scribbled pages of my desk calendar and replace it with my sparkling, fresh 2003 daily calendar refill, I wonder where did the time go? If I really want to know, I can flip through the documented pages and glean some idea of how I spent many hours.

More importantly, I set my sights on 2003 as I turn to page one, January 1 and begin reading for the third year, *My Utmost for His Highest*, Oswald Chambers's daily reading. Like Paul says, "My determination is to be my utmost for His Highest."

Chambers writes: "To get there is a question of will, an absolute and irrevocable surrender on that point." This year I hope to surrender my will to Him, as did Paul and Chambers, whose writings come from his lectures given at the Bible Training College in England, during the years 1911–15. I find them relevant today and most helpful as I read each daily devotion.

I hope to be more attuned to the time and the temperature in 2003: thanks to the B. W.'s ultimatum, Woodrow Cordell installed the Vermont wall thermometer—guaranteed for life—that a friend gave me a couple of Christmases past. This morning I gave it a cursory glance as I descended the back steps to begin my morning walk.

I found it helpful that Charlie Schaeffer has repaired CommerceSouth's time and temperature clock on Broad Street—at least the clock mechanism is working.

I also resolve to be more alert as I drive out my driveway onto North Eufaula Avenue's ceaseless traffic onslaught. As I observe other local drivers along Broad and on the Bluff, the thought comes to me that one thing we need during the New Year is a "defensive driving" class.

I'm reminded—and so is long-time friend Dottie Vezina—of the time our friend Sarah Russell taught such a course to the Business and Professional Women's Club way back when Eufaula was Camelot. (Indomitable Sarah was a powerful personality in her Merle Norman cosmetic shop along Broad Street, but she was an atrocious driver.)

I'm off to a good start this New Year, and I hope you are too, gentle reader. The B. W.'s orthopedic specialist Dr. Francis Moll—of several in her medical trust—has dismissed her, and that's encouraging news too.

Chapter 12

Santa, Cedar Trees & Christmas Spirit

FLYING SQUIRREL CAME TO CHRISTMAS

January 15, 1981

Thank goodness we Methodists don't observe the Twelve Days of Christmas like our neighbors, the Episcopal rector and family, do. Don't get me wrong. I love Christmas like a kid, but Christmas 1980 was just about too much.

It all started Christmas Eve when the third flying squirrel of the season made his appearance known inside our excited household. The Squirrel Who Came to Christmas managed to escape our three sons and hide either among the decorations on our fourteen-foot cedar tree or somewhere among the many nooks and crannies of our old house until the day after Christmas.

The furry little fellow seemed to enjoy the chase about as much as a fox pursued by a band of inebriated hunters. I kept thinking he would run for his life and make it to the outside world, but then we stopped up his entrance hole in the dining room fireplace. Just when we thought he had left, there were the telltale signs on the kitchen counter where the little squirrel dined on a fine coffee cake baked in the shape of a Christmas wreath.

The Squirrel Who Came to Christmas, like two of his friends before, was finally cornered in the bathroom and spirited outside in the wastepaper basket.

Backing up a bit, an X-ray made Christmas Day confirmed the wife had a bronchial infection and our ailing family doctor prescribed via telephone she must be put to bed for two weeks. Her allergist had recommended an artificial Christmas tree, so down came the towering live cedar—on Christmas Day. However, the plastic boughs of holly swagging down the staircase and the big plastic wreath hanging from the balcony outside were still drooping days after the Episcopalians' Festival of Light ceremony on Epiphany.

I was too busy nursing the wife, cooking breakfast and warming up covered dishes friends brought over and chauffeuring kids to take down the last remnants of Yuletide.

I'd never make it as a short-order cook or a helper at one of the fast food restaurants. Cooking breakfast and getting boys off to school is about as nerve wracking as trying to publish a newspaper when the old flatbed press decided to be cantankerous. Omelets are the main thing I can cook, and one son simply does not like my cheese omelet. The fried toast, my other specialty, would get cold before I could flip the omelet and blend the orange juice and pour the water and set the table.

And to make matters worse, it took at least two runs up the stairs to wake up my three sons. The nine-year-old is always grumpy when he wakes up—except on Christmas morning. Upon entering the kitchen, he always wants to know, "What are we having?" My answer, "Bubble and squeak," never sets very well with him, either. And what is bubble and squeak? It's leftover cabbage and whipped Irish potatoes fried into patties for breakfast.

It's a specialty of British diners, and so help me the next time I'm pressed into kitchen duty, I'm going to hide the cereal and dish up bubble and squeak for my unappreciative offspring.

Yes, there are Christmases Past, and then there is this past Christmas. We may just spend the family's Christmas Club check on a Christmas at Williamsburg and give the boys IOUs for gift certificates next year.

CHRISTMAS IS A TIME FOR REMEMBERING

Christmas is a time for remembering. It is of course a high holy day and time to commemorate the birth of Christ the Lord. The Yuletide season is also tinged with nostalgia and it is a time to reflect on Christmases past.

Born on the advent of the Great Depression, I grew up when the economy was in terrible straits. However, my four brothers and a sister didn't know then those weren't the best of times. Our father was a businessman who had been quite successful as a young man and he was fortunate in wooing and winning our mother, a beautiful and talented daughter of a country doctor. Their all-too short life together was one of the world's greatest love stories—not the kind of story that makes a good made-for-television movie.

Ours was a happy home even in the days when banks were foreclosing and our father's business found it hard to operate at a profit. I remember as a boy thumbing through some of his old ledgers stored in an outbuilding, which contained page after page of past-due accounts, never to be collected. There were mortgages signed by poor farmers which were never foreclosed. And well do I remember the rolling store he operated out in the surrounding country.

I loved to make the rounds with the amiable driver who would stop at farmhouses and crossroads where a farm wife would often swap a chicken or eggs or produce for store-bought merchandise. There was a deep chicken coop underneath the long rolling store body. As a child I would come down to the store downtown when the rolling store driver was checking in and my father would let me have any bantam chickens that were bartered by the farm families.

Those were happy times for me and my brothers and our sister, although I know now they must have been tough times for my father and his adoring wife. Like children today, we believed in Santa Claus. Long before Christmas we wrote letters to St. Nick, which weren't mailed to the North Pole or printed in the weekly *Samson Ledger*, where our mother was the work-at-home society editor. Instead, we burned our letters in the fireplace and had full confidence Santa would, somehow, mysteriously read every line. And even in those Depression days, Santa always seemed to deliver. There was the war year when he even found a new bike for me and a beautiful chest of drawers for my younger sister. Wagons and later chemistry sets were part of the Santa loot.

The Smith brothers didn't hang their stockings on the mantle, instead Santa placed our gifts in separate chairs, and each child knew which was his chair without question.

Of course, all South Alabama families cut their own Christmas tree, and our family was no exception. I can remember that Christmas when we selected a lovely holly tree. It didn't need too many decorations, but I recall the beautiful string of electric lights made up of ornaments shaped like oranges or bunches of grapes and miniature Santa Clauses. The house was also decked with boughs of holly. Behind every picture on the wall, it seemed, our mother artistically arranged sprigs of holly.

Good things were baked in the old wood stove, too. The fruitcake was baked weeks, it seemed, in advance of Christmas so it could be wrapped in a wine-soaked cloth and packed with ripe apples and allowed to mellow before the holidays. Well do I remember the year my older brother dropped the bottle of homemade wine he had picked up from a family friend's house and broke it on the front walk.

The Smith house was a beehive of activity before and during the Christmas holidays. Early in the evening, we would build a bonfire in the side yard and shoot firecrackers. When we were small, our father would tie the firecrackers on to the end of a long dog fennel and we would light them from the fire. The Christmas holidays were noisy because kids all over town continuously shot firecrackers as part of the celebration.

As a small boy, my brothers and sister and I delighted in wrapping up such ridiculous things as a sweet potato or a brickbat to place under the big Christmas tree. However, we did our serious Christmas shopping at the dime store which was stocked to overflowing with the most exciting kind of merchandise.

Our city kin in Montgomery always mailed us the biggest package allowed by the U.S. Post Office. Our young aunts and our grandmother showered us with the most delightful gifts, all beautifully wrapped. Cutting the wrapping paper from around that big box is one of my fondest Christmas remembrances. Then our debonair, "rich" bachelor uncle in the city would always send each of us a check for five dollars, a tremendous amount of money. I'd always use it to open a new checking account. While my intentions were good, the five bucks didn't last too long, but my younger brother made deposits of a quarter at a time to add to his tidy nest egg.

Those were some happy Christmases, and so were the ones spent in Eufaula with my devoted aunts during my high school and college days, after my mother died. The parties in Eufaula were great in those days when there was a formal dance at the club and an intermission party. Without fail, I usually managed to pack without my black socks. And I remember the Christmas my younger brother forgot his black shoes and he borrowed Hamp Graves's father's pointed-toe shoes.

The economy, the Depression, or the war didn't keep our family from enjoying a merry Christmas. Christmas was always a happy time, a time of togetherness for our big family.

This Christmas may be best ever

December 19, 2004

The Camerata and Eufaula Men's Chorus concert was the harbinger of Christmas for me, followed by my thirty-second RSVP Christmas recognition dinner.

If the majestic music and the cheerful senior volunteers dressed in red dresses didn't get my undivided attention, the Christmas pageant at church last Sunday with three grandchildren cast as an angel, a wiseman and an animal in the manger scene did. Two grandsons and their preschool singing, "We Wish You A Merry Christmas" was the icing on the cake.

The B. W. and I hosting the *Tribune* staff for an annual Christmas dinner, followed by a children's concert at the church with two grandchildren performing Wednesday, have me revved up for the holidays. It's bound to be the best Christmas ever at our old house.

The magic of Christmases past came to my mind as the newspaper staff lingered, enjoying big slices of a luscious coconut cake and coffee. It happened after Ann welcomed our wonderful guests and recalled the decades past when we hosted the staff.

All week, I've had that first Christmas and moving into the circa 1845 Couric Homestead on Dec. 11, 1966, on my mind. Months after we were married, we moved from a one-bedroom apartment on Malone Alley into the neglected Greek Revival landmark.

I had admired the tall house with its six square columns and peeling white paint. A window unit air-conditioner stuck out through a second story window with a small hose hanging down, dripping condensed vapor on the concrete floor below. In the front hall, near the stairwell, stood a supply of metal bedsteads and old mattresses stacked inside a wooden frame. The place had been divided into four low-rent apartments.

The living room was in the best condition of all the rooms, freshly painted chocolate brown. The landlord and owner had walled in the Victorian staircase to create part of a kitchen on the landing. To give privacy, a door was framed in on the fourth step. It rained Dec. 11 when my friend Ike Taylor moved Ann's wedding gifts and my few pieces of old furniture. The heavens were crying, but we didn't know until our friend Charlotte and her elderly Aunt Bess called on us and suggested the only thing for us to do was to spend Christmas with my new in-laws.

That first night, tired but excited, we managed to erect a bed and were fast asleep when we were serenaded with Christmas carols by a group of our friends who congregated outside our bedroom. They thought we had lost our minds, but we were happy as a partridge in a pear tree.

Since we moved into only one of the ground-level apartments, Ann was innovative and arranged a combination dining room and living room. There she decorated a tabletop Christmas tree with the red and green silk Christmas balls her mother mailed us. The tree must not have impressed Aunt Bess or Charlotte's children, Ben and Eleanor. I overheard Eleanor say to her brother, "Look at all this junk!"

Every year for the past thirty-eight years, Christmas has gotten better. We've never left Christ out of our Christmas, and I resent the greeting card purveyors who have pushed Christ's name off the fold and substituted "holidays."

I'm a hopeless traditionalist who likes to worship God at eleven AM every Sunday, and I love the magic of Christmas in our old home. We still hang our three sons' stockings with care on the mantel, crowded by two daughters-in-law's and six grandchildren's stockings.

Ann again hoodwinked our resident carpenter and his elf into assembling our "fake" tree and hanging our garlands from the dining room mirror. It's still my job to loop the garlands down the stair railing, wiring a gold ribbon near the spindle where the door once stood on the stairs.

A talking moose that chuckles "Ho! Ho! Ho!" and sings, "Santa Claus is Coming To Town" is the new addition to our Christmas memorabilia. The charming gift from Dottie Vezina, which looks like he galloped in from the Maine woods, is turned on by a sensor.

The maid and loyal friend almost had a heart attack when the stuffed animal greeted her with a hearty "Ho! Ho! Ho!" while preparing for the the *Trib's* party. I can't wait for the grandchildren to meet Marvin the Moose.

Looking at the tall, skinny tree, decorated from top to bottom with a collection of circa 1966–2004 ornaments, I wonder if our three sons, now in their thirties, have forgotten those fourteen-foot tall cedar trees we used to cut and decorate, right on the same spot where the antique fake tree still stands.

I hope they've forgotten how I wrestled with giant fresh cedars, with their prickly foliage, and groaned when the tree was too tall for our fourteen-foot ceilings. And I certainly hope the three of them have forgotten the Christmas when we trudged to the Martins's back forty to harvest the Smith family tree and my back got out of whack as I sawed the monster with a rusty blade.

I'll never forget dragging that tree to the station wagon and struggling to tie it on top as the boys enjoyed the outing in the countryside. Nor will I forget the Christmas Day the B. W. became ill and the three sons and I had to take the decorations off the cedar tree and toss the genuine tree—

doctor's orders.

I cherish the memories of Christmases past as I survey the dozens of ornaments—some worn. The little boys pictured in their hand-made Sunday school ornaments, a dozen or more brass ornaments engraved with their names and age, my mother-in-law's silk Christmas balls and elegant ornaments made by Aunt Babe all reflect our family history.

Christmas '04 will be the best one yet—thanks to our six beautiful grandchildren, their parents, our son, Bill, and my B. W.

CHRISTMAS ORNAMENTS BRING BACK MEMORIES

December 19, 1984

The family Christmas tree will bring back fond memories of Christmases past if you pause long enough to look carefully at the wide assortment of ornaments collected through the years.

The large, slightly worn red and green satin balls on our twelve-foot "fake tree," as our children used to call it, remind me of the first Christmas after Ann and I married. We had daringly moved into the long-neglected, antebellum Couric House, which was divided into low-rent apartments.

After a wise, elderly friend paid a visit only days before Christmas and observed the table-top Christmas tree in our sparsely-filled living-dining room, she advised Ann to spend that Christmas at her mother's. On the bright side, I remember being serenaded by curious but supportive friends before we left for Christmas in Springville that year.

Several ornaments, made by the little hands of our three sons, remind me of those following Christmases when the boys and I would go into the woods near Georgetown and choose and cut our own cedar trees. We'd pick big trees that were also tall because there was plenty of room in the living room. Sometimes, I'd miscalculate, and after nailing a homemade tree stand onto the trunk and dragging the cedar into the house, I'd discover it was more than fourteen feet tall, and then I would impatiently whack off a half-foot or so.

I also recall that year when my back got out of whack as I sawed down a cedar in the far back woods of the Martins's Christmas tree farm near Cottonton. After dragging the tree to the car, the tree and I both were fit to be tied.

The ornaments engraved with the boys' names remind me of thoughtful Eufaula friends like Ruthie and Flo who remember us at Christmas. Some are engraved with the year.

The fake tree also reminds me of the Christmas the doctor pronounced the wife is allergic to live trees. We didn't let our Christmas dinner settle before I took the ornaments off the fresh cedar and pulled it out of the house.

Playing Santa Claus was challenging to me, because I didn't like to read instructions written for mechanical engineers, and I'm all thumbs assembling toys with dozens of small parts. And there was always a midnight ride to the Zippy Mart to pick up more batteries for the toys.

Now, it's great to have sons big enough to help assemble the branches of the shop-worn, plastic Christmas tree. They do a better job spacing the dozens of little white lights than I ever did when we used to string the larger colored lights on the tree.

Two decades later, the many, many beautiful and sometimes funny little ornaments also remind me of the decorations we had on our tree when I was a boy. The Smith brothers would go with our father into the woods and find just the right holly tree or cedar that was "bushy-out" enough. Nobody but snobs or rich folks would buy a Douglas fir that had been shipped into Dothan.

The Christmas lights, strung on red and green wire, were shaped like miniature oranges or grapes. Oriental lanterns or Santas were so well made they lasted my entire childhood. In the Depression years tinfoil icicles, which had been carefully retrieved from the tree the year before by our beautiful Mother, were hung on the tree after the lights and glass balls were hung.

I remember reading *The Night Before Christmas* and about Jabbo Dawes, the boy who didn't believe in Santa Claus, to our little boys days before Christmas.

It was always surprising how quiet it was around our normally bustling house on Christmas Eve and how lively it was around the tree early Christmas morning, long before the sun showed its winter face.

Each Christmas is memorable, each has its highlights, but even now our family keeps using the same ornaments, because, I suppose some things shouldn't change too much.

IT'S MORE FUN TO CUT DOWN YOUR OWN
CHRISTMAS TREE

When it comes to Christmas, I'm rather old fashioned. I love all the Old South tradition that goes with the holiday season. I still like for the family to "deck the halls with boughs of holly" and to go to the woods and hunt for a Christmas tree rather than selecting a Canadian balsam or a fancy Scotch pine at the grocery store.

Ever since my oldest son became large enough to hike through the piney woods, he and I have joined our friends, Dick Boyette and his boys, for that eventful trip south of Georgetown to cut down the family Christmas trees. Last Saturday was the long awaited day. As usual, our wives admonished us not to bring back such large trees. And as usual, we didn't pay them any attention after cruising the beautiful woods that border the lake.

This year we decided it would be best to select bigger, taller trees with the understanding we could cut from the top and come up with fuller more symmetrical trees. After an enjoyable trek through the beautiful wooded countryside, we settled on a couple of tall, deep green cedars. When a tree would fall, somebody would yell, "Timber!" and we would shorten the cedar a time or two before loading it on the back of the pick-up truck. After an enjoyable outing in the woods, we finished filling up the truck with branches of holly that were filled with large red berries.

Back home, after unloading our White-House-size trees, we took a break for refreshments. The trip to hunt for the Christmas tree proved rather exhausting and I was able to convince the wife we should soak the trunk in water and put up the tree the next day. Trouble was the tree was so big, I couldn't find anything big enough to serve as a container for the water.

Even though our old house has ceilings fourteen feet tall, it became evident I'd have to whack off two or three feet from the tree. Of course, those store-bought tree stands just simply don't work on these big, native grown red cedars. But a stand for the tree wasn't too much of a problem because I'd saved the one from the years before which I made in desperation out of two by fours.

The doors connecting the entry hall and the parlor had to be opened wide so the bushy cedar tree could pass through. Once erected, it proved to be a beauty. And decorating it wasn't much of a problem because we usually wind up with a thirteen- or fourteen-footer, and some how the wife has been able to collect enough Christmas ornaments to decorate a tree that large.

Yep, when it comes to Christmas trees, I am old fashioned. I don't like those perfectly symmetrical balsam trees shipped from Canada. Those needles just don't look like the cedars or the short leaf pines I'm accustomed to. And I don't want a Scotch pine, even though its stiff dark green needles cover the tree uniformly, it's still an import and it's store-bought.

I have too many fond childhood memories of Christmases gone by. I still remember those trips to the woods with my father and brothers to hunt for the family Christmas tree. And I still like to see branches of holly in the house because my mother always decorated with sprigs of the glossy-leaved, red-berried plant. She used it profusely, and this is still a tradition with my family. Holly and cedar are as much a part of Christmas as fruitcakes, Lane cake, homemade candies and a traditional family dinner.

Yes, an important part of Christmas is the fragrance of cedar and that trip to the woods to hunt for just the right tree.

Santa Was Marvelous Fellow, Even in Depression

December 19, 1974

O ne of my friends told me the other day there are two kinds of people, "Christmas people" and folks who aren't turned on by the Yuletide season. Indeed, as was pointed out, I'm a "Christmas person." I always have been. Why, I believed in Santa Claus years after my younger brother discovered the great holiday hoax.

Times must have been so tough back then even the grown folks needed to believe. The oldest brother, in our family of five boys and a girl, is largely responsible for my clinging to the idea that indeed there was a generous ole fellow who could work miracles, come Christmastime. We wrote letters to Santa Claus, which we burned in the fireplace rather than mailed at the post office. Big brother Jack usually did the burning while the younger kids wondered out loud how marvelous it was Santa could read our smoke signals at the North Pole, originating all the way from South Alabama.

Of course, our father and the Smith brothers always "shopped" for just the right tree in the woods. I can remember one year we chopped down a beautiful holly tree, already decorated with big, red berries by mother nature, this time not for greenery to stick behind the pictures on the wall nor to put on the mantle, but for our family Christmas tree. And my Mother's decorations were something to behold when she finally unpacked the ornaments for the tree. The lights, strung along red and green cord, were in such delightful shapes as miniature oranges, bunches of grapes and a fat little Santa Claus.

Ages before Christmas, we kids had fun wrapping up all sorts of funny things such as sweet potatoes, playing jokes on each other. Somehow, even during those depression years, our parents managed to answer some of our wildest dreams. There were those tough years when I received a big red wagon and my very own bike, and that chemistry set was something really special but times were more prosperous then, "thanks" to WWII.

Like other "Christmas people," I have some wonderful Christmas memories, and I want my boys to experience the joy and little pleasures of Christmastide. Yes, we still cut down our own Christmas tree. My first grader would have it no other way, nor would I. He didn't cotton to those live, cut trees on sale downtown, and an artificial tree is entirely out of the question in spite of the family allergist, Dr. Rufus Lee's polite suggestion. Metal and tinsel trees are pretty, but they don't smell like cedar nor pine.

I'm sure their Christmas memories will include riding in the *Tribune* van to cut down that towering cedar tree and cutting boughs from the short-leaf pines on our lot to use as greenery around our house. They'll probably remember how we always managed to bring home a cedar tree so tall it had to be sawed off at least once before it would fit in our living room with its fourteen-foot high ceiling.

No doubt the three Smith boys' Christmas memories will include the delicious tea cakes, beautifully decorated, and all the other goodies wife Ann cooks up for the holidays, not to mention their grandmother's stacks of cookie tins, filled with home baked gingersnaps, sand tarts, brownies, fruitcake and candied grapefruit and orange peelings colored green. I believe they'll also remember hanging the holly wreath, year after year, from the same little nail on the front door, and they should recall the hanging of our great big wreath from the balcony upstairs and Ann's old fashion swags and red bows on the living room mantle, accented by those mischievous looking little blonde headed elves clad in red that bear such a striking resemblance to our three towheads.

Somehow, I hope they won't remember how their Mama always looked at me when she laid eyes on the over-grown tree, but you see since I'm a Christmas person, I believe in getting excited about Christmas, just like my little boys do.

CHRISTMAS SPIRIT WRAPPED IN RED, WHITE AND BLUE

December 30, 2001

T he spirit of Christmas 2001 was "Glory to God in the highest," wrapped in red, white and blue. The pallet of holiday colors embraced America in the wake of the Sept. 11 attacks.

We had a Merry Christmas in Eufaula with the old, old theme sung in cantatas and concerts and acted out in Christmas pageants: "Glory to God in the highest, and on earth peace, good will to all people."

A big banner reading, "Welcome Home Daddy," and Old Glory swayed with the wind at a modest home on River Road. On West Broad Street, the big round columns of a vintage home were wrapped in red, white and blue lights. Downtown, the traditional live Christmas trees were also festooned with red, white and blue.

There was peace in the valley and on the Bluff, too. The Christmas pageants were, as usual, an important part of the celebration. At my church, the precious Baby Jesus placed in the manger was a beautiful live baby boy. (Some years a baby girl fills the role.) This year, there was no gossip about a hair pulling between moms of the newborns during the casting for the Christmas pageant, although there could have been because there are several newborn baby boys in the congregation.

The angels sang sweetly, and the animals were restless. The reluctant innkeeper was escorted to the manger by his dutiful mom, but the look on his face was miserable, and he bolted. (I admired him for it. All the world may be a stage, but we don't all have to be the hams.)

The RSVP's Christmas banquet also again got me in the Christmas spirit.

An Associated Press feature compared today's patriotism to Christmas after Pearl Harbor. I've tried to think back to Christmas 1941, sixty years ago. A boy of twelve, my friends and I scavenged the countryside looking for old scrap metal—iron and aluminum—to cast into bullets and war machines to help vanquish the WWII enemies and to put money into our pockets to buy Christmas gifts.

This Yuletide embraced suggestions to buy and boost the sagging national economy. As the AP story noted, "times are vastly better than in 1941." That I can vouch for. I couldn't get excited about spending large amounts for Christmas presents. I tried to convey that feeling to my B. W., our household's chief consumer. I convinced her we should buy a much-needed lamp and lamppost for the end of our back walk and consider it our gift to each other. I wound up with a stainless steel sink for the Fourth Estate that wasn't gift wrapped, but it suited the tenor of the times. My other "surprises" under the shop-worn fake tree, decorated with many fractured ornaments from Christmases Past, included necessities, boxer shorts, socks and cotton handkerchiefs. Now, that doesn't sound exciting but it suited me to a T.

Looking back in the *Tribune's* December 1941 bound volume, the edition was filled with war stories and a big, black ad urging Eufaulians to "Remember Pearl Harbor: America has a job to do! Turn your dimes to bullets and your dollars into guns. Buy U.S. Defense Savings Stamps and Bonds."

Well I do remember buying defense savings stamps and collecting them until they totaled $18.75, enough to swap at the Post Office for a Savings Bond.

That same yellowed copy of the local newspaper included an account of the Country Club's annual Christmas dance. It was a "gay affair" with the Auburn Knights Orchestra playing until the late hours. Two Alabama and Auburn leadouts were featured, according to society editor Willie Copeland Couric. All around town, Eufaulians and their guests enjoyed festive Christmas dinners. The R. P. Kennedys hosted a holiday party at Roseland, and the Raymond Trammells entertained at Cross Creek Plantation.

The Christmas party at the Country Club this Christmas was also enjoyable with great food, good company but few of the college crowd—certainly not enough for an Alabama or Auburn leadout. The college crowd during Christmas 2001 didn't dance. They hung out with friends.

It may not have been a jolly Christmas for everyone, but Christmas 2001 was tinged with emotion and filled with love: love of family, fellowman and country. Perhaps it fostered a return to basics, and there is nothing wrong with that.

Now, let's focus on 2002 and pray for peace and a good year.

Chapter 13

Fatherhood

It's a boy!

August 22, 1968

The most amazing thing has come to the Smith home on North Eufaula Avenue. Ever since the stork paid us a visit, there has been activity around the clock.

To the surprise of some, I was a pretty stable expectant father. Not once did I really lose my cool during those many months Ann and I patiently waited for the arrival of our first born. Those who two years earlier had watched my pale, poker face as I marched to the altar to take my nuptial vows just knew I'd wind up in the intensive care room at the hospital when the countdown began.

Ann nudged me from my sleep around twelve AM Wednesday and gently told me it might be time to take her to the hospital. Her quick call to her doctor, Dick Whitehurst, confirmed this. I finished dressing, backed the car up to the back steps, raced the motor and cut on the air conditioner before Ann could dress and close up her already-packed suitcase.

I managed to keep the car in the road as we drove briskly to Barbour County Hospital, where we met the doctor at the emergency room. After an examination, he called to me to pick up the wife's bag and to meet them in the maternity ward. With the greatest of ease and in good professional form, Dr. Dick administered to Ann in the Labor Room as I nervously stood outside. My heart began to pound faster than ever when he looked at the clock and stated flatly we'd have a baby delivered by 3:00.

Dr. Whitehurst must have minored in psychology or done post-graduate work on the Care and Handling of Expectant Fathers. He kept my nerves steady by talking, and he casually reminded me that his assistant, Mrs. Louise King, was the best in the business.

Then when he rolled Ann across the hall into the delivery room, he had Mrs. S. Cooper bring me an admittance form to fill out. Just as I had finished letter, "Joel P.," I heard a spank. Then finally—it seemed like minutes later—I heard a faint little cry.

At this point I was pushing against the delivery room door, straining to hear all the conversation going on inside. "Pretty baby," the doctor said, and I thought to myself, "Oh, it's a girl!" Then the calm doctor referred to the newborn babe as "he" a time or two. For thirty minutes, I waited breathlessly to learn whether I was the father of a son or daughter. Then Ann and the baby were wheeled out, and they told me the good news: It was a boy!

I became a permanent fixture outside the nursery. I couldn't keep my eyes off that little baby. Mrs. Inez Babb and the other nurse's aides seemed to understand. They pulled the curtain back as I watched the "Greatest Show on Earth" as my little son would wave his arms as he cried, just as Ann does when she talks, or as he just slept in his crib.

"Ya'll gonna look the look off that baby," one elderly nurse joked as she observed Ann and me looking through the nursery window.

Now, you better believe I greeted my wonderful mother-in-law with open arms. The good doctor agreed to release wife and baby Sunday morning, and Vassie, the practical nurse, wasn't scheduled to appear until Monday afternoon. The in-laws arrived fully prepared and equal to the task. They had even shopped and prepared food in advance.

Good ole Vassie is now on the job, faithful Mittie Griggs is helping out, and my mother-in-law has cooked, tended to the wee one and done all sorts of man-sized chores around the bustling "mention." There's activity practically around the clock up at our house these days.

You wouldn't believe a little, tiny fellow like my namesake and son could cause such commotion and excitement day after day.

That first birthday party is wild

August 21, 1969

That first birthday party for your offspring is an event to be remembered. For years now, I've heard youthful mothers groan about the frustrations of giving a birthday party for their little ones.

"Sugar Doodle" was one-year-old last Friday. It was my contention that certainly such an important occasion should be celebrated with a party, complete with birthday cake, candle, gifts and little friends. Wife Ann, the practical little mother who has been guest at a tot's party before, vetoed my idea. Now I know why.

The only toddler invited to share this festive occasion with Joel Jr. was Richard Boyette, an active wee one who can out run a junior high school track star. The other guest included little Richard's mother—his invitation hinged on her attendance too—and several other adult friends and kin. (I always thought it was funny the way the adults and the maids outnumber the guests at kids' birthday parties. Now I don't. It takes two adults per child to maintain any hope of order.)

In spite of a couple of head bumpings and a slight hand burn, the "Sugar Doodle" loved his party. And the one little guest, who is a little more mature by several months, had a ball. He couldn't contain himself during the picture taking, which preceded the cutting of the birthday cake. Before the proud papa could light that one small candle, Richard dug into the white, creamy icing and began lapping it up. The honoree then did likewise, with gusto.

During the wild uproar, amid flash bulbs popping and home movie cameras grinding, somebody suggested lighting the candle. Sitting on top of the dining room table, beside the cake, "Sugar Doodle" couldn't resist that flickering candle. Before I could catch his little hand, he had touched the flame. However, after time out for first aid administered by the mother, the celebrating one-year-old got back into the spirit of things and continued to whoop it up, eat ice cream and man-handle his slice of cake as he clutched it in his little right hand.

All in all, it was a wild, wild party. Not only were the two toddlers wild, but the grown folks whooped it up, too.

I used to groan every time I read one of my colleague's personal columns about the day-to-day adventures of his young adopted son. Back in those bachelor days, I vowed I'd never write so much about any son of mine—if I ever had one. Now, I can understand. As a doting father, I could write a daily column about that delightful little boy of mine.

The privilege of being a father is one of the greatest joys in this life. Ever since I first laid eyes on our baby boy, I haven't been the same. Of course, he's changed my world completely—and my outlook, too. Who would have thought I'd change a wet diaper or hear his cry in the middle of the night?

But how wonderful it is to see him early every morning, standing in his bed calling "da da." And when I go home for lunch or home at the end of a day's work, he gives me a greeting that surpasses any ticker-tape parade or red carpet welcome for a visiting head of state.

To watch him progress from crawling to standing alone and walking was marvelous. Soon after the astronauts walked on the moon, he started toddling. At first, he carefully balanced his little arms, much as the moon men did when they made their historic lunar walk. Now he's more confident and can point himself, walking almost directly to a pre-determined object in the room.

And to hear him talk. Like every father's little boy, he is unusually bright in my eyes. When he adds a new word to his growing vocabulary I just know he'll be a Phi Beta Kappa someday. And I get excited when he sees a picture of a dog and says "bow-wow!" I just know he'll be one of the "bluebirds" in the fast reading group when he finally reaches grade school.

It's been a great year, and I know this year will be equally exciting, but I can't honestly say I'll look forward to that second birthday party when more than one little guest will be invited to help us celebrate.

It's another boy!

April 8, 1971

IT'S A BOY!

I'm the proud papa of another little boy. Mother Ann and baby Abb Jackson Smith II are doing just fine. So is our number one son, Joel Jr.

If there are more errors than usual on the editorial page and if some page one headlines don't quite make good sense, it's because the editor is still stretched out and up in the clouds.

Of course, being a good newspaperman's wife, Ann cooperated beautifully. She took the staff literally when they told her not to deliver on a Monday or a Wednesday. She also cooperated with the local school system, the Eufaula Pilgrimage committee and the Eufaula Ministerial Association, by not conflicting with the school board's meeting, the Pilgrimage nor Easter Sunrise Services.

We made the quick dash in the dark of night to Barbour County Hospital at 4:30 AM Tuesday. The blessed event took place two hours later as I waited anxiously outside the delivery room. This time Dick Whitehurst didn't keep me in suspense, and I heard him announce it was a boy.

I also "assisted" the nurses in the birthing of another baby across the hall less than ten minutes after little Jack Smith made his entrance and promptly began to tell the good news to the world. It seemed the expectant mother sped up the birthing process by promptly chewing up and swallowing this special little tablet instead of letting it dissolve slowly.

Nurse King yelled to me to run get a helper from the nurses' station, which I promptly did. I also found an electrical outlet and plugged in the incubator just in the nick of time to receive the tiny black baby born only a few minutes after my baby made his debut.

Now back to baby Jack. This happy fellow weighed in at seven pounds, three and three-quarter ounces and is nineteen and one-half inches long. Several say he resembles his big brother, but his hair, which has a red cast, sticks out. He's a contented little fellow, but he winces every time his papa takes a picture, setting off the strobe light.

Already little Jack has brought joy to the Smith and Sutton clans. All of the Smiths are rejoicing over his proud name. The Suttons just naturally like boys. You see, he's named for his much beloved grandfather, the late Abb Jackson Smith, and his uncle, Jack Smith from Geneva, one of the grandest big brothers ever. Brother Jack is the proud father of three lovely girls but no son to carry on the family name. So you see, our little Jack is a most welcomed little fellow.

We wouldn't have had a little girl!

BEING A REAL TOP POP BIG CHALLENGE TO MEN

June 17, 1971

After five years of blissful matrimony and fathering two sons, I'm beginning to understand the role of a good father. This round-the-clock job of daddying is indeed a full-time proposition.

However, I know of no responsibility or job that could be half as rewarding.

What greater thrill can a man experience than to have his two-and-a-half-year-old son run out to greet him when he drags home after a hectic day at the office?

And what a send-off a little boy can give you when you're rushing off to work. My number one son sees me to the back door and gives me a big hug. He stands grinning, with the door wide open, and waves to me until I pull out of the driveway.

And what a thrill it is to hold a tiny baby, your second son, and to watch him as he changes day by day. Then when he's two months old and smiles when you talk to him there's real communication between father and son. You begin to understand what love is all about. You realize love knows no bounds, that you have an unlimited capacity for love and that second child is just as special as the first.

Then there are trying times when you lose your temper and you find yourself yelling at your little boy much like a wild man. And then you begin thinking, how stupid of me!

Yes, it's a job to discipline a bright two-year-old who is already skilled in changing the subject when you try to talk to him about something unpleasant. It's frustrating to try to impress him with the importance of a certain code for his behavior. Somehow, he doesn't want to understand.

And it's a real test when spankings don't seem to have the desired effect. Yes, I'm an old fashioned papa. I believe in the old adage, "Spare the rod and spoil the child."

I've also concluded you have to become a father before you can fully appreciate your own father. Maybe that's why it was a real joy to me to have my youngest son named for my father. I consider myself quite fortunate to have had such a wonderful, devoted father.

I only hope I can be half the father he was. My fervent hope is I can instill some of his principles and ideals in my sons. I hope I can help inspire my sons to want to succeed in life not because of the material rewards but because of the opportunities to do so many of the good things one should do. And I hope I can teach them, as he taught me, that there isn't much to simply being good. "You have to be good for something," he used to say.

I hope I won't ever get so busy and so wrapped up in my work or in some selfish interest that I can't find time to spend with my boys. Even during those tough days that followed in the wake of the Depression, my father found time to spend with his large family.

In the summertime, he took us swimming in some of the most beautiful creeks you ever saw. He took me with him on business trips when I was just a small boy. And he always treated me as if I were mature far beyond my years. He did the same with his other fours sons and a daughter.

I hope I am able to realize my two sons are distinct individuals with some common characteristics and many differences. I hope I can realize—as my father did—each son is special in his own way. I hope I can understand their individual needs but at the same time treat them equally.

The business of being a good father is indeed challenging. It's also the most rewarding thing that can happen to a man.

'My Three Sons' now live comedy

May 30, 1974

I f somebody else hadn't already thought of the idea, I could write a convincing, true-to-life script for a continuing TV series appropriately titled, *My Three Sons*.

Business picked up at our house over the weekend. My wife, Ann, gave birth to our third son, whom we've named William Sutton after his maternal grandfather. Not deviating from our policy of never disclosing the name of one of our offspring prior to the big arrival, we stayed shut mouth for months, refusing to divulge any names under consideration. However, the third time around, our choice proved to be the overwhelming choice with both sides of the family. "You couldn't have named him anything else!" we've heard more than once.

Little Bill, who weighed in at six pounds and fourteen ounces, came into this world with his eyes wide open—his Mama says he thinks he's still in the middle of remodeling the home place, running the Eufaula Pilgrimage and planning the Historic Chattahoochee Commission's annual workshop. He's a great little fellow, a considerable improvement in looks over his long-nosed, balding old man. His disposition is also remarkable; he's much more diplomatic and cooperative.

After bedding down in the nursery at home, Bill is the center of attention. So are the big boys in an adjoining room. His homecoming was a joyful occasion, though a bit taxing, I'm afraid, for my other two sons, proud Joel Jr., who's five, and jealous Jack, the three-year-old.

They were excited enough when Mama started packing her bag for that eventful trip to the hospital. Joel was as bright as a Christmas tree, and Jack wanted to go along for the ride to pick up the baby, but they both seem to know there's going to be a heap more togetherness around our house.

The demonstrative three-year -old announced he had plans for an extended visit to his "Gendaddy's" house almost immediately when he walked into his mother's room at the "'spital." The big brother, excited about it all, cooled off a bit when he learned the new arrival was a boy. He had a sister in mind.

My three sons are really something.

It looks like I'm going to be the oldest member of the PTA and probably the most inept Boy Scoutmaster ever to wear that heretofore-proud uniform. Already, my spouse has informed me, "You're going to have to learn to fish and hunt," even though I'd told her I've already taught our number one and number two sons everything I know about fishin.' She still contends the boys are going to become discouraged if our little fishing trips aren't more productive. Mama may be a Phi Beta Kappa, but Papa ain't dumb. Besides, I'm counting on the boys' namesakes, Uncle Jack and Granddaddy, to teach 'em about huntin' and fishin'.

In the meantime, I'm proud as a peacock and happy as a lark. That William Sutton Smith is some fine little fellow. I'm sleeping like a baby myself ever since our bright-eyed Bill came home. I'll worry about learning how to teach little boys how to tie knots and build campfires tomorrow. Or maybe I'll swap out with some kids' dad who's a real outdoorsman and let him be the Scoutmaster while I write our troop's publicity releases.

Son's leaving brings on 'empty nest' syndrome

September 6, 1992

It's awfully quiet around our house. Saturday, the wife and I accompanied our third son to Birmingham-Southern College, where he is a freshman. We're beginning to experience the legendary Empty Nest Syndrome. This scenario isn't uncommon in late summer and early fall.

It would have been a particularly long trip home from the Magic City if our number two son, a rising senior, also at 'Southern, hadn't extended spontaneous invitations to five other collegians to be our houseguests following a wedding that Saturday evening.

Now that the weekend passed and our lively houseguests returned to their respective college campuses, it's like a morgue, almost, at our old house. I have to remind my subconscious that noise I hear emanating from the kitchen late at night isn't a ghost: It's the clanking ice cubes dumping out of the fridge's icemaker. It didn't bother me before: I probably surmised those late night or early morning noises were made by one of our sons.

The Empty Nest Syndrome just struck again: As I type this column, sitting in our number one son's bedroom, the carriage to my antiquated typewriter just knocked a glass of ice water off the table, crashing onto the hardwood floor. Bill's Jekyll Island souvenir glass has been trashed. I'm not wallowing in my misery, not yet. I know the worst is yet to come.

Everybody's last is special and most parents' youngest offspring is a little out of control, or so I've observed. Maybe we parents tend to relax more with that last child, or maybe children are getting smarter and smarter and know how to manipulate us.

William Sutton Smith, our youngest son, has led us on a merry chase ever since we parked him in the church school nursery. I knew he was a livewire when one of our church's most gracious ladies, Mildred Neville, presented a delightful Christmas reading to the congregation's children and their parents in the fellowship hall.

Sitting in a rocking chair on top of a makeshift stage, she held the crowd spellbound. That is, until my little curly headed tot broke away and crawled under the platform and also began entertaining the crowd.

Some churchgoers feared I'd snatched his arm out of joint as I spirited the little monster out the back door.

Bill has been my pride and joy, though. He can do all the things well that I can't do. He's the *Trib's* computer specialist. Attending MacWorld Expo in Boston was a highlight for him last summer. Except for the spectacle of it all, I wouldn't have given two hoots for the whole darned trade show, but Bill loved the technical seminars and talking with all the computer experts. He also loves the theatre; I do, too, but you couldn't drag me on the stage, nor upstairs to the lighting and technical switchboard. He loves it all, including designing the theatre program and counting the ticket sales' money.

He and Tammy, our circulation manager, were an awesome combination this summer. She has his number, but he recently conned her into backing a boat trailer down the ramp while they rescued the family boat, half-filled with water, from up the lake. She'd never backed a trailer in her life, nor does she particularly like the wild outdoors. A water moccasin's untimely appearance prompted her to make unladylike utterances; all the while a preacher witnessed the episode.

That's our Bill.

He's happy as a lark on the Hilltop. He likes 'Southern's "hands-on president," Dr. Neal Berte. He greeted us in the parking lot as we arrived in our two-car caravan with many of Bill's graduation presents and tons of various and sundry computers and electronic devices.

The wife and I spoke few words after saying goodbye to Bill at the handsome new Harbert Building, where his orientation began, until we took Exit 205 on I-65 for the Durbin Farm fruit stand. As we quietly ate frozen peach yogurt, another father from Spanish Fort recognized us. The robust, manly gentleman confided he hadn't slept for three nights, anticipating his daughter's departure for college.

Right now I pray that hilltop in Birmingham is big enough for two Smith siblings. It took several different campuses to have room to educate my five siblings and me.

No, I'm not sad our last chick has left the nest. I'd be sad if he didn't want to try his wings.

EDITOR WRITES LETTER TO THREE SONS ON HIS BIRTHDAY

February 14, 1993

Editor's note: If this open letter strikes you, dear reader, as too personal, I apologize. I am aware some fathers and sons can't find the courage to tell each other, "I love you." My intent is to help them break through the silence, as I did years ago.

D ear Sons,

   In college psychology classes you may have learned that "There's a deep hunger on the part of men to feel that they're valued and appreciated by their fathers."

I heartily concur with psychologist Samuel Osherson, the author of *Finding our Fathers*, that this is true.

On this birthday, which nudges me further along into the Modern Maturity set, I hope to convey to you that your father, with all his short-comings, truly loves you, each of you, unconditionally.

For thirty-five years, I have disciplined myself to write a weekly column for the *Tribune*, yet I seem to find it difficult to find time to write you personal letters. And yet, I know how important a short, sincere letter from your father can be. Well do I remember perhaps the last letter my father wrote to me before he died when I was in college.

I've always treasured the message in that handwritten note: "You are precious to me." Since I am a son, too, I've found it reassuring to know my earthly father, like my Father in Heaven, loves me.

At times, after my beloved father died, ten years after my beautiful mother's death, I sometimes felt nobody truly loved me as Daddy did. Of course, as you know, in our close-knit family we love each other. But I also know a father's love is special—just as a mother's love is different.

I want you to know that my father loved each of his six children and had the wisdom not to compare us, at least to each other. He valued each individually and appreciated our similarities and our differences.

In my ineptitude I'm afraid I sometimes compare you three, but there is no question that I love each of you personally and appreciate your unique qualities. However, maybe I've been influenced by my wonderful fraternal grandmother, who would say, when someone was crass enough to ask which child she loved best, "I love the one best who needs my love the most" at that particular time.

It is not my goal in life to leave you a large estate but to encourage and assist you in becoming educated, to practice Christianity and to be good citizens.

I believe one of the great things a father can do for his children is to love

Sons Joel, Bill and Jack helped their father celebrate his eightieth birthday on Feb. 13, 2009.

their mother, and I do. If I am weak and negligent at times, it's because I know your bright, hardworking mother, with all her wonderful qualities, will see to it that you have what you need. I also know she will not mince words, nor neglect discipline.

On this birthday, I don't need nor expect generous gifts. My sons, you are the gifts beyond compare. I have been blessed in knowing I am loved by you, just as my father was loved by me.

If I haven't conveyed to you by word and deed that each of you, in your inimitable way, is valued and appreciated, then I have failed: I have learned nothing about psychology from life. I love you more than you could possibly know.

Role as groom's father is
a challenging proposition

August 6, 1995

Being father of the groom—and best man besides—is a challenging proposition. It's like being part of a well-managed road show when the bride-elect and the prospective groom live on opposite sides of the state.

My middle son Jack's official engagement exceeds my own six-month protracted engagement by a couple of months. It has been a new experience, but now I'm almost qualified to become a groom's consultant, if there is such a thing.

The groom's family involvement began Dec. 17 when we hosted an Open House to introduce our beautiful future daughter-in-law, Barclay, to our extended family and friends. I got so carried away my wife had to have two invitations printed, staggering the time of the party in order to get the crowd inside our house. The excitement was contagious.

It's been fun—sometimes frustrating—shuttling between Eufaula and Mobile five times already, with side trips to Birmingham. In between travels, I've become a certified gemologist and something of an authority on the mother-of-the-groom's dress.

I'd forgotten everything I ever knew about buying a diamond ring and a string of pearls. (When I did my personal shopping twenty-nine years ago, I met the jeweler after store hours so that a gossip didn't catch me in the act of buying an engagement ring.) I learned quickly what to look for in choosing the right diamond at the right price while assisting my son, who also made the big purchase a project.

Buying the groom's gift for the bride was equally challenging. I thought all pearls were snow-white, perfectly round and had the same luster provided by the dutiful oysters. I learned a grain of sand inserted inside an oyster's shell can agitate the obliging mollusk into creating a magnificent pearl. The trick is to find a string of rose, white, cream or silver-white pearls well matched in size.

The lovely bride will greatly enhance the groom's gift.

Shopping for the mother of the groom's dress was the greatest challenge. Friends were frantic Ann would wait too long to make up her mind. One friend, who'd married off two daughters in high style, spent hours searching through catalogues for just the right gown. Every trip out of town became a shopping excursion to find the right dress. I sat patiently at dress shops in Dothan, Columbus and Birmingham while the wife tried on many, many dress-up dresses. The bridal consultant and congenial clerks fluttered as they pulled down many ornate dresses from the racks.

It was a time-consuming process that called for the patience of Job from the groom's father—as well as his mother. I am now eminently qualified to advise mothers of the groom in making their most important purchase. They sell mothers' formal dresses like high-priced hotcakes at The Occasion, an upscale shop in Mountain Brook. The management also knows how to cater to the payee, the groom's father.

I was quickly invited to move to "the hot seat," a Chippendale winged-back chair, as the fashion parade began. Being diplomatic and expert at making big sales, the congenial manager and a couple of clerks asked patronizingly for my input. I was voted down on my first choice, an ivory chiffon dress that took me back to my courting days and ballroom dances.

Watching and listening to young brides-to-be and their doting mothers as Mom tried on dresses for the big occasion was somewhat amusing. None of them asked my opinion as they preened and looked into the mirror, but I could have told one short, fat lady that she made the worst possible choice. She must have floated down the church aisle like a big, puffy cloud.

Family members expressed a degree of concern when I announced I'd dust off my vintage tails. During a road trip to the Port City, I took my formal attire to the tux rental shop. I thought perhaps the waist-high, black trousers might be dated. The fussy, long white haired authority on groom's and groomsmen's attire carefully examined my cutaway coat. His Bostonian accent reached a high pitch when he saw the neat satin lining.

The wide-legged trousers are the exact traditional style the groom selected, he said cheerfully. The "pegged" pants have the "retro" look smart young grooms favor. (I thought "pegged" pants went out with the zoot suit craze.) The solid front detachable collar shirt is a treasure, he said excitedly, but we settled for one matching the groomsmen's.

I'm going to look like a live museum mannequin, accented by my usual pale face, when I step into the Dauphin Way United Methodist Church sanctuary. But I'll feel confident in my own tails.

It will be the first marriage among my three sons. It will be a sacred ceremony I'll endure, but I'll relish the celebration following. It's the second most exciting wedding in my lifetime. But I'll be happy the road show closes with a beautiful new daughter-in-law and a punch bowl and chicken salad sandwiches under a tent.

I'm certain Birmingham-Southern Professor Nicholas is right when he said the marriage of two of his best history majors, Barclay and Jack, is a "marriage made in heaven."

Editor's Note: Pale face reference—heart attack one-and-a-half weeks later.

Father ponders parental advice
for betrothed son

August 13, 1995

What advice, if any, does a father give to his son on the eve of his marriage?

Is it too late to impart knowledge helpful in getting the marriage off on the right foot?

I don't know, but I am experiencing the joy a parent knows with the marriage of his first of three sons to a lovely young lady who meets with full family approval—not necessarily a prerequisite for a successful union of a fine young man and his bride, albeit.

Matrimony is sacred in Eufaula. It also meets with hearty approval and acceptance, generally. We're still a small Southern city with deep roots, where people love each other and share in another's excitement. Friends greet news of an engagement with applause. They also graciously entertain the betrothed couple, their family and friends.

A bachelor family friend of long standing mused, following a round of convivial parties for my middle son and bride-to-be, that it is something of a conspiracy, contrived by the women to obligate the fiancé so publicly that he dare not break the engagement.

Could be, but I prefer to believe it's such a part of the Eufaula tradition that it happens almost automatically. Sometimes, the anxious matrons begin forming a social committee even before the young man gives his ladylove a ring. They're so organized that the cocktail party, buffet or shower goes off without a hitch, even when the guest list is lengthy.

Generation after generation of Eufaulians have been convivial, caring people who celebrate at the drop of a hat. They enjoy the prenuptial festivities and also make the effort to attend the wedding ceremony, and, of course, the reception.

Weddings are such splendid affairs here that the mother-of-the-bride has a choice between the fellowship hall at the church, magnificently appointed Shorter Mansion or historic, imposing Kendall Manor. Several professional caterers are available to serve an elaborate spread. However, this is an aftermath of new prosperity in Old Eufaula.

When I came to town, before the river was impounded, weddings were just as big and important social occasions as they are today, but the mother-of-the-bride's friends pitched in and did a superb job of spreading chicken salad sandwiches by the dozen, which were frozen for the non-catered reception. They also arranged beautiful flowers. The ladies worked in teams: They each had a basket of tools and their specialties. The results were another gala reception fit for a queen. The florist generally decorated the church.

Today, a society wedding is gauged by the number of tents sheltering the reception. "That was a three-tent affair," an observant woman might tell her friend.

The manner in which the bride and groom leave their reception for the honeymoon is also worthy of comment. Limos are now old hat in Eufaula.

Departure via helicopter or cabin cruiser—if the reception is a lakefront affair—might surprise gleeful guests. All this fanfare is accompanied by a burst of fireworks lighting up the evening sky.

But back to my quandary as to what advice a father gives his betrothed son: Remember that marriage is an honorable estate, just as the minister says. It is also a bedrock institution in Alabama at a time when the family is endangered. A dutiful son gives a father hope for the present and the future.

His marriage, not entered into unadvisedly, is truly cause for joy. It is also society's assurance the family will remain a bedrock institution.

My advice, son, is to be steadfast in your faith. Stay close to the church the rest of your days. Love your devoted wife with all your heart. Be good to each other, as your wise grandfather advised your mother and me.

From this day forward, be faithful to your wife. Think of God first, others second and yourself third. These things done, you can fully expect a wonderful, rewarding—though challenging—life. God bless you and your wife, and all the other young married couples that give us hope for the future and for eternity.

Chapter 14

Cuba, Cairo & Points Between

Editor grateful for Egypt Experience

November 2, 1994

"Experience Egypt. Live it fully for your entire stay. Revel in its changing kaleidoscope of sight and sounds. Become an intimate of its people, culture and history. See Egypt for everything it is—for its Pharaonic splendor, its Eastern mystery and its modern life. And Egypt will become a part of you as it inevitably must . . ."

That is the invitation the American Egyptian Cooperation Foundation extended to me and five other members of the National Newspaper Association: NNA Chairman Michael Parta, *New York Mills (Minn.) Herald*; Sue Dutson, *Millard County Chronicle*, Delta, Utah; Dalton Wright, the *Daily Record*, Lebanon, Mo.; Jay Jackson, *Van Buren County Democrat*, Clinton, Ark.; and Diane Everson, *Edgarton (Wis.) Reporter.*

Flying via Egypt Air from Cairo to New York Friday, Oct. 28, after a five-day study mission in Egypt, I am grateful for having had the opportunity to participate in the study mission. My hope is that in some small way, I too, am a peacemaker, recalling President Bill Clinton's comment, as he flew to Cairo, "to stand by the people who are standing up for Middle East peace."

Above: Joel Smith is ready to board the VIP van that transported a delegation of six NNA members around Cairo in 1994. Below: A highlight of Smith's career was attending an international press conference in Cairo, where he snapped this photograph of President Bill Clinton and Egyptian President Hosni Mubarak.

(I don't have an inflated opinion of my minute role.)

I am touched by the successful efforts of America's, Egypt's and other Mideastern peacemakers' dedication. I stand tall today as an American, after participating in President Bill Clinton and Egyptian President Hosni Mubark's press conference in Cairo. I am proud of our president, even though some other journalists thought it odd for Mr. Clinton to go to the Middle East late in a hard fought mid-term election campaign. Two years ago, President Clinton would say this day (Friday) that he could not have imagined himself visiting Cairo, the signing of the Israeli-Jordanian peace treaty, visiting Kuwait, Saudi Arabia and Syria.

After my sojourn in Egypt, I greatly admire President Mubarak, his ministers of foreign affairs, culture, economy and foreign trade, international cooperation, state for administrative development, his chief of staff for the armed services and his deputy prime minister. We were privileged to meet and interview them. I was impressed with their candor, their appreciation of America, their intellect, knowledge, dedication to the democratization of Egypt and generosity.

Several cabinet members presented us with gifts, papyrus paintings and brass plates. Gen. Sala Halaby, chief of staff, Egyptian Armed Services, presented me with an engraved brass plate handsomely displayed inside a velvet-covered presentation case.

In turn, I presented Minister of Foreign Affairs Amr Moussa with a box of stacked pecans and gifts of Mann's fishing lures to other ministers and hosts. Mr. Moussa, a cordial impressive gentleman, knows Alabama was in "the Old South." He changed his schedule to accommodate us, after it was announced President Clinton would visit Cairo. He is an extremely busy man, planning for Clinton's visit and the Casablanca Conference, yet he was gracious and gave us an up-to-date briefing and answered our questions.

This has been a rewarding experience. (One of my fellow coffee club members said I should have held up a sign reading "the *Eufaula Tribune*: smallest newspaper in the world covering the Clinton-Mubarak press conference.")

I do feel I have been immersed into the Egyptian culture and its history—

past and present. The study mission included a guided tour of the Cairo Museum by its curator and an interview with its director, a dinner cruise down the Nile and a visit to the Pyramids of Giza.

Equally important, I learned first-hand about the Middle East peace effort on several tracks and also the democratization of Egypt, our most staunch friend in the region. I feel we are part of a global society and that there is hope for the present and optimism for the future.

I appreciate visiting ancient-modern Egypt with her great promise. I realized I am fortunate to look beyond the narrow confines of home, although this makes me more deeply appreciative of being an American living in my hometown, Eufaula.

Czechoslovakia trip shows communism's failings

Oct. 2, 1994

"I'm a coffee house philosopher," Vladimir Cinke, our guide, says as we leave Prague en route to Kunta Hora.

"You are too," Bobby Dixon adds, looking at me. My traveling companion refers to the Eufaula Holiday Inn's 10:00 Coffee Club, as our mini-van glides past industrial suburbs.

"This is pre-war Europe here," Cinke says as we pass dingy plants, some plants making adjustments and some that are shut down. "Russia was never interested in waging war with the USA—just with the weaker [countries]. We were the victims to compromise," he says philosophically.

The seasons are changing and pears and apples are ripe on the branches as we enjoy a sunny day driving past fields of sunflowers, maize and pine forests. Bikers pedal along the picturesque road where red cannas, mums and roses bloom inside the tiny gardens fronting quaint homes. It's also the season to "collect" mushrooms in the collective farms. The Czechs can now move out, Cinke says.

In every hamlet, historic churches with onion-shaped, Gothic domes dominate the townscape. "The older people go to church," he explains. "It's a little eccentric for young people."

Reaching Kunta Hora, the old silver mining town the size of Eufaula, we park in front of a handsome, Baroque (1899) school building and visit St. Barbara Church (1390). As we pay admission and admire the cathedral's stained-glass windows—some added as late as 1903 and 1913—I conclude the church is a museum. It is Sunday and the elders in this sleeping town attend early church. Ten percent of the Czechs are Catholic, five percent Protestant and eighty-five percent have no religion.

Kunta Hora's population was formerly 50,000 but the Czech capital, like Atlanta, has attracted Kunta Hora's youth, leaving the town a "living" museum.

Dixon, our wives Mary and Ann and I admire the treasures of Gothic Bohemia in the perfectly preserved medieval town, said to be the most remarkable Bohemian city beside Prague. I wonder if the Bluff City on the Chattahoochee would have become a latter day "Kunta Hora" if our river hadn't been impounded. While our Greek Revival and Victorian architecture isn't very old compared to the towns of Bohemia, it is in far better condition. Their once magnificent downtown centered around an ancient well, and the historic homes decayed almost beyond restoration under communism. Today, tourism is the town's lifeblood.

As we walk past the impressive pest statue, erected to thank God for the town's escaping a pest epidemic, a sign explains they have an historical society. The buildings are in a natural, drab state of preservation. The exception is around the new—since the communists left—square where storefronts are painted in an array of colors. The Queen's Club, a casino, is ensconced inside an historic building.

As we return to Prague, our linguist guide sounds like a conservative: He recalls President Clinton, the Populist, played his sax in a club last November while Ronald Reagan rang a bell in Prague's Wenceslas Square.

The excursion, while pleasurable, is proof-positive communism was a miserable failure.

Cuba struggling with shrinking Russian ties

November 4, 1990

"If all those people get on one airline, it would be the Great Goose created by Howard Hughes," quipped a fellow journalist as we waited in the Miami airport en route to Cuba. Most were Cubans returning to Havana after visiting relatives in the States.

Many carried mesh bags filled with patent medicine and numerous articles purchased from Wal-Mart—items scarce in their homeland. One woman, carrying a bunch of artificial flowers, explained she would place them on her father's grave. It was her first visit to Cuba in twenty-five years, since taking refuge in the United States.

The Charter flight on a Haitian plane leased from Peru was uneventful, but seeing the masses of people crowded along the fence and outside Jose Martin Airport, watching anxiously for relatives, was heart stirring. Many had come to welcome family members they hadn't seen since the revolution when Castro came to power.

"Poco! Poco!" an immigration official commented to our host, Jose Delgado, the personable staff member with the Minister of Exterior Relations Department, as I filled out still another form.

Suddenly, our group of ten Alabama journalist was immersed into the communist Cuban culture. Cuba is a treasury of mobile antique cars, our guide commented, as we surveyed the '50s model Fords and Chevrolets in the airport parking lot. The Tourismo Taxis were Russian-made.

The beautiful island of Cuba, where Christopher Columbus landed in 1492, has two million people and is struggling now that economic ties with Russia are shrinking. Many of my opinions changed after spending last week in Cuba.

Travel to Cuba is extremely limited for Americans—limited to journalists and those doing research. U.S. sanctions that isolate Cuba economically deprive it of U.S. dollars, even though our "hard" currency is circulated freely. Those sanctions are working; yet, I wonder, after interviews with

Cuban economics and governmental officials, how long communism will last in that depressed Caribbean island nations.

Key dates help us understand Cuba today:

1492: Discovered by Columbus

1510: Spanish colonization begun by Diego Velazquez

1519: Founding of Havana

1868: Beginning of the Wars of Independence

1902: Beginning of The Republic

1959: Triumph of the revolution when Castro came to power

1961: Literacy campaign. Officials now claim virtually everyone "writes and reads."

1976: Socialist constitution

"Mr. Imperialist," I read from a billboard on our first tour of Havana, "we are not afraid of you." The billboards communicated one message, the Cuban people another.

As we toured Old Havana, focusing on three squares, we experienced another side of Cuba. There was music in the square; it was "Saturday in the bazaar" and children, many dressed in costumes, were having a great time. Venders were selling fruits and vegetables in outdoor markets.

Old Havana has 190 historic buildings and eighty-eight monuments. The seventeenth century Square of Arms has two imposing buildings: the Intendencia Palace and the Palace of the Captains (now the Museum of the City of Havana). A Cuban baroque touch contrasts with the light, spacious galleries around the inner patio filled with tropical plants.

The handsome statue of Columbus in the palace patio prompted our guide to quote the great discoverer: He said Cuba was the most beautiful island "eyes have conceived."

We were also informed the island was ruled from this palace from 1898 until 1902, when the Platt Amendment gave the United States the right to interfere whenever U.S. Interests were affected.

"Many presidents took all the money," our guide added. Batista, first a general, then president, brought about "the generation of Fidel." While another sign proclaimed "Socialism or Death," one Cuban said, "Cubans want to change whatever is not running properly. Some of the socialist methods in some fields do not work out here very well."

Would Cubans like to see a change from socialism? "A minimum number of people—we Cubans call them worms—would like to see a change," one Cuban journalist answered, and after thirty-one years, he continued, "there are those living on the other side of the channel."

A philosopher, Angel Thomas Gonzalez, added, "We never had the opportunity to learn democracy in Latin America. We try to think of socialism as a very European way: We are Caribbean's [way]."

After spending a week in Cuba, I'm convinced the masses are suffering, yet governmental officials, Communist Party members and foreign visitors and tourists—and there are many—enjoy a good life. The European and Canadian tourists Castro's government is courting might very well communicate to the unhappy masses that capitalism offers a better way of life.

"Are you a journalist searching news or bringing money to our king?" the elevator operator at our circe-1939 hotel, El Presidente, asked, looking up from his book, *Babbit.* "The king won't let Eastern block change catch on here," he told another Alabama journalist.

I am, and was, a journalist who gathered enough news to write a book about Cuba filled with many conflicting chapters.

Brazilians cheered as if Pelé were playing

August 25, 1996

I'm glad I honored my commitment made more than a year ago to attend the seventeenth World Methodist Conference in Rio de Janeiro, Brazil, Aug. 7–15. I accepted the bishop's appointment as a delegate only weeks before my open-heart surgery.

This experience warmed my heart, and a member of my Sunday school class says I look none the worse from the experience.

Riding in to Rio from the airport late at night, my wife and I were partially screened from miles of Rio's slums, but finally seeing the lighted

130-foot statue of Christ the Redeemer high above Corcovado Mountain was inspiring. And so was seeing the magnificent mountains and the lighted Copacabana Beach setting for our hotel that had known better days.

Taking communion during the opening ceremony at Rio Centro with 3,000 Methodists from around the world was equally inspiring. Bishop Richard Looney from the South Georgia Conference was one of the "servers from the nations."

Also inspiring was joining 15,000 Brazilian Methodists who packed a covered stadium on Saturday afternoon for a three-hour celebration. As the Rev. Karl Stegall, Montgomery First United Methodist minister, says: "You would have though that the Brazilian Christians were cheering for Pelé in the 125,000-capacity soccer stadium next door."

Some of the Brazilians had spent more than thirty hours traveling by bus to Rio. Remember, Brazil is larger than the United States. Many of the people from all over Brazil were so excited I'm sure they didn't hear half what the speakers said, and neither did I. I don't understand Portuguese, but "Great is Thy Faithfulness" sung in Brazil's native language is magnificent when led by a choir composed of 1,000 children and adults dressed in colorful robes. The delegates from the four corners of the world and visiting Brazilians spoke many different languages, but they silently prayed in the language of love as they gave their gifts totaling $206,000 to fund the Brazilian Street Children Ministries.

The Brazilian Bishops conducted the highly-charged rally and Bishop Adriel de Souza Maia delivered the main message, saying his hope was that the world conference, "in the splendor of its accomplishment, be a mature, historical event to ponder and deliberate over the advance of the World Methodist Church.

"All around us the changes and innovations are coming about hastily. Technology and science progress by themselves, boldly and visibly. Confronting this mosaic of growth, the Methodist Church must explore new paths, be sensible, creative and flexible, opening new routes to bring the message of the redemption of Jesus Christ to a perplexed man. However, the church must hold fast its inherent principles."

Dr. Donald English, World Methodist Council executive committee chairman, in his keynote address asked: "Be sensitive to God's will as it is made known to us," and he urged us "to be children of obedience. There is a need for the church to set a different example."

"We must see the world with the outlook of Jesus," added Dr. Joe Hale, World Methodist Council general secretary. "We have learned that peace is a moving target that has to be moved in every generation."

"Could we replace the ancient heritage of war with a new heritage of peace?" he asks. Certainly, the World Methodist Conference is a move in that direction. I was blessed to be a delegate.

No fanfares celebrate Cuban communism

November 11, 1990

Just before voting in Tuesday's election, I heard the stirring "Fanfare for Freedom" played on Peach State Public Radio. To my knowledge, no composer has written a "Fanfare for Communism." After spending a week in communist Cuba, I know why: There's little to stir one's soul in a communist country.

It's only ninety miles from Miami to Havana, across a turquoise channel, but the United States and Cuba are poles apart with the U.S. Treasury continuing to impose an economic embargo against Castro's Cuba.

After spending the week of Oct. 19–26 in Havana, it is my considered opinion—following meetings with numerous government officials and talking with rank-and-file Cubans—communism isn't working in Cuba. It's not that President Fidel Castro and his Freedom Fighters haven't tried hard enough to make socialism work.

The economy is extremely depressed, and predictions are things will get worse before they get better. Cuba is having to depend less and less on the Soviet Union since the USSR's economy is also in shambles. Food is rationed and personal gasoline use has been cut thirty percent as a result of declining Soviet oil deliveries to the island.

Even so, Dr. Jose Luis Rodriquez, deputy director of economics, says, "Capitalism is not an option in the future," while admitting, "We have not developed a perfect socialist society."

He and other officials were more open that I had expected, while conferring with us ten Alabama journalists. "We have to adjust to reality," Dr. Rodriquez continues. "We have to deal with some level of private property and private workers."

He was speaking to us in a Spanish count's former mansion. And as was the custom, we were served thick, sweet coffee in demitasse cups. Eight percent of the land is privately owned, he explains, and 28,000 small firms have private workers in the cities.

Joint ventures, with foreign partners, are much talked about, especially in the state-operated tourism industry. The government is building a modern stadium and athletic complex and "five-star" hotels to accommodate the 1992 Pan-Am Games.

I predict socialism will undergo some radical changes during the next few years. A case in point: "We have to adjust to reality," Dr. Rodriquez says. "We have to deal with some level of private property and private workers."

Cuba would like to have "a solution to the problem: to reestablish a good relationship with the U.S., but not as formerly," the dean of the Havana University Journalism School says candidly. Oscar Oramas, vice-minister for foreign affairs, speaking in an ornate conference room, ensconced inside another former private mansion, says, "We have been accused of so many things . . . of being a proxy of the Soviet Union. Now, we don't want to follow the Soviet Union's path." The former U.N. ambassador observes, "I don't see in the very near future a change [in U.S. relations] nor a more flexible attitude toward Cuba."

The most negative thing I found in Cuba was the press. Visiting with journalists from *Granma*, the Communist Party's national newspaper, radio and television, was demoralizing. The newspaper converted to weekly publication because the Russians cut their newsprint supply drastically. The Cuban writers made it clear they would never publish anything that would "damage the Revolution."

"We are guardians of the Revolution," one explains proudly. We Alabama journalists went away, resenting the Cuban writers calling us their colleagues. They don't have freedom of the press. And they don't mind.

No, communism hasn't inspired a composer to write a stirring piece of music interspersed with flourishes of trumpets, but if I could write music I could compose a dirge for Castro's handmaidens. The suffering Cuban masses deserve better than what communism has to offer.

Memory of Haiti poverty haunting

September 28, 1994

Like people of good will everywhere, I was relieved the entry of Americans into Haiti wasn't the bloody confrontation it could have been. Of course, I'm not naïve and didn't believe our "humanitarian assistance" wouldn't be costless in terms of lives.

While I didn't relish the thought of another police mission for U.S. troops, I do identify with the plight of the poor Haitian people. That may sound odd coming from a white, Anglo-Saxon from the American South, but I've been interested in that tiny republic that shares about one-third of the island of Hispaniola with the Dominican Republic ever since visiting the West Indies in the late 1950s.

Two friends and I used to Southeastern Peanut Association's Miami convention as a springboard to visit the World's Fair in Cuidad Trujillo in the Dominican Republic. Let me hasten to explain to our young readers who won't find Cuidad Trujillo on the map. It didn't disappear, but after the benevolent dictator's demise, the good people of Dominica renamed the beautiful city overlooking the emerald waters of the Caribbean to Santo Domingo.

Unlike the Barbour County Fair, nobody came to the tiny island's World Fair—except a handful of other adventurous souls and me. I was fascinated with the Caribbean's islands in the sun. Our plane touched down first in

Port-au-Prince where we vacationed in nearby, affluent Pationville—before reaching our final destination.

It's been more than thirty-seven years since I set foot in Haiti, but I remember it like it were yesterday. Why oh why did I convince my affable friends we should take a side trip to Haiti, en route to the World's Fair?, I wondered as we passed through customs and our taxi rode us through the most pitiful capital city imaginable.

The only modern, inviting facility in sight was the gambling casino. Papa Doc's presidential palace didn't look like any pictures of palaces I'd ever seen. In 1957 during my visit, Francois Duvalier, popularly known as Papa Doc, was president and had his own dictatorial style. There hasn't been a democracy there since Haiti won its independence from France in 1804, the first country in the Americas, after the United States, to win freedom from colonial rule.

As we know from watching the 6:00 news, the great majority of Haitians are of African descent. Some five percent make up a powerful mulatto minority who include the elite. I was fascinated hearing the Haitians speak beautiful French.

I was also impressed with Haitian folk art. The tiny country had a movement going to teach the natives to unleash their creativity, painting and sculpting interesting figures from native woods. My first exposure to the Haitian arts was the first evening poolside at our tropical resort. I spied a young artist, standing quietly nearby, just beyond the lush landscape, holding up two folk paintings. Later, in a mountainous area we haggled with the natives and bought impressive sculptures, which I later displayed along with my folk paintings at my beach house.

We went native on a Saturday night and attended a voodoo ritual. Led by a priest, called a houngan, the worshipers invoked the Loa by drumming, dancing, singing and finally the priest spitting rum first on a fire and then on the dancers. It may have been contrived for the meager tourist trade, but the dancers were ecstatic: In a trance, they danced until a state of exhaustion. Voodoo is the early religion of Haiti, and some vestiges of such cults were still practiced in Eufaula when I came here thirty-six years ago.

Running out of travelers checks, we made a trip to the bank in Port-au-Prince. This was an experience: The banker told us we couldn't scratch through our local bank's name and add our American bank's name—a practice common back home then. Not to worry, a department store executive cashed our checks, which he mailed back to the U.S. When I mentioned he didn't really know our checks were good, he shrugged and replied, "It's only money." This transaction, like the voodoo dancing and the starkness of the capital city, impressed me.

I saw pitiful women squatting by the roadside cooking food to sell. I'd never seen such poverty. The Haitians' plight has bothered me ever since.

Across the mountain range in the Dominican Republic things were considerably better. The resort hotel was on a par with Miami's, the trees along the seaside boulevard were pruned, and the World's Fair buildings were impressive. They were built by foreign businesses or governments and designed to serve as a city hall, library, etc. once the fair closed down. I saw "dancing waters" keeping time with music at the World's Fair. I also used some of my high school Spanish to tell our taxi driver to take us to Christopher Columbus's tomb.

Signs everywhere—even on the end of the diving board—saluted their benevolent dictator and I felt I was shadowed because I had little enough sense to list my occupation, newspaper editor. Dictators like the press even less than American presidents.

I'm staying tuned in now in the wake of the Haitians' gunfight with the Marines. I read about the Haitians, spurred on by the firefight with our Marines, ransacking police stations, carrying off guns. Where will it all end? Will our service become another army of occupation as they did in 1915, staying nineteen years?

History and religion come into focus in Turkey

July 8, 2001

This summer I've continued my quest to experience the world, a boyhood dream. Last July, I packed a small American flag to take on my trip to Scotland since I had misgivings about spending the glorious Fourth of July in another country.

The Alumni College tour director had scheduled an Italian dinner the night of July 4, 2000. To my delight we were surprised with a first-class All-American Fourth of July dinner at our historic Stirling, Scotland hotel. Happily, the B. W.'s and my thirty-fifth anniversary cruise in the Mediterranean ended in time to be home for the Fourth.

I agree with Dr. Roy Crowe's remark he made at the July Fourth Community Service: "America is the greatest nation on earth, those who have gone out of the country know." Yes, I do, but my experience from world travel has also taught me the world's many peoples in other lands love their countries, too.

At this late date in my lifetime as my childhood dreams continue to come true, I'm beginning to understand something about global stewardship. I'm following the coverage of Milosevic, the former Yugoslav president's, appearance before the U.N. court in The Hague, the home of my former college roommate. I'm also concerned the Middle East cease-fire seems to be failing.

Our seven-day Mediterranean cruise and two-day Venice extension was an opportunity to relax on shipboard and to experience some more of our fascinating world. The weeklong international cruise was a compromise because it didn't include Istanbul, a place I've dreamed of visiting. However, I now have an appreciation for the ancient coast of Turkey and the Turkish people.

Turkey may have been my favorite country. Kusadasi was our gateway to Ephesus, a city created by the Ionians in the eleventh century B.C. and later taken over by the ever-expanding Roman Empire. Perhaps it was only logical I would like the Turkish people after a splendid guided tour of Ephesus.

It's one of the greatest reconstructed sites in the ancient world. This is the region that also saw the likes of Cleopatra, Mark Anthony, the Virgin Mary and John the Apostle. Kusadasi and its citizens are imbued with charm. Our port of call has grown into a sprawling tourist center because of its natural and man made beauty and because of its close proximity to Ephesus's unbelievable ruins.

I was struck with Turkey's natural beauty as the Splendor of the Seas docked in the colorful port of Kusadasi. I always observe the flora and the fauna and was impressed with the pine trees that look similar to our short-leaf pines, but most especially with the fig trees that grow wild along the roadways. Seeing their green fruit and the ripe peaches in the markets made me want to plant some fig and peach trees out at the Fourth Estate.

The History and Religion of Rome was the title of our fascinating tour. After a drive through the beautiful landscape we passed by the Magnesia Gate and entered the fascinating administrative section of Ancient Ephesus. The excavation of these ruins is fascinating.

It isn't hard to pause while looking over the classic marble ruins and imagine what a magnificent city it must have been during its golden days, with its Apartment House with five terraces, the Steam Baths of Scolastika, the Temple of Hadrian and the impressive Library of Celsus. Obviously this ancient city of 250,000 enforced its building codes.

Soon after being settled by the Ionians they built a tremendously impressive marble temple overlooking the sea to honor their goddess, Artemis. The temple was four times larger than the Parthenon and was one of the Seven Wonders of the World.

Sailors dropping anchor at this ancient port of call were required to bathe at the harbour bath before coming into the proud city. At the beginning of Christianity, the Ephesians were still worshipping their goddess, Artemis. It has been written that Saint John and the Virgin Mary spent their last days there. We visited the House of the Virgin Mary, where she reputedly spent the last days of her life. The site was made famous by the travels of Pope Paul VI and Pope John Paul II. Outside is the Fountain of Our Lady

During a 2001 Mediterranean cruise, Joel and Ann Smith visited the ruins of the ancient city of Ephesus, where they are pictured in front of the library façade.

where the faithful take water from the fountain at the foundation. This is only twenty minutes away from Ephesus.

I was also impressed with the ruins of St. John's Basilica, which was a great church in its day. The wind was blowing when I visited the impressive site, which Pope Paul also visited in 1967. St. John's grave is marked with four small classic columns and a marker reading St. Jean in Mazari The

Tomb of St. John. Writers say St. John died in Ephesus.

Ali, our knowledgeable guide, took us to a steam engine train museum for a delightful luncheon outdoors. Musicians and dancers in native Turkish dress entertained as we enjoyed barbecue and caramel flan for dessert.

A lecture on carpet making was interesting, and we learned handmade carpets are passed from generation to generation. Our guide Ali's wife had eight carpets in her dowry. I was so impressed with the traditional art of Turkish weaving and the quality of the carpets that I badgered Ann into buying a small runner, which I tucked away in my carry-on bag and dragged through customs.

Turkey enjoys 330 days of sunshine, and from the way the tourists were spending, I believe the economy is strong. Certainly, Kusadasi has some of the best salesmen anywhere on the globe I've visited. They are attractive, gracious and they speak excellent English. I didn't have the heart to bargain too much because they have so much class.

Kusadasi is thriving because cruise ships regularly dock there so visitors from all over the world can see the magnificent, unbelievable ruins of nearby Ephesus–the result of one hundred years of excavations.

Turkey is one of the most beautiful, fascinating places I've visited. I loved the ancient treasures and the beautiful arts and crafts in the shops near the waterfront. I also liked their cultured and affable people.

Index

A

Abraham, Pegge 90
Adams, Albert 276
Adams, Anne 220
Admiral Moorer Middle School 203, 206
Airport Restaurant 94
Alabama Academy of Honor 215
Alabama Bancorp 31
Alabama Breneau 122
Alabama Citizens' Committee for Better Schools 55
Alabama College at Montevallo 180
Alabama Department of Archives and History 105, 129
Alabama Federation of Women's Clubs 55
Alabama Highway Department 155
Alabama Historical Association Newsletter 56
Alabama Historical Commission 100, 102, 106, 129, 135
Alabama History and Heritage Festival 61
Alabama Legislature 38, 109, 151, 153, 161, 162
Alabama Power Co. 45, 96
Alabama Press Association 60, 261, 264, 267, 269
Alabama Sports Hall of Fame 67
Alabama State Capitol 107
Alabama Supreme Court 38, 40
Alabama United States Volunteer Infantry 131

ALAGA Antique Car Club 222
Allen, Jim 204
Allied Sports Distributors 240
Along Broad Street 54, 59, 60, 121
American Buildings Co. 41, 155
American Institute of Architects 44
Andrews, George 37, 194
Ann Lowe Originals 207
Ante-Bellum Mansions of Alabama 129
Anthony, Mark 340
Apalachicola 68, 232, 237
Archibald, Charlie 35
Arinder, Max 88
Arlington National Cemetery 203
Askew, Frances 220
Auburn University 38, 44, 45, 115
Aunt Mamie 176–177
Austin, Will 99

B

Babb, Inez 308
Bachman, Fred 23
Backtracking in Barbour County 77, 107
Bainbridge Boat Club 186
Baker, Alpheus 119
Baker, Russell 95
Bankhead, J. H. 36
Barbour County Courthouse 147
Barbour County Fair 336
Barbour County Hospital 187, 224, 307, 311
Barbour County Improvement Association 53

Barbour County Medical Society 224
Barbour County Probate Office 89
Barbour County School 32
Barbour, James 118
Barkmeyer, Alma 286
Barr, Bob 243
Barron, N. G. 33
BASS 63, 65
Battle, Cullen Andrews 119, 120
Battle, Emory 72
Bay County High School 184, 285
Beasley, Jere 38, 153
Beauvoir Country Club 176
Becker, Jane Godfrey 287
Beck, M. L. 172
Berte, Neal 317
Bevill Center, The 45
Bible Training College 275
Big Bass Capital of the World 63
Birmingham City Auditorium 156
Birmingham Country Club 164
Birmingham News 120, 159, 167, 253, 258, 278
Birmingham-Southern College 31, 32, 315
Bishop, Sanford 243
Black Belt 59
Blackmon, Charles 61
Blackmon, Mrs. Ray 117
Blackmon, Ray 16–18, 117
Blair, Joe Neal 23
Bland, Bettie 93
Blinov, Ben 26, 33
Blinov, Mary Lou 92
Blinov, Veniamin Dmitri 26, 88

Blondheim and Mixon 44
Blondheim, Charlie 43
Blondheim, Martha 83, 92, 116
Bloomer, John W. 120
Bloom, Sig 252, 253
Blount, Winton 122, 156, 204
Bluff City Bachelors Club 71
Bluff City Barber Shop 159
Bluff City Inn 14, 49, 85, 91, 94, 185, 186, 266
  Barber Shop 156
Booker, Tina 64
Bowden, Ben 99
Bowden, Bobby 276
Bowden, Mary Ann 99
Bowick, Bobby 149
Bowman, Angie 221
Boyer, Jo 224
Boyer, John 43
Boyette, Dick 23, 71, 88, 175, 300
Boyette, Jane 23
Boyette, Richard 309
Bradley, Jim 242
Bradley, W. C. 247
Bragg, Braxton 119
Brewer, Albert 150, 151, 217
Brierfield 107
Brooks, Roland 280
Brown, Carl 279
Brown, Elizabeth Via 207
Brown, Jeff 212
Brown, Jerry 61, 213
Brown, Leroy 64
Brown, Mack 145
Brown, Molly 167
Bryant, Bear 276
Buck Abbot's Café 266
Buckingham, Nash 61
Bullock, Edward Courtenay 48, 97, 107, 116, 117
Burch, Jesse 231
Burger, Warren E. 229
Burnham, Denson 66
Burtz, Bobby 92
Bush, George H. W. 209, 272
Bush, George W. 200, 209, 272
Bush, Laura 211
Butler, Pierce 25
Buzzard Baptists 64
Byrd, George 231

Byrd, Robert C. 229

C

Cabinet Room 122
Café Dupont 165
Callahan, John W. 247
Calvary Baptist Church 63, 64
Camerata Chorus 88, 94
Cameron, John 267
Camp David 206
Camp Rucker 195
Carnegie Library 56, 90, 118
Carolinas 119
Carter, Dan T. 38, 161
Carter, Jimmy 225
Carter, O. B. 122, 158
Castro, Fidel 271
Catherine II 26
Cedar Creek 120
Centennial Commemoration Pageant 116
Chamber of Commerce 69, 73, 78, 88, 234
Chambers, Solita Hortman 93
Champion, Becky 243
Chancellorsville 120
Chapman, Jacque 23
Charleston 99
Charoen Pokphand USA 200
Chattahoochee Indian Heritage Center 111, 113
Chattahoochee Poochie 91
Chattahoochee River 18, 22, 35, 49, 67, 68, 69, 79, 87, 91, 93, 118, 235–237, 237
Chewalla Creek 231
Chewalla Mill 234
Chewalla Motel 174
Chewalla Restaurant 91
Chickamauga 119
Chief Eufaula 113
Children of the Confederacy 97, 117, 186
Choctawhatchee 96
Choctawhatchee Regional Library Service 55
Christ Child Circle 40, 55, 94
Cinke, Vladimir 328
Citizen of the Year 55
Citizens Bank 50, 216
City Board of Education 121

City Hall 134
City of Eufaula, The 241
Civilian Air Patrol 115
Civil Rights Movement 52
Civil War 107, 109–111, 126–131, 131, 235
Clapham 275
Clark Compound 51
Clark, Dot 97
Clark, Floyd 88
Clark, Fred M. 49–51, 78, 97
Clark, James S. 38, 49, 216, 217
Clark, Jimmy 23, 46, 91, 94, 122, 155, 156, 215, 216, 239, 266
Clay, Gen. Lucious 37
Clayton 109, 159, 208
Clayton Anti-Trust Act 36
Clayton, Gen. 119
Clayton, Henry D. Jr. 36, 117, 119, 162
Clayton Highway 155
Clayton, Jewel Gladys 117
Clayton, Lee Johnston III 19, 20–22
Clayton, Preston C. 19, 38, 59, 88, 93, 161, 218, 220
Clayton Record 207
Clayton, Victoria 117
Clearings in the Thicket: An Alabama Humanities Reader 61, 213
Cleopatra 340
Cleveland, Attorney Grady 117
Cleveland, Mary 117
Clinton, President Bill 272, 325, 326, 327
Clio 31
Clothier, Jane Bailey 286
Cloverdale High School 204
Cloverleaf Salve 31
Coast Guardsmen 115
Coffee Springs 166
Cold War 206
Cole, Lewis 208
Cole, T. C. "Dooley" 34, 35
College Hill 21, 85, 97
Columbia University School of Journalism 54
Columbus 13, 64
Columbus Ledger-Enquirer 112, 136, 255, 288

Columbus Symphony 88
Comer, B. B. 31
Comer, Braxton Bragg 36
Comer, Donald 46
Comer, Donald III 23, 32
Comer, Edward 16, 33
Comer, George Legare 37
Comer, Jane Stephens 32, 46
Comer, Montine 29
Commercial Club 78
Confederate Museum 116
Confederates, Confederacy
79, 97, 103, 104, 116,
116–118, 118, 131, 186,
233
Conner, Gwen 222
Conner, Jim 275
Conner, Louise 70, 212, 214
Cook, Caroline 117
Copeland, Caroline Elizabeth
18–20
Copeland, William Preston
19, 29
Cope, Motier 89
Cordell, Woodrow 289
Corps of Engineers 186, 216,
236
Cossey, G. H. 217
Country Club 34
Couric, Charles Maturon 220
Couric Homestead 165
Couric, John 222
Couric, Katie 199, 220, 223
Couric, Pauline 222
Couric, Willie Copeland 222,
262, 305
Cowikee Mills 32, 92, 157,
234
Cowikee Mills Band 194
Cowikee Mills Educational
and Charitable Foundation
106
Cowikee Park 90
Crawford, Thurston 241
Creek Indians 111
Creek Indian War 98
Cronenberg, Allen 135
Cross Creek Plantation 99
Crowe, Roy 339
Crow, Magnolia 89
Cruise, Capt. James 56
Cuidad Trujillo 336
Culpepper, Curly 140
Culpepper, Tom 35, 174, 256

Curio, Col. Bob 126

D
Daily World 249
Dale's Lounge 257
Dallas 79, 151
Dalton 119
Daniel, Rodger Jr. 145
Daughters of the American
Revolution 222
Dauphin Way United Meth-
odist Church 322
Davis, Jefferson 90, 104, 107,
117, 145
Davis, Winnie 90, 117
Dawes, Jabbo 299
Dean, Jeanne 106
Dean, Jennie Kendall 97,
104, 116
Dean, L. Y. III 105
Dean-Page Hall 79
Dean, Yank IV 23, 87, 90, 93
Declaration of Independence
131
DeGraffenreid, Ryan 159
DeLesseps, Edgar H. 249
Delgado, Jose 330
DeLoach, John 277
DeMille, Cecil B. 116
Demopolis High School 40
Dent, Annie Young 117
Dent, Hubert 117
Department of Transporta-
tion 75
desegregation 81, 96, 121–
122, 156–158, 265, 272
Deutsche Bank 199
Dialysis Clinic 222
"Dixie" 117
Dixie Shoe 155
Dixon, Billy 88
Dixon, Bobby 88, 328
Dixon, Mac 252
Dixon, Sharon 65
Dodson, Alan 64
Dogwood Inn 94
Dole, Senator Bob 270
Dollar, Johnny 149
Dozier, Albert 78
Drake, Basil 286
Duke University 219
Dutch Town 16
Dutson, Sue 325

E
Earnest, O. B. (Buck) 243
Eblen, Bing 87
EBSCO Industries 31
EB&T 90
Edwards, Marvin 13, 73, 92,
97, 117, 128
897th Bomb Squadron 123
Eiland, Fred 70
Eisenhower, Dwight D. 114,
285
1103rd Corps Support Bat-
talion 125
1128th Transportation Com-
pany 56
Ellisor, Joe 77
Ellisor, Thad 77
Elton B. Stephens Expressway
32
Elton B. Stephens Library 32
Embers Restaurant 72, 186
Emfinger, John 64
Encyclopedia of Southern Cul-
ture 198
England, Gordon 206
English, Donald 333
Enterprise 63
Eppes, Nell 92
Eufaula Adolescent Adjust-
ment Center 155
Eufaula Adolescent Center 40
Eufaula Alcoholics Anony-
mous 94
Eufaula Arbor Day 46
Eufaula Art Association 42
Eufaula Arts Council 32
Eufaula Carnegie Library 94,
128
Eufaula Carnegie Library
Board 55
Eufaula Chamber of Com-
merce 106
Eufaula City Auditorium 94
Eufaula City Council 50,
100, 239
Eufaula City Hall 45
Eufaula City Schools 121,
122
Eufaula City Schools Board
203
Eufaula Coffee Club 66
Eufaula Community Center
65

Eufaula Cotton Mill 234
Eufaula Country Club 36
Eufaula's Downtown Action
  Plan 100
Eufaula's Favorite Recipes 88
Eufaula Geriatric Center 18
*Eufaula's Gracious Lady:
  Caroline Copeland Clayton*
  59, 95
Eufaula Heritage Association
  42, 56, 77, 94, 105, 128,
  134, 222
Eufaula High Band 117
Eufaula High School 121,
  125, 186, 216
Eufaula High Times 59
Eufaula Historical Museum
  105, 256
Eufaula Historic District De-
  sign Review Manual 100
Eufaula Historic Preservation
  Commission 100
Eufaula Housing Author-
  ity 49
Eufaula Jaycees 67, 89
Eufaula Little Theatre 17
Eufaula Men's Chorus 94
Eufaula Military Co. 19
Eufaula Milling Co. 87
Eufaula National Wildlife Ref-
  uge 67, 92, 94, 216, 239
Eufaula News 130
Eufaula Pilgrimage 56, 89,
  103, 127
Eufaula Planning Commis-
  sion 49
Eufaula Post Office 44, 45
Eufaula Recreation Depart-
  ment 67
Eufaula Regency 107, 108,
  233
Eufaula Renaissance 49
Eufaula Rifles 119
Eufaula Sesquicentennial 38
Eufaula Tribune 7, 18, 54, 60,
  65, 88, 95, 118, 130, 215
"Eufaula Waltz" 89
Eufaula Wharf Company 241
Euphrates River 58
European Common Market
  137
Everett, Terry 243, 271
Everson, Diane 325

Exterior Relations Department 330
Ezzell, Donnie 280

F

Falwell, Jerry 177
Fannie, The 241
Faulkner, Jimmy 137, 159
Fay, Marjorie 286
Fendall Hall 79, 91, 106, 135
Ferguson, Ma 144
54th Alabama Infantry Regi-
  ment 119
Finding our Fathers 318
fireballs 132
First Alabama Infantry Regi-
  ment 119
First Baptist Church 36, 61,
  77, 80, 129
First Federal Savings and
  Loan 50
First Methodist Church 55
First Presbyterian Church 43,
  80, 87
First United Methodist
  Church 39, 51, 57, 85, 87,
  219
Flewellen, Avner 117
Flewellen, Lenora Salter 62
Flewellen, Louise Sparks 29
Flewellen, Mary Fontaine 19
Flewellen, Robert H. 55,
  58–62, 93, 95, 112, 117,
  121
Flewellen, Robin 62
Flewellen, Sarah Hardaway
  117
Flewellen, Williams T. 19
Flint Waterway 237
Florida Flambeau 185
Florida State University 159,
  179, 184, 278
Folmar, Emory 211
Folsom, Big Jim 159
Ford, Gerald 226
Fort Rucker 285
Fort Sumter 108
Fortune's Seafood 87
Four-H Club 193
497th Bomb Group 123
Foy, Carrie Ellen 204
Foy, Humphrey 96
Foy, Mary Ross 23, 29, 233
Foy, Ross 88

France 115
Franklin, Ben 272
Friends of Fendall Hall 135
From the Bluff 60
Frost, Anderson 53
Frost, David Jr. 51–54
Frost, Fred C. 54
Frost, Major 53
Ft. Benning 57
Ft. Bragg 125
Ft. Gaines 63, 64, 186, 216,
  227, 231, 234, 241, 243,
  245
Ft. Lauderdale 179
Ft. Mitchell 111, 112, 113,
  231
Ft. Pickens 108
Ft. Pillow 119

G

Gallup Poll's Ten Most Ad-
  mired 33
Garbo, Greta 71
Garden Club of Eufaula 55
Garrison, Bill 88
Garrison, Ed 223
Garrison, Frankie 117
Garrison, Margaret 94, 220
Geneva County 25, 176
Geneva County Reaper 159,
  167, 185, 249, 258, 271,
  278
George, Rebecca 286
Georgetown 109, 202, 230
George, Walter F. 245
George W. Miller, The 241
Georgia 19, 119
Georgia State Democratic
  Executive Committee 227
Georgia Tech 44
Gettysburg 120, 131
Gingell, George 13
Goggans, Harry 91
Gone With the Wind 183
Gonzalez, Angel Thomas 332
Good Times, The 95
Goodwin, John 232
Gore, Al 272
Governors Park 92
Graddy, Becky 23
Grant, U. S. 117, 131
Graves, E. H. 78
Graves, Hamp 13, 35
Gray, Fred 53

Gray, Henry B. III 218
Gray, Mary 23
Gray's Anatomy 19
Great Depression 181, 234, 284
Greer, Murray 35
Grierson, Benjamin H. 85, 109, 117, 126–128, 233
Griffin, Glenn 33
Griggs, Mittie 92, 308
Grizzard, Lewis 188–189, 281
Growing Up 95
Grubb, Archie 24, 33, 67
Grubb, Bill 21
Grubbs, Haywood 72

H

Habitat for Humanity 40
Hagood, John 24, 94
Hague, Parthenia Antoinette 127
Halaby, Sala 327
Hall, Jane 90
Hammond, Ralph 129
Harbert Building 317
Harbour, Al 50, 58
Harper, Jennifer 206
Harrison, Sherry 23
Harrison's Mill 109
Hart, Franklin A. 37
Hart, John 106
Hart-Milton House 106
Harvey, Paul 79
Hasty, Son 34
Hatfield, Bitsey 140
Head, William 14
Heflin, Howell 70, 272
Henry County 231, 288
Heritage of Barbour County, Alabama 53
Hester, Gaston 23
Hicks, Jerald 90
Highland Bank 31
Hines, Henry 64
Hines, Jeff 64
Hinton, Eleanor 23
Historic American Buildings Survey 106
Historic Chattahoochee Commission 155
Historic Preservation Commission 134
Hobbs, Truman 268

Holiday Inn 16, 33, 42, 88, 239, 266, 328
Hollins College 54, 55
Holmes, Louie 139
Holy Redeemer Catholic Church 85
Holy Trinity 236
Hortman, Solita 186
Hotel Washington 157
House of Representatives 137, 161
Houston, Billy 40
Houston, Celeste 40
Houston, Gorman 20, 46, 116, 186, 252
Houston, Gorman III 39, 219
Houston, J. Gorman Jr. 38, 40, 106, 218, 220
Houston, Martha 23, 219
Houston, Mildred Vance 23, 39–41, 219
Houston, Toni 23
Huff, Dale 89
Hughes, Howard 330
Humann, Jane 48
Humann, Phil 48
Humphrey, Hubert H. 156
Huntingdon College 163
Hurst, Joe 226

I

Iacocca, Lee 41
Ides of March 21
Indians, Indian Wars 109, 111–113
Infant Sock Mill 124
Ingram, Bob 139, 143
Introduction of War Personalities 117
Iraq 57
Irby, Paula 62
Irby, Russell 21
Irwinton 109
Irwinton Bridge Co 232
Irwin, William 231
It's a Wonderful Life 64
Ivey, Kay 211
Iwo Jima 37, 123

J

Jackson, Bill 33
Jackson, Jay 325
Jackson, John 94, 279

James, Dave 280
Jaxon, Jay 45, 50, 54, 60, 117, 125, 135, 200, 221
Jeff Davis Hotel 97
Jefferies, Martha 252
Jelks, William D. 30, 35
Jennings, Bobby 48, 271
John McNab Bank 78
Johnson, Anderson 53
Johnson and Wales University 99
Johnson, Frank M., Jr. 121, 158
Johnson Outdoors 240
Johnson, Robert 94
Johnston Jewelry 89
Johnston, Young 216
Jones, Emmett 15
Jones, Frances D. 223
Jones, J. J. 178
Joy, Willard 42

K

Kay, Minnie Ruth 72, 74, 88
Kelley, J. T. 285
Kendall Manor 22, 79, 85, 97, 116, 234, 244, 323
Kendall, Marrie Holleman 30
Kennedy, David 130
Kennedy, Jacqueline Bouvier 207
Kennedy, John F. 156
Kennedy, Robert Jr. 130
Key, Alexander 89
Keystone Readers Service 32
Killian, Principal Albert 252
King, Danny 279
King, Janie 280
King, Louise 308
King, Martin Luther 24, 53
King, Troy 211
Kite, Debbie 260
Kiwanis Club 55
Knight-Ridder Newspapers 184
Koscielski, Craig 99

L

Laing, Earl 23
Lake Eufaula 20, 22, 61, 63, 87, 88, 92, 93, 234, 237, 239, 242, 243, 245, 266, 288
Lake Eufaula Festival 46, 103

Lakepoint Lodge and Marina 94
Lakepoint Resort State Park 38, 45, 87, 92, 154, 239, 266
Lakeview Community Hospital 200, 279
Land, Cathie 89
Lanier, Sidney 235
LDR International 100
Leathers, Dan 91
Lee, Alice 215
Lee, Barbara 221
Lee County 153
Lee, Jan 23
Lee, Janet McDowell 30
Lee, Mrs. H. R. 117
Lee, Nelle Harper 70, 212
Lee, Robert E. 117, 120, 131
Lee, Rufus 187, 303
Lee's Drive-In 186
Lee vs. Macon 122
LeMaistre, Jeannette 66
LeMaistre, Sam 23, 33, 65, 74, 88, 93, 239
Lewis, Richard 84
Lewis, Tom 78, 79
Liberty Ships 115, 195, 285
Lingo, Al 147, 155, 159
Little, George 42, 89, 117, 216
Little, Lois 24, 89
Lockwood, Bobby 33, 66, 88
Lockwood, Dorothy Ann 90
Lockwood, Susan L. 121
Logue, Lib 23, 89
Logue, Neal 24
Lomax, Tenant 120
Long, Bill 23
Longfellow Literary Society 186
Looney, Bishop Richard 333
Lore, Seth 77, 81, 232
Louisville 109
Lowe, Ann 207
Lowe, Jack 208
Lowe, Janey Cole 208
Lunsford, Charles 106

M

MacMonnies Fountain 85, 94
Malone Alley 41, 165, 175
Mangum, George M. 35
Mangum, Viola 72

Mann, Hazel 24
Mann, Sammy 16
Mann's Bait Company 63, 239
Mann, Tom 62–65, 91, 209, 238, 239
Marianna 109, 240
Martin, Jim 134
Martin, Lou 62
Martin, Mary Wallace 24, 90, 94, 256
Martin, Willie T. 275
Mattox, Leckie 92
May Day Queen 136
McCoo, Marilyn 223, 225
McCoo Memorial Children's Library 224
McCoo, T. V. 223
McCoo, Waymon 223, 225
McDowell, Archibald M. 36
McDowell, Carrie 77, 104, 116
McDowell, Charles S. 36
McDowell, C. S. 117
McDowell, Jennie 116
McIntosh Treaty of 1825 112
McKee, Judd 94
McKenzie, B. B. 117
McKenzie, Betty Flournoy 117
McKenzie, Dan 48
McKenzie, James K. 117
McKenzie, Lillian Luke 46–49, 92
McKenzie, Martha 48
McKenzie, Robert 37, 88
McNab Bank Building 85, 94
McNair, Chris 157
Means, Marianne 152
Mercer University Press 61
Merrill, Bertha Moore 30
Methvin, Bob 35
Methvin, Mary Lou 27
Miller, Alice 140
Miller, Ann Martin 140
Mills, Gary 131
Minn Kota 240
Mississippi River 119
Mitchell, Ann 23
Mitchell, Blake 57
Mitchell, John 156
Mitchell, Logan 57–59
Mixon, Paul 61
Mobile 57, 233

Mobile Bay 285
Moll, Francis 290
Monahan, Caroline Couric 221
Monahan, Jay 221
Monroeville 70, 215
Montgomery 97, 219
Montgomery Advertiser 139, 177
Montgomery Civic Center 220
Moore, Ira 80
Moorer, Billy 23, 157, 213, 224
Moorer, Joe Park 37
Moorer, Lillie 93
Moorer, Rosa R. 117
Moorer, Thomas H. 30, 37, 157, 203, 213, 272
Moorer, W. D. 203
Mooty, Lois 23
Moreland 189
Morgan, Annie 145
Morgan, Ted 279
Mostellar, Helen 140
Motley, Robert 24
Moulthrop, Moss 77, 113
Mount Willing 203, 205
Moussa, Amr 327
Mubarak, Hosni 272, 326, 327
Mueller, Edward A. 246
Mulkey, Marcus V. Jr. 265
Mullen, Sid 91
Murfreesboro 119
Murphy, James D. 41–43, 105

N

NAACP 52
Napier Field Band 114
Nason, Jim 87
National Guard Armory 97, 116
National Newspaper Association 205, 227
National Trust for Historic Preservation 105, 128
Nazariah, Iraq 58
Neal Logue Company 114
Nelson, Harry 57
Neville, Anna 23
Neville, Bill Jr. 155
Neville, Mildred 316

New Birth Center Church of God in Christ 53
New Madrid 119
New York City 199, 205
New York Times 86, 95, 147, 274, 287
Nimitz, Chester W. 37
Nixon, Richard M. 37, 122, 155, 206, 272
Nobel Peace Prize 225
Nolin, Doug 90
Normandy 113
Norman, Merle 290

O

Oakley, Melvin 94, 189, 281
O'Hara, Scarlett 183
Old Creek Town Park 92, 222, 230
Old Eufaula Jail 94
Old Fairview Cemetery 90
Old Glory 92
O'Neal, Emmet 208
O'Neal, Walt 160
Opelousas 249
Operation Desert Storm 125
Opothle-Yaholo 112
Oramas, Oscar 335
Osherson, Samuel 318
Owen, Robert 21
Oxbow Meadows Environmental Learning Center 243

P

Pacifico, Al 187, 188, 281
Panama Canal 206
Panama City 115, 178, 184, 185, 195, 285, 287
Paper, The 258
Pappas Building 85
Parchman Prison 189
Parker, Dan 24, 91
Parker, Eugene C. 242
Parker, Gene 23, 88, 96
Parker, Solita 92
Parta, Michael 325
Parton, Dolly 209
Paterno, Joe 276
Pate's Royal Theater 278
Patrick, Bette Ferrell 117
Patrick, W. R. 117
Patterson, John 138, 159
Patton, George 66

Paul Harris Fellow 60
Paul, Waters 23
Pearl Harbor 195, 203, 204, 304, 305
Peckerwood Club 186
Peck, Gregory 214
Pennsylvania 56
Pensacola 119
Perilous Journeys: A History of Steamboating on the Chattahoochee 246
Perry, Hugh 93
Perry, Sis 24
Persons, Gordon 38
Peterson, Barney 123, 124
Peterson, Betty 252
Peterson, Billy Neil 124
Peterson, Dale 123
Peterson, David 135
Peterson, Ila 123, 124
Peterson, Lemuel Byrd 123, 124
Petry, Louise 24
Phi Beta Kappa 168, 174, 310, 315
Phi Kappa Phi 175
Philippe, Louis 220
Pickett, Gladys Christo 285
Pierian Club 55
Pony Express 90
Poon, Emma 170
Pope, C. J. 109, 234
Porter, Martha Ann 221
Portman, John 45
Posey, Tom 33, 72, 89
Powell, Jack 89, 94
President's Cabinet Committee 122
Preston, C. 117
Price, Sarah Margaret. *See* Smith, Sarah Margaret (sister)
Princeton Survey Research Associates 184
Provisional Congress 107
Public Involvement Meeting 75
Publishers Auxiliary 210
Pulitzer Prize 213
Purcell, Doug 101, 242

Q

Quarterback Club 72

R

Randolph Avenue 68
Rane, Tony 72, 186
Ransom, Virginia 221
Reagan, Ronald 227, 228, 272
Rebel, The 72
Reconstruction 53
Reeves, Ben 35, 145
Reeves, Charlotte Adams 145, 164
Reeves, Mac 24, 87
Reeves Peanut Company 94
Reifenberg, Jo Ann 30
Resaca 119
Reston, James 274
Revolutionary War 98
Richard Russell Bridge 94
Richards, Betty 83
Richardson, Ed 88
Richardson, Elliot 156
Richmond 107
Riley, Lawton 23
Riley, Patsy 211
Rio de Janeiro 332
River and Harbors Act 242
Riverkeeper's Guide to the Chattahoochee 244
River Road 14
Rivers of Alabama 244
River Tavern 241
Roadkill Party 98
Roberts, Bill 23, 63
Roberts, Clara 92
Roberts, Earl 89
Roberts, G. A. 117
Robinson, Annie 94
Robinson, Sam 35, 88, 92
Rodriquez, Jose Luis 335
Rolls Royce 42
"Romance and High Adventure" 213
Roosevelt, Franklin D. 195, 285
Roseland Plantation 98
Ross, Willie 13
Rotary Club 34, 46
ROTC 66, 125
Rove, Karl 210, 272
Royal Theatre 195
RSVP 40
Rudderman, A. M. 33, 74
Ruddy, Christopher 206

Russell, Margaret Lee 22, 220
Russell, Richard 245
Russell, Sarah 92, 290

S

Sam's Barbecue 189
Samson Ledger 169, 278, 293
Sanford Street Elementary
   122
Santo Domingo 336
Sasser, Mildred Houston 219
Satterwhite, Herbert 88
Savannah 119
Schaefer, Terry 220
Schaeffer, Charlie 290
Schaffeld, Bob 89
Schaub, Jule 35, 89
Schneider, David 100
Schultz, George 156
Scott, Ray 63, 65
Scott, Travis 286
secession 233
Sellers, Grandmother 194
Sellers, Joel Carter 263, 278
Sellers, Rose Drane 178, 277
Selma Times-Journal 267
Senate Intelligence Commit-
   tee 200
Sessions, Jeff 200, 243
Seth Lore 89, 244
Seven Sinners from Seale 139
Sexton, Hilda 89, 94
Shalala, Donna 76
Shelby, Richard 200, 243
Sheppard Cottage 88, 106
Sherman, W. T. 119
Sherrill, Chris 99
Shorter, Eli II 129
Shorter, Eli Sims 98, 130
Shorter, John Gill 35, 98,
   107, 111, 130, 218
Shorter, Major Henry 117
Shorter Mansion 29, 42, 77,
   79, 89, 90, 93, 98, 105,
   128, 128–131, 222, 223,
   323
Shorter, Mrs. 117
Shorter, Wilenya Lamar 129
Simpson, Albert 71, 175
Singer, Bette Ferrell Patrick
   116
Sixteenth Street Church 157
Sizoo, Ton 287
Slade, Ed and Margaret 220

slavery 233
Smith, Abb Jackson (father)
   177, 180, 277, 282, 312
Smith, Abb Jackson II (son)
   7, 201, 311, 314
Smith, Alberta 130
Smith, Ann (wife) 94,
   145, 146, 160, 163–165,
   167, 169, 172, 174, 187,
   207, 262, 264, 279, 281,
   295–303, 307–317, 329
Smith, Babe (aunt) 24, 96,
   115, 124, 165–167, 175,
   195
Smith, Bill (son) 199
Smith, Bob (brother) 175,
   283
Smith, Cile 207
Smith, David (nephew) 199
Smith, Doug (brother) 115,
   124, 283
Smith, Gene 262
Smith, Jack (brother) 115,
   195, 283, 285, 312
Smith, Janice 23
Smith, J. Craig 157
Smith, Joel
   family of 174–181,
      282–284, 322–324
   heart surgery 187–189
   international travel
      325–342
   newspaper career 158
   on President's Cabinet
      Committee 122
Smith, Joel Jr. (son) 7–10,
   95, 96, 201, 229, 309, 311,
   314, 326
Smith, L. C. 171, 278
Smith, Lee and Elizabeth 186
Smith, Marcus 91
Smith, Maury (brother) 115,
   192, 283
Smith, N. D. Eubanks 130
Smith, Rose (mother) 180,
   282
Smith, Sally 24–25, 96, 124
Smith, Sally Rawlinson 178
Smith, Sarah Margaret (sister)
   96, 115, 124, 166, 283
Smith, Sarah Mixon Rawlin-
   son 166

Smith, Saul Pierce 166
Smith, Sherri M. L. 245
Smith, Willard 13
Smith, William Sutton (son)
   314, 316
Southern Bell 96
Soviet Union 206
Spanish-American War 131
Spanish Fort 317
Sparkman, John 204
Sparks, Chauncey 29, 37, 61,
   78, 137, 145, 159
Sparks, Lou 90
Sparks State Technical College
   45, 89, 154, 266
Speake, Charlie 99
Spence, Terry 277
Spirit of the South, The 117
Spradley, Wayne 288
Springville 164, 168
Springville High School 173
Springville United Methodist
   Church 164
Spurlock, Mrs. O. R. 117
Stafford, Butch 87
Stars and Bars 116
State Department of Educa-
   tion 184
State Docks Industrial Park
   41, 217, 237
State Mental Health Board 38
State Teachers Examination
   25
Stations of the Cross 93
St. Barbara Church 329
steamboats 246–247
Stegall, Karl 333
Stephens, Elton B. 31
Stern, Edward 109
Stewart, Jimmy 64
St. Francis Bend 230
St. Francis Point 42, 61
St. James's Episcopal Church
   200
St. Julian Hotel 90, 104
Stokes, Ron 56
Strang, Carl J. 55, 56
Strang, Florence Foy (Fonnie)
   23, 54–56, 92, 93, 106, 128
Summerville Land Co 232
Superior Pecan Company 94

Sutton, Ann Moxley 163, 164, 167–169. *See also* Smith, Ann (wife)
Sutton, Evelyn Beck 165
Sutton, W. E. G. 165, 171, 172, 174, 263
Symposium Club 40

T

Tallahassee 184
Tapley, Clarence 148
Tasker, Robert 87
Tatum, Donald B. 126
Tavern, The 32, 90, 94, 106, 110, 232, 243
Taylor, George 186
Taylor, Wyndell 90
Teal, James 147
Techsonic Industries 240
Ten O'Clock Coffee Club 16
Think Like a Fish: The Lure & Lore of America's Legendary Bass Fisherman 63, 240
Third Alabama Infantry Regiment 120
39th Alabama Infantry Regiment 119
This is Your Life 173
Thomas, R. D. 117
Thomas, Sim 38, 114, 216
Thornton, W. H. 117
Tidewater 231
Tigner, Charles 139
Tip Top Café 171, 278
Tito 284
Today Show 199, 222
To Kill a Mockingbird 70, 213, 214
Tom and Tina Outdoors 65
Torbert, Clement C. Jr. 218
Town House 72, 186
Townsend, Vincent 156
Trammell, Annabel 89, 99
Trammell, Seymore 145
Tree That Owns Itself 78, 88
Truman, Harry 124, 173
Tucker, Earl 249
Turning Point 226
Tuscaloosa 119
Tuskegee Light Infantry 120
T. V. McCoo High School 121
Twin Springs 98

U

Union Springs 122
United Daughters of the Confederacy 48, 97, 103, 116, 186, 222
United States Naval Academy 38
United Way 88
University Hospital 62, 187, 188
University of Alabama 37, 45, 66, 119
University of Alabama Birmingham 45
University of Alabama Law School 137, 219
Upshaw, Elizabeth McKeithen 24, 90, 130, 223
Upshaw, Fanny Shorter 130
Upshaw, Herman L. 130, 262, 265
Upshaw house 77
U.S. 431 38
U.S. Corps of Engineers 185
U.S. Fish and Wildlife 67, 239
U.S. Marine Corps 37
USS *Missouri* 37
USS *United States* 66

V

Vance, Lucia Edwards 40
Vance, Oscar 140
Veterans Administration 124
Vezina, Dottie 290, 297
Vicksburg 119, 131
Vicksburg & Brunswick Depot 86
Vietnam 42, 115, 158, 203, 206
Vining, Charlie 89
Virginia Tech 276

W

Wainwright Shipyard 195, 285
Waldron, Jim 248
Walker, Anne Kendrick 77, 107, 110, 118, 233
Walker, Solomon 98
Wallace Act 239
Wallace, Betty 145
Wallace College 276
Wallace, Cornelia 204
Wallace, George C. 32, 33, 38, 96, 138, 140, 146, 151, 153, 154, 158, 159, 161, 204, 216, 217, 218, 228, 266
Wallace, Gerald 145
Wallace, Jack 145
Wallace, Lurleen B. 38, 61, 143, 144, 154, 217, 266
Walter F. George Lock and Dam 63, 237, 245
Walton, Robert 98
Walworth, Susan 125
War Between the States 30, 48, 97, 108, 116, 117, 131
Ward, John and Levy 177
Warner, Lee 135
Washington Times 206
Waterfowl Refuge Association 67
Water Patrol Post 155
Watts, Thomas 111
Weedon, Hamilton M. 30, 233
Wellborn House 32, 90
Wellborn, Thomas Levi 98
Wellborn, William 98
Westling, Louise 52
Weston, Charlie 32
Westover Plantation 98, 99
Wharton, Morton B. 36, 77, 129
Whitehurst, Dick 307, 308, 311
White Oak 88
Wilbourne, Billy 89
Wilkinson, Mrs. T. G. 117
Wilkinson, Thomas G. 25, 122
Williams, Benny 149
Williams, Dick Sr. 33
Williams, Hank 277
Williams, John Henry 156
Wilson, Charles 131
Wilson, Ester 222
Wilson, Jim 49
Wilson, Woodrow 36
Winn, Billy 112
Winslett, Carson 231
Wiregrass 59
Witness to Injustice 51
Woodbury, Phillip 224
Word, Emest 40

World War I 131, 172
World War II 37, 66, 97,
    113–116, 116, 123–124,
    194–196, 204, 278, 284,
    302, 304
Wright, Dalton 325

Y

Yale University 219
Yoholo-Micco 113
Young, E. B. 232
Young, Edward 109
Yufaula (Indian village) 109